Sixty Years with Japanese Prints

H. George Mann

Sixty Years with Japanese Prints, by H. George Mann

Julia Meech and Jane Oliver, Editors
Margery Cantor, Impermanent Press, Designer

Robbie Capp, Copy Editor
Theresa Duran, Index Editor
Thomas Hummel, Crash Paper, Liaison with Printer

Printer and Binder: Artron
Printed in China

Cover: Chōkyōsai Eiri (act. 1790s–early 1800s). *The Flowers of Edo: The Master of Yanagibashi (Edo no hana Yanagibashi natori)*. Japan. Edo period, c. 1795. Color woodblock print with mica ground. 36.8 x 25.2 cm. The Mann Collection

Frontispiece: Utagawa Kunisada (1786–1865). *The Actor Nakamura Utaemon III as the Monkey Trainer Yojirō (Yojirō)*, from the series *Great Performances (Ōatari kyōgen no uchi)*, in a kabuki version of the puppet play *Recent Riverbed Rivalry (Chikagoro kawarano tatehiki)* (also known as *Horikawa* or *Oshun Denbei*) by Tamekawa Sōsuke, Tsutsukawa Hanji and Nakawa Shimesuke, performed at the Nakamura-za theater, 1807/08. Japan. Edo period, c. 1808; possibly 1814/15. Color woodblock print with mica ground. 39.3 x 26.8 cm. The Mann Collection

Library of Congress Control Number: 2020922924

ISBN 978-0-578-80411-8

This publication is printed on 150 gsm New-G matte art paper made in Japan. New-G matte is acid-free in compliance with the minimum durability requirements of the American National Standard for Information Sciences—Permanence of Paper for Printed Library Materials, ANSI Z39.48-1992.

The book is set entirely in Arno, an Adobe typeface created by Robert Slimbach in 2007. Arno is a typeface family designed in the tradition of early Venetian and Aldine book types.

Contents

Acknowledgments

IN CRAFTING A NARRATIVE OF MY DECADES of fascination with ukiyo-e, I have depended on contributions from a wide range of individuals and institutions.

I am deeply appreciative of those who granted permission for publication of images in their collections and assisted in other ways. They include the Allen Memorial Art Museum, Oberlin, Ohio (Selina Bartlett); The Art Institute of Chicago (Susan J. Lerner); Bridgeman Images (Jacob Daugherty); the Freer|Sackler at the Smithsonian Institution (Jennifer Berry); Asian Art Museum of San Francisco (Laura Allen, David Armstrong and Jay Xu); The British Museum (Timothy Clark and Alfred Haft); Brooklyn Museum (Joan Cummins and Monica Park); Honolulu Museum of Art (Pauline Sugino); The Metropolitan Museum of Art, New York; Museum Angewandte Kunst, Frankfurt (Stephan von der Schulenburg); Museum of East Asian Art, Cologne (Bettina Clever); Museum of Fine Arts, Boston (Carolyn Cruthirds, Anne Nishimura Morse, Jennifer Riley and Sarah Thompson); the Nelson-Atkins Museum of Art, Kansas City, Missouri (Yayoi Shinoda and Marc Wilson); Städel Museum, Frankfurt (Regina Freyberger); Tokyo National Museum (Sugawara Atsuo of DNP Art Communications Co., Ltd., with the assistance of Sachie Numajiri of Mita Arts Gallery Co., Ltd.); University of Illinois at Chicago Art Study Collection (Julie A. Duignan); and The Weston Collection (Roger Weston and Mami Hatayama).

I am grateful to all the friends and acquaintances who provided photos reproduced in this memoir, including: Robert Sawers and Mia McCauley, for a shot of my wife and me viewing Hiroshige prints in New York; Julia Meech, for various pictures, including those of visits to our home by members of the Japanese Art Society of America; Anisabelle Berès, for the façade photo of Galerie Berès; Tom Cottle, for his wonderful shot of Tom and his dad examining a Neolithic Chinese pot; Gloria Gaines Callen, for a photo of her father, John Gaines; Jo-Ann Pinkowitz, who sent pictures of her mother, Dorothy Edinburg; Jaron Borensztajn and Ilya Drukker-Tikotin, for sharing pictures of Felix Tikotin, Jaron's grandfather and Ilya's uncle; Yu-Ying Brown, who provided a previously unpublished photo of her mentor, Jack Hillier, taken at the British Library; Jan Lewis Slavid, for a photo of Ray and Mike Lewis attending an auction in Switzerland; Janice Katz, Roger L. Weston Associate Curator of Japanese Art at The Art Institute of Chicago, for an image that captures her "at work"; Ray Kaempfer, for a nostalgic picture of his father, Heinz Kaempfer, taken on his seventy-fifth birthday in 1979; Donald Jenkins, the retired director of the Portland Art Museum and the former associate curator of Oriental Art at The Art Institute of Chicago, for his photo taken at the 1973 opening of "The Ledoux Heritage" at Japan Society; Allan Reich, for his beautiful picture of the sea, taken at Benesse Art House on Naoshima in 2019; Andreas Marks, Mary Griggs Burke Curator of Japanese and Korean Art at the Minneapolis Institute of Art, for the photo of Dick Gale; Michael Fornitz, for the photo of his Sukenobu erotic print; Kurata Katsuhiro, for providing shots of the evening my family spent at the Yomiuri Shinbun teahouse in Tokyo; David Packard, for the photo of Harry Packard; Yamaguchi Keizaburō and Yamaguchi Katsura, for a photo of Irma Grabhorn and Professor Yamaguchi; and thanks to Eric Köhler, Elaine Merguarian and Margot P. Ernst, who assisted with the acquisition and identification of other photos. Each of the above has enriched my experience of remembering. A warm "thank you" to all.

Over the years, I have come to know a number of print dealers in Europe, Japan and the United States, and the knowledge and insights gathered from each (not to mention the magnificent prints acquired from or through them from time to time!) have added to my pleasure and understanding. These include Ayako Abe, Huguette and Anisabelle Berès, David and Ken Caplan, Merlin Dailey, Mary Diamond, Herbert Egenolf, Israel Goldman, Sebastian Izzard, Roger Keyes, Kondo Sentarō, Roland Koscherak, Richard Kruml, Gary Levine, Raymond Lewis and his daughter, Jan Lewis Slavid, Katherine Martin, Joan B. Mirviss, Nagatani Toshizō, Nishi Saijū, Geoffrey Oliver, Anders Rikardson, Robert Sawers and Carolyn Staley.

The extraordinary vision of other Western collectors has informed my own, including: Walter Amstutz, Pierre Barboutau, Louis Black, Lee Dirks, John Gaines, Richard P. Gale, Paolino Gerli, Edwin Grabhorn, Charles Haviland, Louis Ledoux, John Mellor, James Michener, Lilla Perry, Hans Popper, Otto Riese, Alexis Rouart, Theodor Scheiwe, Werner Schindler, Adolphe Stoclet, Felix Tikotin, Ernest Le Véel and Henri Vever and many others who owned prints now in our collection.

Many collections can now be accessed online, including those of Buckingham (The Art Institute of Chicago); Bigelow, Morse, Spaulding and others (Museum of Fine Arts, Boston); Michener (Honolulu Museum of Art); Happer, Havemeyer, Ledoux and others (The Metropolitan Museum of Art, New York); Duell and Ross (Harvard Art Museums); Freer (Freer Gallery of Art); and Ainsworth (Allen Memorial Art Museum). I have spent countless hours over the years studying the prints in those collections, enthralled by their beauty and variety. The website <ukiyo-e.org>, initiated and maintained by John Resig, makes access even easier.

I return often to scholarly auction and exhibition catalogues, the compendia of private and museum collections and other monographs published by scholars, including: Asano Shūgō, John T. Carpenter, Timothy Clark, Julie Nelson Davis, Matthi Forrer, Margaret Gentles, Andrew Gerstle, Helen Gunsaulus, Jack Hillier, Sebastian Izzard, Donald Jenkins, Janice Katz, Roger Keyes, Kikuchi Sadao, Richard Lane, Samuel Leiter, Howard A. Link, Andreas Marks, Julia Meech, James Michener, Narazaki Muneshige, Jane Oliver, Harold (Phil) Stern, Suzuki Jūzō, Sarah Thompson, Ellis Tinios, Osamu Ueda, David Waterhouse, Ann Yonemura and many others. The truths and history recorded in those works are always enlightening. John T. Carpenter, Timothy Clark, Paul Griffith, Sebastian Izzard, Janice Katz and other scholars also have provided valuable insights on prints in our collection, as well as in museums and other public and private collections. Hayashi Rie and Suzannah Yip provided significant historical information for this memoir.

For his translations of poetry and inscriptions on selected prints and for other contributions to the collection catalogue, I am especially grateful to Alfred Haft. The enjoyment of the prints is so enhanced by his efforts. I also thank John Carpenter and Yoshinori Munemura for assisting with selected translations and to Akiko Yano for clarifications on Ryūkōsai Jokei. Other experts who have helped solve provenance puzzles include Joachim Brand, Anne Nishimura Morse and Martin Stahl. Geoffrey Oliver plumbed his vast collection of auction catalogues to track provenance of many prints with indefatigable enthusiasm, generosity and patience. I could not have ferreted out those sources without him. I owe him a special "thank you."

Maurice Cottle, Donald Jenkins and Roger Keyes played significant and complementary roles in my adventure. Maurie imbued in me a curiosity about ukiyo-e that has never been quenched. Donald taught me to "read" prints critically while focusing on their beauty and cultural significance. And Roger, in visits and in correspondence over many years, contributed his scholarship, discerning eye, understanding of history and broad knowledge of collections all over the world. Donald located the "unexpurgated" version of my first Sugimura, and Roger identified the issues surrounding my Kiyomasu and those in the Nelson-Atkins Museum and Museum of Fine Arts, Boston. These "sages" (if I may) have shared an infectious exuberance that continues. I am deeply grateful that Donald Jenkins agreed to contribute his reminiscences and observations of my years of collecting. The "Primitives" exhibition and symposium he organized at The Art Institute of Chicago, in 1971, were critical to my move into "serious" collecting.

Unquestionably, I could not (and would not) have embarked on this project without the initial and continuing encouragement of Julia Meech and Jane Oliver, two warm, experienced and determined (I might even say "relentless") specialists I have known and admired for many of my decades of chasing ukiyo-e. Their contributions to the ukiyo-e field through auction and exhibition catalogues and other publications are well-known and widely admired and appreciated. They have corrected, reorganized, shortened, expanded and otherwise made my memoir more complete. Jane took on the catalogue entries, bibliography and glossary, as well. I am forever grateful to them both. Margery Cantor's design skills have brought this project to life. And my thanks to Robbie Capp, for her superior work as copy editor; to Thomas Hummel, of Crash Paper, who assisted in printing decisions; and to Aron Gent, for his patience and his painstaking and elegant photography of our collection.

But the major force behind this effort is my wife of forty-seven years. Roberta has been alongside me at auctions and exhibitions, at journeys to collectors and museums and on visits to dealers around the world. She has encouraged me and supported me and, truth be told, restrained me when appropriate. And I love her.

H. George Mann
Highland Park, Illinois, USA
January 2021

Foreword

Donald Jenkins

GEORGE MANN AND I HAVE BEEN FRIENDS for almost fifty years now, and what brought us together was a Japanese print. We were in Chicago, George's hometown, where he had begun his lifelong career as a lawyer several years earlier. I had only recently come back to Chicago, where I had once been a student, from my native Northwest. I was named Associate Curator of Oriental Art at The Art Institute of Chicago with the charge to take the place of Margaret Gentles, who had been Keeper of the Clarence Buckingham Collection of Japanese Prints for twenty-six years but was suffering from cancer.

Apparently, George had seen something in the press regarding my appointment, and it came to his mind when he bought a print of a subject he had never seen before. He hoped I might be able to explain it to him. I was able to tell him what it was, namely *shunga*, which most Japanese-English dictionaries translated as "obscene" or "pornographic" pictures, even though the more accurate reading given the *kanji* characters used would be "spring pictures." In any case, we agreed that such a word would be more appropriate for George's acquisition. When he left my office that day, both of us knew that we had made a new friend.

That neither of us had seen a *shunga* print before had something to say about the changing relations between the United States and Japan, but I will wait until later to go into that knotty subject. One thing was sure, however—we were in the midst of experiencing more about Japanese art than any prior American generation. In fact, the two of us were in some ways helping create that development, and Chicago was a perfect place to take part in it.

By 1970, George had acquired about sixty prints, thirty-five of them in his collection to this day. Clearly, he had learned a great deal, but he would need every bit of knowledge at his disposal given the challenges of the field. In April of 1971, he attended his first auction, where he met several of the most noted collectors of the time.

In the meantime, I was working on "Ukiyo-e Prints and Paintings: The Primitive Period, 1680–1745," an exhibition held in late 1971 at The Art Institute of Chicago in memory of Margaret Gentles. Of the 190 works of art, twelve came from overseas, six from Japan. Moreover, the two-day symposium at the opening of the exhibition in November was equally international in its makeup. It included Japan's two most famous ukiyo-e scholars of the time, Shibui Kiyoshi and Narazaki Muneshige.

Clearly, the exhibition could never have taken place without Japan's wholehearted participation, which was particularly impressive when one remembers that it had just emerged from a disastrous war. In 1945, its cities were in ruin, a million and a half of its soldiers dead, and much of the population starving. Japan was occupied by the U.S. Army, with support from British Commonwealth forces, from August 15, 1945 until April 28, 1952, seven years later, when it regained full sovereignty.

By 1971, however, relations between our two countries were changing, and citizens from both nations were beginning to reach out to learn about the other. This became evident in the number of people, many from some distance away, attending our symposium. Among them were Mary Griggs Burke from New York, who was just beginning to build her collection of Japanese art, the art dealer and collector Harry Packard, who flew in from Tokyo, and Rand Castile, newly appointed as director of Japan House Gallery in New York.

As far as I know, no other Japanese print collector has ever written a book like this one. It is the *experience* of collecting prints that most concerns George. For those who are not close to him and fear that the book might be too pedantic for their tastes, I must make it clear from the start that George could never be pedantic. Yes, he is a collector, but he is also a son, a husband, a father and a friend, all of which have important places in his writing.

George Mann and I became friends in ways that might seem unusual given the many years we never saw one another. On the few times our paths did cross, we always knew that nothing had changed between us, and that was because both of us were so deeply attached to the same period of Japanese art, the period of the "Floating World"—a unique culture that arose among a limited group of people living in Edo (the earlier name of Tokyo) roughly from 1680 to 1800. Though some people may question my attachment to that form of Japanese art, given everything else I did during my many years at the Portland Art Museum, my true devotion to it is obvious for anyone who is familiar with my last major exhibition, "The Floating World Revisited," in 1993.

As for George's commitment to ukiyo-e, there could be no question for anyone who has had the pleasure of viewing his collection.

In 1973, I organized an exhibition for Japan House Gallery of prints that had once been in the collection of the great Louis Ledoux. George was a lender. This may be the appropriate time to recall the words Ledoux wrote in the foreword to Part One of his monumental five-volume catalogue in 1941:

> In the past these prints have been loved separately by others; for a moment they are together, dear to me; and before the storms of time scatter them, as well they may, their loveliness should be recorded for the study and solace of those who care for beauty. . . . [He] into whose keeping have come for a time works of art that are rare and perishable as well as lovely is merely their custodian and feels it a duty not only to transmit all that he has learned about their meaning but to share likewise with others . . . the joy that he himself has had in loveliness.

I know that George feels the same way.

NOTES TO THE READER

Japanese and Chinese names generally are cited in the traditional order: surname first, followed by the personal name. Japanese artists and literati commonly are referred to by the personal, art or literature name: Hokusai (for Katsushika Hokusai); Eiri (for Chōkyōsai Eiri). Those who have adopted Western name order are so listed: Hiroshi Sugimoto and Osamu Ueda, for example.

The diacritical mark is used to indicate a long vowel in Japanese, except when the word has entered the English lexicon: Tokyo, Osaka, Kyoto.

"Mann catalogue no. x" in parenthetical citations refers to the catalogue entry of a Mann Collection print in this volume, unless clarified otherwise (Gerli cat. no. x).

Sixty Years with Japanese Prints

H. George Mann

I STARTED WORK ON THIS MEMOIR many years ago as a record of the fascination and excitement I have experienced over sixty years—1961 through 2020—of studying, acquiring and sharing woodblock prints of Japan's Edo period (1615–1868), called ukiyo-e. (In Japan, sixty is an important milestone, the completion of the zodiac cycle and a time of reflection and renewal.) In recounting the activities of those decades, I wanted to cover the depth and breadth of my ukiyo-e adventures—mistakes and regrets, as well as surprises and successes.

Beginnings

It all began in 1959.[1] My school friend Tom Cottle (b. 1937) and I left Chicago for Paris on July 13 for a rambling drive through France, around the continent and then over to England, Ireland and Scotland. Tom had just graduated from Harvard College and I had just finished my first year at Columbia Law School. (Tom later earned his MA and PhD degrees at the University of Chicago and became a clinical psychologist and sociologist at Boston University.) We visited many of the customary cultural and tourist sites everywhere we stopped.

We were on the road for several weeks, driving from Paris to Lyon, through the Loire Valley and on to the Riviera. We crossed the border into Italy, stopping in La Spezia, Padua, Venice, Florence and Rome. After turning north and visiting Cortina d'Ampezzo, we continued into Austria, Switzerland and Germany. Along the way, we saw a poster announcing an important exhibition of Japanese prints, and Tom suggested that we stop. Tom's father, Maurice H. Cottle, MD (1898–1981), displayed ukiyo-e on walls in their residence in Chicago and in their vacation home in Union Pier, Michigan. I had already seen enough Japanese prints at the Cottles and wasn't interested in seeing any more. Tom reminded me recently—I had completely forgotten—that we had a "serious argument" over whether or not to visit the exhibition, which concluded with my decision not to go. After a few more days on the road, we separated: Tom went on to Brussels and I took the car to Amsterdam, where I arranged to have it shipped to New York. I flew to Scotland for a brief visit (I *had* to see the Old Course at St. Andrews), and then we reunited in London. Our six-week journey that started with our arrival in Paris on Bastille Day ended without ukiyo-e.

When we returned to the States, my curiosity about the colorful images hanging at the Cottle home was rekindled on one of my informal visits. Our families lived just a half mile from each other on the north side of Chicago, yet, in rather different worlds. My father came from a meager background and built a strong and successful business manufacturing clothing. Neither of my parents graduated from college. Our family occasionally enjoyed a Chicago Symphony Orchestra performance, and I remember seeing Arthur Rubinstein play Chopin when I was about eight years old. I took piano lessons until I was about ten and went to children's concerts during grade school. Tom, on the other hand, grew up in a highly cultured home where music and art were paramount. Tom's mother, Gitta Gradova (born Gertrude Weinstock, 1904–1985), was a musical prodigy who became a world-renowned concert pianist. Rachmaninoff and Prokofiev, among many celebrated colleagues, considered her peerless. Her abrupt decision to retire and concentrate on her family caused a lifetime of regret, although she continued to practice intensely and to play privately within her wide musical circle (fig. 1).

Gitta's husband, Maurie, raised in England and France before emigrating to Chicago with his parents, was an eminent rhinologic surgeon and charismatic professor. He was the founder and first president of the American Rhinologic Society in 1954 and was instrumental in establishing the International Rhinologic Society in Kyoto in 1961. He was also an accomplished and devoted musician, having contributed to his medical-school fees from the proceeds of gigs with his banjo. He liked to play his Stradivari or Guarneri violin at regular evening musicales at the Cottle home. Famous musicians and composers were always dropping by to participate—among them, Toscanini, Heifetz and Horowitz, Gitta's greatest friend. (I once drove Isaac Stern to their house after a Chicago Symphony concert, nervous I would have an accident and damage him and his violin.) Photos with dedications from admirers in the international music world sat on the two pianos in the Cottle music room.

In addition to his music, Maurie loved, and seriously collected, Chinese and Japanese art (fig. 2). He had been stimulated by exposure to the British Museum and the Louvre as a young man and began collecting in the 1920s. He was a warm and articulate man who communicated his enthusiasms readily to anyone who expressed even passing interest. One evening, in December 1960, a year after my European adventure with Tom, I asked Maurie about their Asian art.

ALL PHOTOS ARE COURTESY OF H. GEORGE MANN, UNLESS OTHERWISE NOTED.

FIG. 1. Dust jacket of *When the Music Stopped: Discovering My Mother,* a 2004 memoir of Gitta Gradova by her son, Thomas J. Cottle

OPPOSITE: FIG. 2. Thomas J. Cottle and his father, Maurice, examine a Chinese Neolithic pot from the Cottle Collection. 1959. Courtesy of Thomas J. Cottle

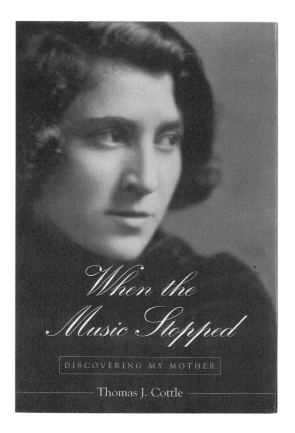

He led me on a tour of precious Chinese porcelains from the fourteenth to the nineteenth centuries, Tang and Song pieces from earlier eras—and, of course, Japanese prints and paintings of the Edo period. Cabinets were opened, storage boxes were removed and treasures were displayed. All of the objects intrigued me with their fluid lines and wonderful colors.

Much of the ukiyo-e I remember seeing on the walls of the Cottle home or in Solander-type boxes was modest. One of the hanging prints turned out to be a reproduction of a design by Ichirakutei Eisui (act. 1790–1823). That became apparent to me a few years later when I convinced Maurie to remount it and discovered its modern paper as we unframed it. In 1967, he did buy a print from the British dealer Robert G. Sawers (b. 1934)—a beautiful bust portrait by Kitagawa Utamaro (1753?–1806); the courtesan Matsuyama of the Wanya, shown holding a pipe, is from the series *Five Beautiful Women in a Competition of Personal Charm* (*Gonin bijin aikyo kurabe*) that Bob acquired at the auction of prints owned by Lilla Simmons Perry at Sotheby's, London, in July 1966. Perry (1882–1971), who lived in Los Angeles, visited Japan in 1936 in search of ukiyo-e.[2] Maurie also owned a brightly colored Torii Kiyonaga (1752–1815) pillar print of a woman running in a breeze beneath wisteria that he

displayed in their vestibule. (Try as I might, I could not convince Maurie to take the print out of the sunlight.)

The Chinese material is what drove Maurie Cottle. His Tang horses, camels, court ladies and other figures were especially captivating. In February 1973, Bob Sawers brought his good friend Giuseppe Eskenazi (b. 1939), who would become the preeminent European dealer in Chinese art, to Chicago to meet Maurie. A month later, Giuseppe sent Dr. Cottle a proposal detailing a plan to sell the collection. The Cottle Collection of Chinese art was offered in a catalogued sale/exhibition at Eskenazi Ltd. in November–December 1973. The sale was the second in the new Eskenazi premises, which opened at Foxglove House, Piccadilly in early 1972.

During Christmas vacation from law school in 1960, just after Maurie gave me that enthralling tour, I bought a copy of James Michener's *Japanese Prints: From the Early Masters to the Modern* (Rutland, VT and Tokyo: Charles E. Tuttle Company, 1959). I began poring through images in Michener's book, captivated by their design and quality. (The Cottles did not own prints anything like those in the Michener catalogue, except for the Utamaro from Lilla Perry and the Kiyonaga described above.) A week later, in January 1961, returning to New York to complete my final semester of

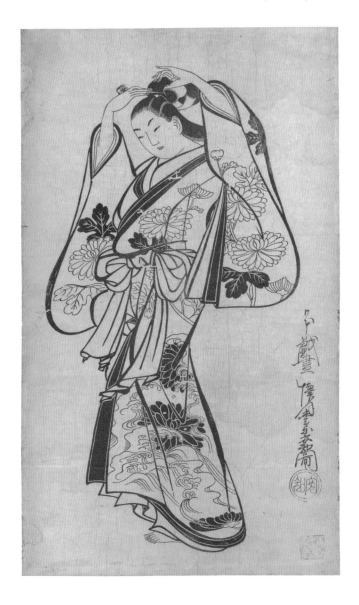

law school at Columbia, I arranged an appointment at The Metropolitan Museum of Art to see Japanese prints.

When I arrived at the museum, I was escorted to a conference table in the print study room and was left there alone. I selected prints from lists in loose-leaf notebooks, sending request forms to storage on a dumbwaiter. After several minutes, a box containing my requests arrived on the same dumbwaiter. There were no photos in the Met's loose-leaf notebooks and little, if any, didactic information on the mats or on separate documents. Among the works I saw were several by artists of the Kaigetsudō school published between 1710 and 1715, all of which had been in the collection of Louis Vernon Ledoux (1880–1948) and which the Met bought in 1949 from Roland Koscherak (1899–1987), a prominent New York dealer in Tibetan and other Asian arts (figs. 3 and 4). I think I made my choices because the names of artists whose prints had intrigued me in the Michener book rang bells. What I hadn't expected was how holding them in my own hands and seeing them, even with untutored eyes, completely bowled me over. Then and there I decided I wanted the thrill of learning about and collecting Japanese prints for myself.

Security at my Met visit was effectively nil. Even as a novice, never having owned a Japanese object, never having visited a dealer or a museum collection until that day, I was surprised by the manner in which the prints were presented. In hindsight, I can say that the storage of those rare masterpieces (there are only forty-two or so authenticated Kaigetsudō works extant) was appalling. The hinging of the paper edges to the mats was haphazard (some were completely loose and, worse yet, some were attached by only *one* hinge), and there was no interleaving of glassine paper to protect against dirt and damage. I was very timid about touching those rarities and handled them gingerly.

By the summer of 1961, when I graduated from law school and returned to Chicago to prepare for the Illinois bar examination and to begin practicing at the law firm McDermott Will & Emery, my interest in ukiyo-e was stronger. I had made my way through Michener's book several times and had experienced the enlightening visit to the Metropolitan Museum. I wanted to jump in. Maurie Cottle recommended a visit to Nagatani, Inc., a shop selling Japanese and Chinese art and artifacts at 848 North Michigan Avenue in Chicago, established by Nagatani Toshizō (1905–1994) in 1944. Nagatani had been a U.S. representative of the Japanese firm of Yamanaka & Co., which had branches in Chicago, New York and Boston, among other cities, before it was seized as "enemy property" by the United States government earlier in the year.[3] The Cottles purchased many of their Chinese pieces from Nagatani.

I remember vividly the day I visited Nagatani's shop in June 1961. I mentioned the Cottle name and received a warm welcome from Nagatani, a soft-spoken and kind gentleman. The shop was one main room, cluttered with objects (mostly Chinese, as I recall). Saitō Minoru (c. 1929–2009), Nagatani's longtime assistant, stayed in the background. I asked to see nineteenth-century landscapes. Nagatani went to the

OPPOSITE: FIG. 3. Kaigetsudō Anchi (act. c. 1714). *Courtesan Placing a Hairpin in Her Hair.* Japan. Edo period, c. 1714. Woodblock print. 57.8 x 32.4 cm. The Metropolitan Museum of Art, New York, Harris Brisbane Dick Fund and Rogers Fund, 1949, JP3106

FIG. 4. Kaigetsudō Dohan (act. 1710–16). *Courtesan for the Third Lunar Month.* Japan. Edo period, c. 1714. Woodblock print. 56.5 x 30.5 cm. The Metropolitan Museum of Art, New York, Harris Brisbane Dick Fund and Rogers Fund, 1949, JP3102

back room and brought out an impression of *Shower below the Summit* (*Sanka hakuu*; 1830s), from Hokusai's series *Thirty-six Views of Mount Fuji*, but I demurred because the price was $500. More than twenty years later, in 1983, I purchased *Shower below the Summit* from the Swedish dealer Anders Rikardson at a price many times what Nagatani had asked (fig. 5). I felt more comfortable when Nagatani offered me *Drum Bridge and "Setting Sun Hill," Meguro* (1857) from Hiroshige's series *One Hundred Views of Famous Places in Edo* (fig. 6). The print was priced at $100 and in good condition, with intense color. I must admit I was unaware that it was not an early state—it lacks shading under the bridge and a more elaborate title cartouche. Thus, on Wednesday, June 7, 1961, two days after my first day of work at McDermott Will & Emery (at which I spent my entire forty-year career in the law), I purchased my first Japanese print, a placid scene of travelers in their own private worlds crossing a bridge in heavy snow, not knowing or caring who is passing.

I was hooked.

Soon after I bought that Hiroshige snowscape, I had it framed and glazed and hung it in my bedroom, always keeping the shades closed. I am not sure when I "retired" the print from wall display, but it was probably around 1964, at the time I purchased my first archival storage box, like those I'd seen at the Cottles, from Spink and Gaborc in New York—for $14.[4]

OPPOSITE: FIG. 5. Katsushika Hokusai (1760–1849). *Shower below the Summit* (*Sanka hakuu*), from the series *Thirty-six Views of Mount Fuji* (*Fugaku sanjūrokkei*). Japan. Edo period, 1830s. Color woodblock print. 25.6 x 36.9 cm. The Mann Collection, acquired March 1, 1983

FIG. 6. Utagawa Hiroshige (1797–1858). *Drum Bridge and "Setting Sun Hill," Meguro* (*Meguro Taikobashi Yūhinooka*), from the series *One Hundred Views of Famous Places in Edo* (*Meisho Edo hyakkei*). Japan. Edo period, 1857. Color woodblock print. 35 x 23.7 cm. The Mann Collection, acquired June 7, 1961

Family History

What awakened the interest of a career-minded young man to this new focus? Certain elements of my family history are relevant.

My mother, Belle (1910–2001), and her two brothers, Maurice (1901–1988), a lawyer, and Howard (1898–1964), a physician, both with graduate degrees from the University of Chicago, and my maternal grandmother ignited my love for travel and culture. My maternal grandparents, Harry George (Tzvi Gdalya) Scheinberg (c. 1867–1937) and Toby Rubin Scheinberg (c. 1871–1952), later anglicized to Shanberg, came to the United States from Jalowska, near Bialystok, Poland. My grandfather preceded my grandmother, who arrived with two sons and one daughter in 1903. My mother, the youngest of five, was born in Chicago. My grandfather was a cabinet-maker, in truth, an artisan, in Poland and brought his skills to the United States. I still have the mahogany shaving mirror he crafted over one hundred years ago and used daily. Unfortunately, I never knew him, because he passed away just days before I was born on April 10, 1937. I was given his name at birth and, like my grandfather, who was known by his middle name "Gdalya," I've always been called "George."

My grandmother Toby insisted that her family speak English in their new home, rather than Yiddish, the language of the "old country." She studied English and current events in citizenship classes at O'Keeffe Elementary School, across the street from her apartment in the South Shore neighborhood of Chicago. After she "graduated," she continued citizenship courses, receiving multiple "diplomas," year after year, until she died in 1952. She left a handwritten will, entirely in English and tucked into her bible.

My mother's elder brother, A. Howard Shanberg, MD, graduated from the University of Chicago Medical School in 1922 and did postgraduate work in medicine in Vienna. Because of polio contracted as a child in Jalowska that left him with a withered leg requiring a brace, and because of a heart attack early in his career, he was only able to practice medicine briefly. He spent his days reading, mostly European classics. On occasion, while we still lived in the neighborhood (until 1948), he would give me his opinions on the importance of ideas and serious study. He was melancholy and frustrated by his ill health and his inability to be a vibrant force in society. But it was he who traveled back to Bialystok and Jalowska in 1929 (on his honeymoon) to visit and film a record of his birthplace. The brief record of his visit is now in the Steven Spielberg Film and Video Archive at the United States Holocaust Memorial Museum in Washington, DC. His interests in literature and history had a strong influence on me, as did my grandmother's interest in learning.

While I was still in grade school, our family traveled to Arizona and Florida, but we spent almost all of every year in Chicago. My older brother, Sheldon (b. 1933), graduated from public high school in Chicago in 1950 and went on to the Wharton School at the University of Pennsylvania, in Philadelphia, graduating in 1954. Then, he joined my father in the clothing manufacturing business and eventually became the chairman and president of that company. He lives with my sister-in-law about five miles from me, in Glencoe, Illinois. His interest in the visual arts is not as fervent as mine (he is not a collector), but he owns a spectacular Man Ray rayograph.

Our father, Henry Mann (1907–2001), was still named Yaney Iddishmann when he entered grammar school in Chicago around 1912. He told me that his first teacher said, "You can't have a name like 'Yaney' in this school. Your name is Henry." In 1931, at the age of twenty-four, he changed his last name from Iddishmann to Mann. His parents and siblings also changed their names to "Mann" around the same time.

Soon after Dad graduated from high school in 1925, he took a job with Reich Dress Company in Chicago. He became a nearly equal partner in the business, which continued to thrive until 1953, when it closed. Soon after, my father established Henry-Lee and Co., a more efficient clothing manufacturing business, now specializing in designer jeans under the leadership of my nephew, Robert T. Mann.

My parents were very devoted to each other and to their children, grandchildren

and great grandchildren (fig. 7). They died within six months of each other in 2001. My parents strongly supported the Jewish United Fund and other Jewish charities. When I was very young, my mother volunteered at Michael Reese Hospital, where both my brother and I were born. As a major research and teaching hospital on the South Side of Chicago, it was one of the oldest (founded in 1881 and closed in 2009) and largest in the city.

My mother and her family were extremely close. We gathered, with our cousins, aunts and uncles, at my grandmother's home nearly every Friday after dinner for family "discussions." My parents and all of my aunts and uncles were fluent in Yiddish, but, as mentioned above, my grandmother insisted we use English "now that we live in America." Conversation was always spirited, and the kids were often included and expected to participate. Only when the conversation turned to a subject deemed inappropriate for the *kinder* (children) did the discussion switch over to Yiddish. (It was then that the cousins started to pay strong attention, hoping to hear and understand something we were not supposed to get.) Generally,

FIG. 7. Belle S. Mann and Henry Mann. 1990

we discussed "current events" and were often "grilled" by our Uncles Howard and Maurie on what we were studying in school. All the cousins (there were ten of us) loved being there and being together. My parents and three of my mother's four siblings and their families lived within two or three city blocks of one another. My Uncle Maurie and his family lived several miles away.

I had seven cousins on my father's side—but my father's family was not as close as my mother's. His parents, Hyman and Kate, were born in Europe, but met and married in the United States. My father's younger brother, Jack, was very observant and studied for the rabbinate before entering the clothing manufacturing industry. Their older sister, Bertha, my aunt, married and moved to Indianapolis. My paternal grandfather died when I was four years old, and I have no recollection of him. My paternal grandmother was a stern, strong woman who, unlike my maternal grandmother, preferred to speak Yiddish. She was an outstanding cook whose strudel was the best I ever tasted!

Until age eleven, I attended O'Keeffe Elementary School, the same school where my grandmother took her citizenship courses at 69th Street and Merrill Avenue. After my immediate family moved from the "old neighborhood" to the North Side of Chicago in 1948, I remained in public school through the ninth grade, but graduated from secondary school in 1954 at the Latin School of Chicago, a private school founded in 1888.

I was a strong student in secondary school, transferring to the Boys Latin School of Chicago after my freshman year at public high school. I had placed fourth among first-year students in the Illinois state-wide Latin contest. My freshman class in public high school numbered several hundred, but the sophomore class at the Boys Latin School had only seventeen students. In my junior year, the Boys and Girls Latin Schools merged, and when I graduated in 1954, the class numbered thirty-two. I was not even a casual reader then, but I was conscientious. In my senior year, I won an award for a paper arguing that John Milton had plagiarized *Paradise Lost* from an obscure Dutch author.

I went on to Harvard College, where I received my undergraduate degree in 1958. To stand out at Harvard felt daunting, and I slacked off when I got there. In those days at Harvard, it was fairly easy to get Bs and Cs, the range into which I settled. I majored in economics, took no courses in fine arts and did not consider writing a senior thesis, something that about half the class did. Instead, I indulged in too much bridge and beer and too many excursions to nearby women's colleges. I compressed weeks of reading assignments into a few days during the "reading period" before exams, getting through *War and Peace* in four days and fifteen plays for a course entitled "Drama Since Ibsen" the night before the exam. The only museum I visited when I was at Harvard was the Busch-Reisinger Museum, and then only because I wanted to see the organ on which the renowned concert organist E. Power Biggs played Bach so beautifully.

When I arrived at Harvard in 1954, at age seventeen, I moved into Matthews South dormitory (in Harvard Yard) with Daniel Swett, a close friend from Chicago. At that time, freshmen were permitted to choose their roommates. Dan lived across the street from me in Chicago and had graduated from Evanston Township High School. We played golf at the same club. Our housing at Matthews had a great room and two separate bedrooms. After our freshman year, we moved to Lowell House (one of the

Houses for upper classmen) and lived in a suite, again with separate bedrooms. For our junior and senior years, we had a third roommate, Alan Steinert, whose home was close by in Cambridge. Dan, now living in Boca Raton, Florida, and I have remained very close, but I have less contact with Alan Steinert.

I was thoroughly impressed (even intimidated) by many students at Harvard. Most were highly intelligent, with better secondary-school training and a very deep commitment to their educations. Socially, I felt like an outsider. There were many students from eastern private boarding schools (Andover, Exeter, Groton, St. Paul's and the like) and they seemed to live in their own world from which middle class, midwestern, Jewish kids were excluded. While I and a few of my Jewish classmates could (and did) join the Hasty Pudding Institute of 1770, where we had occasional drinks and meals, not one of us was considered for membership in any of the elite "final" clubs, such as the Fly, the Owl or the Porcellian.

In my fourth college year, I decided to apply to law school. I did not want to join my father's clothing business or enter the Army—the only two post-college paths that seemed available. My uncle Maurie, my mother's older brother, was a lawyer, and he encouraged me to join his profession. My LSAT scores were high enough that, notwithstanding my middling Harvard College performance, I was accepted at Columbia Law School. I enrolled there in the fall of 1958.

I entered Columbia with renewed determination to succeed—even excel. I was a prolific note-taker and diligently prepared for exams. I applied myself and finished well. And I enjoyed it! Other than my trip to the Metropolitan to see Japanese prints in January 1961, I don't remember going to other museums in the city. It was only after law school that frequent trips to New York almost always included the Met or the Guggenheim. In the fall of 1961, after graduation from law school, I do believe I went to see Rembrandt's *Aristotle Contemplating a Bust of Homer* (later renamed *Aristotle with a Bust of Homer*) that the Met recently had purchased at auction for the then-unheard-of price of $2.3 million. To put the escalating cost of art in perspective, the Louvre and Rijksmuseum made a joint private purchase of two Rembrandt portraits in 2015 for €160 million ($180 million).

Chasing: 1960s

During the Sixties, I acquired as many as sixty prints, of which fewer than forty remain in my collection, which now numbers around one hundred eighty.[5] The prints I bought in that decade came from a variety of sources.

Mary Diamond

After the first purchase of the Hiroshige snow scene from Nagatani in 1961, described above, I turned to the S. H. Mori Gallery that occupied part of the ground floor and lower level of the Chicago Club building at 83 East Van Buren Street, just west of Michigan Avenue. My first mentor, Maurie Cottle, encouraged me with occasional gifts from his collection. I began to stop by the Mori Gallery on Saturday afternoons to engage in long discussions about prints with the owner, Mary-Morris Van Schaick Diamond Stein (1909–1996)—known to everyone as Mary Diamond. I realized I was joining a new community, in which I felt at home. Although I was deeply committed to the practice of law, which absorbed my days and many evenings, I was succumbing more and more to the allure of ukiyo-e.

The S. H. Mori Gallery was, besides Nagatani, the only ukiyo-e dealer in Chicago at that time. Mary Diamond acquired the gallery when Mori Shigehisa died, around 1957. An elegant woman, Mary was slight and delicate. She often dressed in clothes tailored from exotic Asian-inspired textiles, wore elaborate makeup and always was perfectly coiffed. She used a long cigarette holder that she flourished dramatically. Aloof and secretive, Mary cultivated the mystique that she had more knowledge and experience than she really had. She was insulted when I wanted to return an "Eisui" I bought from her in 1964 that turned out to be "wrong"; the image of the courtesan Kisegawa of the Matsubaya holding a fan, had been quite convincing to a beginner like me. Again and again, Mary refused to take the print back, even though Bob Sawers and every other expert to whom I showed it pronounced it a reproduction. Although the price was only $375, she would not accept a return, even for a credit.

Mary had very round, artistic handwriting that she preferred to use (rather than type) for her statements, a number of which I still have. I also have her copy of the Sotheby's catalogue for the 1963 Mellor sale in London, which she attended, that shows her distinctive hand. The Mellor Collection, consisting of over six hundred lots, was billed by Sotheby's as the "most important to be dispersed by auction [in England] since well before the last war." John Mellor, a successful brewer, acquired most of his prints between 1926 and 1940, when there were many more opportunities to buy fine impressions.

Unlike Nagatani's shop, which was cluttered with a large number and variety of objects, the Mori Gallery was spare. Mary displayed framed prints in the ground-level space with its large window onto Van Buren Street. She often invited me to the lower level to look at prints at a stylish Frank Lloyd Wright (1867–1959) pine desk. Wright made the small desk and accompanying chair for S. H. Mori around 1915 (figs. 8 and 9).[6] Mary "inherited" them, when she acquired the gallery in 1957. I almost never made an appointment—I just wandered in, seldom finding others in the shop.

One time I brought along David C. Ruttenberg (1910–2003), a crony of my father who was an early and ardent collector of photography and contemporary painting (see figure 129). He later served as a trustee of The Art Institute of Chicago and as the chairman of the photography acquisition committee at the museum, to which he donated scores of photographs, primarily the work of Walker Evans. David also owned a small Jackson Pollock that he bought in the 1950s (allegedly for $400) and sold "too soon." Encouraging me to "broaden my horizons,"

FIG. 8. Frank Lloyd Wright. Armchair for S. H. Mori Gallery, Fine Arts Building, Chicago. c. 1915. Oak with pine seat. 66.5 x 55.8 x 48.2 cm. University of Illinois at Chicago Art Study Collection. Gift to the University from Mary Diamond Stein, 1969

FIG. 9. Frank Lloyd Wright. Writing Desk for S. H. Mori Gallery, Fine Arts Building, Chicago. c. 1915. Oak with stained pine top. 60.4 x 106.9 x 60.4 cm. University of Illinois at Chicago Art Study Collection. Gift to the University from Mary Diamond Stein, 1969

FIG. 10. *Enma-ō, King and Judge of Hell.* Japan. Muromachi period, 16th century. Wood with gesso and traces of polychrome and inlaid crystal eyes. 48.3 x 46.4 cm. Brooklyn Museum, Gift of Mr. and Mrs. H. George Mann, 79.277

FIG. 11. Roberta and George Mann's daughter Elizabeth Malkin Lund (b. 1967), age six, with *Enma-ō*

OPPOSITE: FIG. 12. Katsushika Hokusai. *Ushibori in Hitachi Province (Jōshū Ushibori)*, from the series *Thirty-six Views of Mount Fuji (Fugaku sanjūrokkei)*. Japan. Edo period, 1830s. Color woodblock print. 25.3 x 36.8 cm. The Mann Collection, acquired November 26, 1962

26

David asked me which of the contemporary prints hanging at Mary's shop I liked. Then he bought it for me! (I don't remember the artist and I gave it away years ago.)

Although Mary Diamond dealt primarily in both ukiyo-e and contemporary woodcuts, she might return from a trip abroad with other Japanese objects. One Saturday afternoon, I was in the gallery when a sixteenth-century, Muromachi-period wood figure of *Enma-ō, King and Judge of Hell,* was uncrated. Although completely unfamiliar with Japanese sculpture, I bought it on impulse and displayed it in my home for over fifteen years. The age and authenticity of the sculpture were certified later by Mathias Komor (c. 1909–1984), the legendary Hungarian-born New York dealer in "oriental and other antiquities." The *Enma-ō* was donated to the Brooklyn Museum in 1979 (figs. 10 and 11).

Another treat I found at the Mori Gallery in the 1960s is an extraordinary all-blue (*aizuri-e*) *Ushibori* from Hokusai's *Thirty-six Views of Mount Fuji* (fig. 12). The gradation (*bokashi*)—a painterly effect of hand shading—from dark to light blue was amazingly smooth. My first thought was, *"This can't be real. It's just too perfect."* I hesitated until a year later, 1962, when I decided to take a chance on it for $275. Most of the impressions of *Ushibori* I knew from catalogues showed a flaw in the reeds below Mount Fuji, a result of distinct gouges in the woodblock. In some cases, the marks are quite obvious. However, the one Mary was offering showed no evidence of damage in the woodblock, and that very perfection raised a doubt in my mind. Later, I was

FIG. 13. George Mann at home with Mary Diamond's print case. November 8, 2019

struck by the similarity between the *Ushibori* I acquired and the Ledoux example in the catalogue published by his widow (see Louis V. Ledoux, *Japanese Prints—Hokusai and Hiroshige—In the Collection of Louis V. Ledoux* [Princeton University Press, 1951], cat. no. 18). They share an anomaly: a very narrow ¹/16-inch (0.15 cm) wide and 2-inch (5 cm)-long area at the bottom near the right edge lacking color, suggesting that they were both pulled from the same block. Apparently, the block was either a bit shaved or worn at that point and was not fully inked when the prints were pulled. The Ledoux print also had no evidence of block damage in the reeds below Fuji.

When the American scholar Roger Keyes (1942–2020) did an appraisal of my collection in the late 1960s, he valued the *Ushibori* at "$0," as a reproduction, but later, the Tokyo print dealer Nishi Saijū (1927–1995), who was everybody's guru in those days, said it was genuine. Now it's accepted as being among the best surviving examples and is often in demand for exhibitions and publications.

When Mary Diamond retired and closed her gallery in the late 1960s, I bought her Victorian-era print case, an elaborately carved mahogany piece on legs, with a retractable easel above, but never learned its provenance (fig. 13). She donated the Wright desk and chair to the University of Illinois at Chicago, in 1969.

Roland Koscherak and a Toyokuni

In April 1964, I contacted Roland Koscherak, the New York dealer who sold six Kaigetsudō prints (and other masterpieces) from the Ledoux Collection to the Met in 1949. Mary Diamond had told me Koscherak had an Utagawa Toyokuni of interest, and I fantasized that he might have Ledoux prints—more than fifteen years after the death of that great collector. I was planning a trip to New York on business and arranged to meet Koscherak at the Irving Trust Company at One Wall Street, where he stored prints, to see the Toyokuni and other items he had to sell.

When he offered the Toyokuni print to me, and on the invoice for my purchase, Koscherak made it absolutely clear that the *Sawamura Sōjūrō III* from the series *Images of Actors on Stage* (*Yakusha butai no sugata-e*) was not a first edition. It lacks the title cartouche and varies from the more fully realized state (fig. 14). But I bought the print anyway, and it was only after I received the print in Chicago that I did the necessary research. With the help of Margaret (Peggie) Gentles (1905–1969), the Keeper of the Buckingham Collection at the Art Institute, I was able to compare the Koscherak print with a published image of the first state, as well as with other Toyokuni holdings at the museum. Less than two weeks after the print arrived, I returned it to Koscherak, explaining my change of heart: I did not want an example that lacked the title cartouche. Koscherak graciously accepted my return and held my payment as a credit. About two months later, he offered me a Katsukawa Shunchō (act. c. 1780–1801)

beauty print (Mann catalogue no. 61) which, while not in top condition, is charming and extremely rare (I have never seen another one), and I bought it.

Koscherak was a knowledgeable dealer, with high ethical standards and good taste. I respected him for having been selected to represent the heirs in the sale of the Ledoux Collection, and I was disappointed that I never had another opportunity to acquire important ukiyo-e from him.

As an aside, the Toyokuni that I returned to Koscherak in 1964 turned up in a 1967 catalogue of Kegan Paul, Trench, Trubner & Co., London, *Japanese Prints, Drawings and Paintings,* a copy of which Bob Sawers sent me after he visited the Cottles in Chicago that year. That Toyokuni found its way to Kondo Sentarō (1933–1985) of the Red Lantern Shop in Kyoto, who sent it to me on approval in 1973; I rejected it for the third time (fig. 15).

But that was not the only time I encountered an "incomplete" or "unfinished" Toyokuni actor print. In early 1987, I sent nine prints to Christie's for the April 22 sale *Fine and Important Japanese Prints from Various Collections;* six sold and three were unsold, in auction parlance "bought in." Among the prints I sold that day was a

FIG. 14. Utagawa Toyokuni (1769–1825). *The Actor Sawamura Sōjūrō III as Shimada Jūsaburō* in the kabuki play *Faithful Courtesans in Yoshiwara,* from the series *Images of Actors on Stage* (*Yakusha butai no sugata-e*). Japan. Edo period, c. 1795. Color woodblock print. 35.9 x 24.1 cm. The Metropolitan Museum of Art, New York, The Howard Mansfield Collection, Rogers Fund, 1936, JP2720
This is an example of the more fully realized state of the print.

FIG. 15. The "incomplete" Toyokuni from the 1967 Kegan Paul, Trench, Trubner & Co. catalogue *Japanese Prints, Drawings and Paintings,* p. 66, no. 85. 35.5 x 24 cm
Sawers, then Koscherak, then Kondo offered this print to George Mann.

FIG. 16. Utagawa Toyokuni. *The Actor Sawamura Sōjūrō III as Ashikaga Yorikuna* in the kabuki play *The Chastity of the Yoshiwara-bred Courtesan* (*Kimigatete Yoshiwara sodachi*), performed at the Miyako-za theater in the seventh lunar month, 1795. Japan. Edo Period, c. 1795. Color woodblock print. 33.4 x 22.8 cm. Arthur M. Sackler Gallery, Smithsonian Institution, Washington, DC: The Anne van Biema Collection, s2004.3.86

FIG. 17. Ray and Lois Michal (Mike) Lewis (second from right and far right) bidding at auction at Kornfeld & Klipstein, Bern, Switzerland. June 1973. Photo: Kurt Blum fotograf swb bern, Courtesy of Jan Lewis Slavid

Toyokuni of Sawamura Sōjūrō III as Ashikaga Yorikuna, in a kabuki play performed at the Miyako-za theater in the seventh lunar month of 1795. The print went to Anne van Biema (1915–2004), who donated it to the Arthur M. Sackler Gallery in Washington, DC (fig. 16). (In Ann Yonemura's *Masterful Illusions: Japanese Prints in the Anne van Biema Collection,* 101, Julie Nelson Davis describes the "spectacular pattern" of the actor's wide-sleeved robe as expressive of the luxury enjoyed by the character in the play, the Ashikaga shogun.) I loved the print in 1972 when I bought it at the Hans Popper sale (lot 241), and I loved it when I sold it fifteen years later at Christie's. But like the incomplete Toyokuni *Sōjūrō III* that I returned to Koscherak in 1964, it appears to lack color on the inner robe, on the fan and on the *tabi* socks. This design might have been made for *Images of Actors on Stage,* but I have not located another impression, with or without additional color or a title cartouche. Seeing it now in the van Biema catalogue, after all these years, I wish I had kept it.

Raymond Lewis

At the same time as I was communicating with Roland Koscherak in April 1964, I also tried to initiate a relationship with Raymond Lewis (1923–2005) of R. E. Lewis, Inc. in San Francisco (fig. 17). I suppose I had heard of Ray from Peggie Gentles at the Art Institute or from Mary Diamond at Mori Gallery. I must have telephoned Ray, because he wrote on April 14 to say he had sent me seven prints that day by REA Express: three Sukenobu book pages; three Katsukawa–school small, narrow prints (*hosoban*) of actors; and an Eisui image of lovers. Prices ranged from $10 to $225. In less than a week, I returned all seven and wrote to Ray as to why I had rejected them. That letter is still an embarrassment to me: I claimed that I did not want Sukenobu book pages—when they were exactly what I had asked for; I misidentified a "Shunshō" as a "Shunkō"; and I questioned whether some of the prints had been "washed." I was way off base. In his response, Ray suggested, very politely, that "if you are out this way it would be good if you could see what we have at the time. . . . Otherwise I think that at this distance our exchanges are likely to be more frustrating than rewarding." It was not until October 1972, some eight years later, that I bought a print from Ray—and what a print! But more on that later.

Roger Bluett

Late 1963 through early 1964 was frenetic. Mary Diamond had given me an extra copy of the 1963 Mellor catalogue and encouraged me to subscribe to auction catalogues from Sotheby & Co. in London. I bought four prints from E. Weyhe on Lexington Avenue in New York (publishers of three of the five volumes comprising the Ledoux

Collection catalogues), none of which remain in my collection. I bought six prints from Mary Diamond, along with a hanging-scroll painting of a lone boatman on a raft, signed "Hiroshige"—later rejected by various cognoscenti as not being the work of Hiroshige. (I later sold it at auction.) Of the several ukiyo-e I bought from Mary, only two, a Shunshō of Ichikawa Yaozō II and a Sukenobu book illustration of a girl playing with a cat, remain with me (figs. 18, 19).

In the summer of 1964, I traveled to London hoping to purchase a few prints. For reference, I brought along the Sotheby's Mellor catalogue. I visited Bluett & Sons, active buyers at the Mellor sale, hoping to find Mellor prints. And I did. Roger Bluett (1925–2000), the third generation of his family in the business, sold me an Okumura Toshinobu image of three beauties, each representing one of the great cities of Japan: Edo, Kyoto and Osaka. This "lacquer picture" (*urushi-e*), lot 8 in the Mellor catalogue, was expertly hand colored and embellished with brass filings. But the print was heavily darkened and toned and the poses of the beauties, while traditional, were rather stiff. Eventually, I disposed of it. I continued to have some contact with Bluett's, and the firm acted for me in a number of Sotheby's sales in London over the next few years.

Robert Sawers

On the 1964 trip to London, I also visited Kegan Paul in Russell Square. That firm was also active in the Mellor auction, but Robert Sawers, their newly hired manager, told me their print stock was in disarray. Contemporary works were mixed with old, genuine ones and facsimiles. Bob was reluctant to show anything, and I was hesitant to root around in stacks of prints containing reproductions. But I made a new friend and the relationship with Bob has lasted to this day (fig. 20). Everyone in the ukiyo-e and antique book worlds knows him as an enthusiast and expert source for good material. I once asked Sam Fogg, a London dealer in Medieval and Islamic art, if he knew Bob. Sam smiled and reminisced that, when they were both young, they would visit Sotheby's to "buy a book for a pound in the morning and sell it for two pounds in the afternoon."

I am not certain when Bob made his first trip to Chicago. However, in the summer of 1967, he accompanied Giuseppe Eskenazi to see the Cottle Collection of Chinese antiquities. (As I mentioned earlier, Eskenazi sold the Cottle Collection six years later.) In the fall, I called Bob in London, asking that he send on approval several prints I'd seen in a Kegan Paul catalogue he left with the Cottles. Bob told me, years later, that my phone call was the first he had received from America!

FIG. 18. Katsukawa Shunshō (1743?–1793). *The Actor Ichikawa Yaozō II in an undetermined role.* Japan. Edo period, c. 1768. Color woodblock print. 32.5 x 15.1 cm. The Mann Collection, acquired March 14, 1964

FIG. 19. Nishikawa Sukenobu (1671–1750). *Girl Playing with a Cat,* from *River Grasses, a Picture Book* (*Ehon kawanagusa*). Japan. Edo period, 1747. Woodblock-printed book illustration with hand coloring. 23.3 x 12.8 cm . The Mann Collection, acquired March 14, 1964

FIG. 20. Bob Sawers at the exhibition of the Mann Collection, Ōta Memorial Museum, Tokyo, in October 1994. The print, once owned by Sawers, is by Katsukawa Shunkō (1743–1812) of the actor Matsumoto Kōshirō IV as the sumo wrestler Kaminari Tsurunosuke (see Mann catalogue no. 51).

Bob posted three prints from London in a thick package wrapped in waxy water-proof paper. The individual sheets were matted, the mats wrapped in thick plastic sheeting secured with waterproof tape. Around them were stiff Masonite boards stuck together with more tape. The shipping documents declared a very low valuation on the contents to minimize the likelihood a customs agent would open the package. The risk, of course, was not the possibility of incurring import duties (as works of art, prints could be imported into the U.S. without duty), but the possibility of damage. Sawers and other dealers with whom I traded were very comfortable sending prints by mail, and I never suffered any loss or damage from shipments, whether by government post or private service. That said, Bob told me he once rolled an important pillar print into a four-inch cylinder and placed it in an empty toilet-tissue tube for safe keeping. He left it on the dresser in his hotel room, where the diligent maid tossed out the roller (and the pillar print), assuming it was trash.

Of the prints from Bob, one I donated to The Art Institute of Chicago and two remain in my collection. I am very fond of the compelling image he offered from the Mellor Collection of a fierce tiger stalking past bamboo that was attributed later to Nishimura Shigenaga (fig. 21). I have come across two variants, one in the Art Institute and one from the collection of Otto Riese (1894–1977), now in the Museum Ange-wandte Kunst in Frankfurt (figs. 22 and 23). Because the hand coloring of early prints is often quite variable, these differences did not concern me and, at the time, I did not notice any others.

Almost ten years later, in June 1976, Roger Keyes wrote to me from Lausanne, where he was cataloguing Dr. Riese's collection. Roger recalled that the bamboo

FIG. 21. Attributed to Nishimura Shigenaga (c. 1697–1756). *Bamboo and Tiger*. Japan. Edo period, c. 1725. Woodblock print with hand coloring. 32.5 x 15.4 cm. The Mann Collection, acquired October 23, 1967

OPPOSITE: FIG. 22. Attributed to Nishimura Shigenaga. *Bamboo and Tiger*. Japan. Edo period, c. 1725. Woodblock print with hand coloring and lacquerlike embellishment. 33.5 x 15.4 cm. Ex Otto Riese Collection © Museum Angewandte Kunst, Frankfurt am Main. Photo: Uwe Dettmar

The most noticeable variation among the three prints of *Bamboo and Tiger* is in the coloring of the bamboo: the Riese print has a stylized cloud and brushstrokes above the tiger's head; the Art Institute version has added bamboo leaves.

FIG. 23. Attributed to Nishimura Shigenaga. *Bamboo and Tiger*. Japan. Edo period, c. 1725. Woodblock print with hand coloring and lacquerlike embellishment. 29.9 x 14.7 cm. The Art Institute of Chicago, Clarence Buckingham Collection, 1925.1953

leaves at the tops of the Riese and Mann versions are the same, but clearly differ from the leaves on the one in the Art Institute. He postulated that my print and the Riese example were made from recut blocks and that the Art Institute's was the original state. Concerned, I took my print to Osamu Ueda (1928–2011), then the Keeper of The Clarence Buckingham Collection of Japanese Prints at the Art Institute.[7] On the light box we saw immediately that the top inch or so of the Art Institute version is a melded restoration imperceptible to the naked eye, on which the restorer had painted bamboo leaves that do not match those in the other two undamaged impressions. Relieved, I wrote Roger with the good news.

嵐雛助

流光齋英昌

34

The second print from Bob Sawers that I kept is by Ryūkōsai Eishō, now considered a different artist from Ryūkōsai Jokei (act. 1776–1809) (fig. 24 and cat. nos. 154–159). I find Ryūkōsai work fascinating—the faces are so individual and expressive, like Sharaku's dramatic "large heads."

AN ALTERED EROTIC PRINT

In June 1969, Bob Sawers, on another of his by then frequent trips to Chicago, offered me a striking erotic image (*shunga*) of a young samurai embracing a courtesan, with an attendant watching (figs. 25a, b). The intimacy of the couple is so intense that it is difficult to see where the designs on the robes of one figure separate from those on the other in the pyramidal arrangement. I jumped at the opportunity to buy my first Sugimura Jihei, one I had never found reproduced in references available to me.

OPPOSITE: FIG. 24. Ryūkōsai Eishō (act. mid-1790s?–early 1830s?). *The Actor Arashi Hinasuke II* in an undetermined role. Japan. Edo period, c. 1796–1801. Woodblock print with stenciled coloring. 29.6 x 18 cm. The Mann Collection, acquired October 31, 1967

FIG. 25a. Attributed to Sugimura Jihei (act. c. 1681–98). *Samurai Embracing a Courtesan, Observed.* Japan. Edo period, 1690s. Woodblock print. 27 x 37.2 cm. The Mann Collection, acquired June 24, 1969

FIG. 25b. Detail of the alteration

Donald Jenkins (b. 1931), who had succeeded Peggie Gentles in 1969 as the associate curator of Oriental Art and the keeper of The Clarence Buckingham Collection of Japanese Prints, was equally taken with it (fig. 26). Later that year, Richard Lane (1926–2002), the enigmatic American scholar who lived in Kyoto and was devoted to the study of early ukiyo-e, with an emphasis on *shunga*, came to see my prints on a rare trip to Chicago.[8] It's possible he came to confer with Jenkins on the catalogue for the upcoming (1971) "Primitives" symposium at the museum. When Lane examined the Sugimura Jihei at my apartment, he never let on about the extreme "conservation" that I was yet to uncover, although I suspect he was well aware of it.[9]

In the fall of 1970, Donald Jenkins told me he had just seen another example of the Sugimura Jihei in Japan that was "significantly different" from mine. Back to the lightbox and jeweler's loupe. Donald's discovery of an unexpurgated design made us realize that the paper fibers outlining the genitalia on the image I bought had been shaved, and the courtesan's robe had been painted in to mask the change (see figure 25a above). In a letter to Bob Sawers on November 18, 1970, I expressed my dilemma: Do I keep a doctored print or return it? I concluded that if Louis Ledoux chose to publish his similarly altered Sugimura Jihei—he calls it "made more suitable for exhibition"—it was fine for *me* to own one, as well.[10]

A TOYOKUNI BEAUTY EMERGING FROM HER BATH

At the June 28, 1972 Sotheby's, London sale *Fine Japanese Colour Prints,* which I did not attend, Bob Sawers, on my behalf, bought lot 65, an atmospheric Toyokuni of a young woman behind a bamboo blind after her bath, a picture alluding to the famous poet Ono no Komachi (fig. 27). Outside is a lacquered black night sky, sprinkled with

FIG. 27. Utagawa Toyokuni. *Komachi Washing the Manuscript* (*Sōshi arai Komachi*), alluding to the "manuscript-washing" episode (*Sōshi arai Komachi*), one of seven episodes associated with the Heian-period poet Ono no Komachi, from the series *Fashionably Casual Images of the Seven Komachi* (*Fūryū Nana Komachi yatsushi sugata-e*). Japan. Edo period, c. 1790. Color woodblock print. 35.9 x 24.1 cm. Photo from *Ukiyoe taikei*, vol. 9 (1975), no. 2

Bob Sawers purchased this print at a Sotheby's, London auction in 1972, on George Mann's behalf, but Mann returned it to Sawers, who sold it to another collector. It was published three years later in *Ukiyoe taikei* (Compendium of ukiyo-e). The seal of the collector Alexis Rouart (1839–1911) is in the lower right.

mother-of-pearl (*aogai*) simulating stars. The print, formerly in the Rouart Collection, looked compelling in the black-and-white catalogue illustration. When I received it from Bob by mail, I was less sure. "I am a little bit leery of the lacquer and mother-of-pearl on the Toyokuni," I wrote him. "By the way, I was a little shocked at the price we had to pay . . . and I would bet that had I been present I would not have gone that high." The hammer price of £1600 ($3,985 at the then current exchange rates) was high indeed for a Toyokuni at that time. Bob graciously took it back and easily sold it. Looking back, I am amazed I rejected it. In the intervening forty-five years, I have seen only one other impression—in poor condition.

As a footnote to my long association with Bob Sawers, I might mention that he loved playing golf (and drinking fine burgundies) almost as much as he loved buying, selling and talking about ukiyo-e. In the fall of 1977, he accompanied his good friend, the artist Gordon House, to the States. Gordon, a successful graphic designer, was responsible for the record cover of *The White Album* and the back cover of *Sgt. Pepper's*, both by the Beatles. He was showing his prints and paintings in various cities and had come to Chicago with Bob to see the installation of his work at the van Straaten Gallery. Bob relayed that he and Gordon "fancied" a round of golf, so I entertained them at Bryn Mawr Country Club one afternoon. It rained so hard that we dubbed our game "Shōno Golf" after the well-known print by Hiroshige, *Driving Rain, Shōno* (Mann catalogue no. 126). From London, Gordon sent a thank-you note with his take on our Shōno experience (fig. 28).

Passing on a Kanbun Beauty

Another great friend of Bob Sawers was David Newman (1936–2012), a London dealer in Japanese art who enjoyed a reputation as a charmer, always up for a drink and a laugh. He and his wife, Paula, lived in a quirky apartment on Sackville Street, off Piccadilly, and they seemed to lead a rather carefree life. I probably met David in

Date
8 October 77

Ref

Gordon House
109 Highbury New Park
Islington
London N5 2HG

01 359 2040

Mr & Mrs.
H George Mann
107 Deere Park Drive South
Highland Park
Illinois
60035

Kindly reproduced by permission of R. Sanders, London Collection.

From the last Tōkaido (Bryn Mawr) set .   Dwarf Oban (small) .   Wet September 1977

A storm at Shōno American style.

The figure on the right shows Sawers-san taking a shaky ⑥ iron shot through "Bryn Mawr's" famous differing planes of wind blown bamboo which show the variety of grey only seen in really poor impressions of this print.

Running towards the final green can be seen the two club champions of days long gone by, Mann-san, colleague (manufacturer of bamboo furniture) and one soaked caddy (unknown).

It should be noted that the trimmed censors seal on the lower left hand margin depicts also one of the many golf balls gone astray that day.

The name of the club seen on the roof at the right is omitted in the second edition.

In Thanks to Mr & Mrs Mann for their kindness. gordon House

FIG. 29. *Standing Beauty.* Japan. Edo period, c. 1656–78. Hanging scroll; ink, color and gold on paper. 145.8 x 39.6 cm. The Art Institute of Chicago, Frederick W. and Nathalie C. Gookin Endowment, 1989.207

London in the 1970s. The Newmans often joined us for dinners—when Roberta and I were in London or when they visited Chicago.

David did not deal in Japanese prints, but did handle ukiyo-e paintings. On one of his regular trips to Chicago to see James Alsdorf (1913–1990), Chairman of the Board of Trustees of the Art Institute from 1975 to 1978, and his wife, Marilynn (1926–2019), David showed me a photograph of a Kanbun-era hanging scroll of a standing beauty (*bijin*). This was not for the Alsdorfs, so I had a chance at it. I was taken by it, but did not feel comfortable pulling the trigger.[11]

Instead, I gave the photograph to the associate curator of Oriental Art at the Art Institute, Yutaka Mino (b. 1941), but never heard back. About a year later, Yutaka presented the painting to the Committee on Asian Art, and the purchase was approved (fig. 29). On July 23, 1989, David sent me this characteristic note:

> Dear George,
> A belated thank you for your part in bringing the Kanbun
> *bijin* to the attention of the Institute, and its subsequent acquisition. I hope this
> is the beginning of a new period, as past efforts of mine and others always fell on
> stoney ground with *ancien régime!* . . .
> Again, many thanks, yours as ever,
>
> David and Paula

Janette Ostier

Following my visits to Bluett's and Kegan Paul in 1964, I left for Paris. There, I visited the gallery of Janette Ostier (1921–2014), another dealer active at the Mellor sale. Located in the elegant Place des Vosges (the oldest planned square in Paris), the shop was everything one would expect to find in a classic French gallery of Japanese art. It was small and cluttered with paintings, furniture, lacquer and other objects in every corner and on every surface. Until the 1980s, Sotheby's, London, published the names or code names of buyers in the price lists circulated after auctions, so I knew that Mme. Ostier had purchased prints in the Mellor sale, which was much my focus at the time. She acquired a bust portrait of Segawa Kikunojō III in the role of the fox maiden, Okyaku, disguised as a wet nurse (Mellor catalogue lot 314). When I went to her shop, she offered it to me for $800, about 30 percent above the price of $616 she had paid for the print. In my naiveté, I decided the markup was excessive and declined. In 1970, I found another impression (not nearly as bright and fresh as the

Mellor/Ostier one), which I bought for three times her asking price and almost four times the hammer price for the print in the Mellor sale (Mann catalogue no. 87).

Finding Roberta

As mentioned earlier, after Columbia Law School, I joined McDermott Will & Emery, a midsize Chicago law firm, where I specialized in corporate and securities law. In 1968, I became an income partner and two years later, an equity partner. Eventually, I was appointed to the Management Committee and then to the chairmanship of the corporate and securities group and held various other positions there until my retirement in 2001. The firm grew from forty-one lawyers when I joined to over a thousand, and from a single office in Chicago to offices in ten cities around the world. I had been in practice for two years when I first met Roberta Lee Goldman Malkin (b. 1941).

Roberta and I knew each other from the golf club where my family and Roberta's first husband and his family were members, and where Bob Sawers, Gordon House and I were to play golf in the rain. Roberta says she became aware of me when she heard I had driven a motorcycle through a window at the club on July 4, 1963. I had

FIG. 30. Suzuki Harunobu (1725?–1770). *Young Man Writing a Poem under a Maple Tree.* Japan. Edo period, 1760s. Color woodblock print. 28.3 x 21.5 cm . The Mann Collection, acquired October 5, 1972

This image is an allusive picture (*mitate-e*) to a classical theme updated with Edo-period figures. The man is writing a line from a poem by the eighth-century Chinese poet Bai Juyi that is a remembrance of heating wine in a heap of burning maple leaves and brushing away green moss to inscribe poems on rocks. For the poem, see Mann catalogue no. 35.

been celebrating the holiday by trying to learn to drive a "big bike," but lost control. Although I suffered a lot of damage to my pride (and some wounds that required stitches), I was back at work in a few days, but the country-club window and the motorcycle were wrecks.

At that time, Roberta and I led different lives. She was married by age twenty-one, and, when I had my motorcycle "accident" in 1963, her first child was on the way. I was a twenty-six-year-old bachelor, devoting most of my time to practicing law. Roberta is bright, warm, charitable, patient, refined and beautiful. Her daughters, Debbie, Julie and Liz, were born in 1963, 1965 and 1967, respectively. Roberta and her husband separated in 1969 and divorced in 1971. Later that year, Roberta and I had our first date.

From time to time, I had Sunday evening dinner with Roberta and the girls at the club or at "child-friendly" restaurants near her home in Skokie, north of Chicago. I lived in a high-rise apartment building on Lakeshore Drive, about fifteen miles away. It was important to me to develop a relationship with the girls, and I treated them with genuine affection and interest. Julie, about eight years old, was particularly shy and unapproachable. At one dinner, I casually folded a piece of paper into an origami bird while Julie watched with singular concentration. When I finished, I asked her, softly, if she would like the bird and she nodded "yes." That was our first communication and it seemed to have broken the ice. I remember showing prints to Roberta and the girls. Liz particularly liked a recent purchase from the Popper sale in 1972 of a Harunobu—a young man writing a poem under a maple tree—because of the color of the leaves (fig. 30).

Roberta and I married on July 1, 1973 (fig. 31). About a month after the wedding, we moved to a 1939 vintage house in Highland Park, a suburb twenty-five miles north of my office in downtown Chicago. Suddenly (it seemed), I was living a dramatically changed life. In a period of three years, I had gone from a bachelor in a one-bedroom apartment, where my monthly electric bill was $9, to "married with children" in a five-bedroom house in Highland Park, where my monthly electric bill was considerably greater. I was balancing constantly demanding career matters with family matters, which were even more consuming. Our son, David, was born in 1975.

And, oh yes, ukiyo-e.

Gerli Sale, 1971

I must backtrack a bit here.

The sale at Sotheby's, New York, on April 28, 1971, of the Japanese print collection of Paolino Gerli (1890–1982), an importer of Italian textiles, was an extraordinary event for me, because it was the first auction I attended. It was there that I met Richard Pillsbury Gale (1900–1973), the great Minneapolis collector whose prints are now at the Minneapolis Institute of Art (fig. 32). Bob Sawers introduced me to Amy Poster, then the curator and chair of the Department of Asian Art at the Brooklyn Museum, and her husband, Robert (Bob) Poster, and we have been close friends since (fig. 33).

The Gerli sale was also the first U.S. auction "everybody's guru," Nishi Saijū, attended. Harry G. C. Packard (1915–1991), Nishi's good friend and associate, accompanied him. Packard was an American contractor who settled in Japan after World War II and developed expertise in Japanese art. In 1975, he sold and donated an astounding four hundred pieces to The Metropolitan Museum of Art in New York.[12]

FIG. 31. George and Roberta Mann wedding, July 1, 1973. George with (left to right) Liz, Roberta, Julie and Debbie. Photo: Arthur Shay, Deerfield, IL

Among the other leading ukiyo-e dealers at the sale were Huguette Berès (1913–1999) and David Caplan (b. 1934). Berès, Caplan, Nishi and Sawers, collectively referred to by auction-house staff as "The Ring," customarily sat together at sales, usually in the front row, and rarely were seen bidding against one another.

In the morning session of the Gerli sale, I sat with Dick Gale, my new acquaintance. I asked what he thought of the very first lot: an oversize perspective print of a brothel in the Yoshiwara pleasure district, by Okumura Masanobu (fig. 34). Donald Jenkins had viewed it before the sale and described it as "grubby" in a letter to me of April 16, 1971. Gale's reaction was lukewarm. I have located several others of this

design, including those in the Museum of Fine Arts, Boston (06.1002), and the Museum für Kunst und Gewerbe, Hamburg (Inv. IE. 1900,32), reproduced by Rose Hempel in *Japanische Holzschnitte* (1961), no. 6. None approaches the quality or condition of the Gerli Masanobu. I was thrilled when it was knocked down to me and continue to be whenever I look at it.

Also at the Gerli sale, perhaps for the first time, I considered buying a *Fine Wind, Clear Morning* (*Gaifū kaisei*), or "Red Fuji," Hokusai's most celebrated image of that mountain. Before the auction, Bob Sawers had offered me a very nice one: full size, without a center fold, with good, not super, rust color. But, based on the Sotheby's estimate (and the fact that the Gerli Red Fuji had a "very faint centerfold"), I thought I could buy the Gerli print for less than the $2,500 Bob was asking for his. To my dismay, the Gerli print sold for $4,000. I approached Bob after the sale and agreed to his original price. Always the astute businessman, Bob responded that in light of the price realized for the Gerli print, he was raising the price of his. Foolishly, I declined. On March 19, 2019, a Red Fuji sold for $507,000 at Christie's, New York—and that was not even the highest price paid for that image.

I have had countless opportunities during the past fifty years or so to acquire a Red Fuji and continue to mention its elusiveness in these pages because I am still kicking myself for the chances missed to acquire what the Japanese consider the prize Hokusai print. At the Louis Black sale at Sotheby's in 1976, I sat alongside Ray Lewis, who was acting as my agent. When Black's glorious Red Fuji came up, Ray jabbed me, "You should buy that!" The cartouche was very clear and the coloration on the mountain a pinkish red, although the print had a slight center fold from being mounted in an album. I accepted the catalogue description that the softly colored red was "faded," and I did not bid. It went, for what I recall as $25,000, to the savvier Nishi Saijū for his "very best friend"—himself. At the time, I was unaware of the subtle differences among the various states of this powerful design. Years later, I learned from Roger Keyes that the few known examples, like Black's, with a pinkish mountain and soft green trees at the base, showing no evidence of the swirl marks made by the printer's *baren* tool, are the most desirable. [13]

FIG. 32. Richard P. Gale. Minneapolis Institute of Art Archives

FIG. 33. Roberta Mann (far left), Bob Sawers, Amy and Bob Poster at dinner in New York City after a Christie's sale, autumn 1988

東武大和絵画工

蒔月堂丹鳥齋

奥村文角政信正筆

FIG. 34. Okumura Masanobu (1686–1764). *Large Perspective Picture of a Second-floor Parlor in the New Yoshiwara, Looking toward the Embankment* (*Shin Yoshiwara nikai zashiki dote o mitōshi ō-uki-e*). Japan. Edo period, c. 1745. Woodblock print with hand coloring. 41.9 x 65.6 cm. The Mann Collection, acquired April 28, 1971

新吉原堂二階座敷古平見通 大浮絵

通塩町赤本問屋草十下 奥村屋源六板元

Conference on Ukiyo-e Primitives

The symposium on ukiyo-e "Primitives," held at The Art Institute of Chicago, November 4, 5 and 6, 1971, was another turning point for me. The speakers comprised many of the most important ukiyo-e scholars of the day: Jack Hillier (1912–1995), Roger Keyes, Richard Lane, Narazaki Muneshige (1903–2001), Shibui Kiyoshi (1899–1992), Suzuki Jūzō (1919–2010), Harold P. ("Phil") Stern (1922–1977) and David Waterhouse (1936–2017) (fig. 35). I attended all of the presentations. Remarks in Japanese by Narazaki, Shibui and Suzuki were accompanied by abbreviated (and cryptic) summaries in English. As he had done in 1969, Lane came to my apartment a few miles from the Art Institute and commented on my small but growing collection of about forty prints. On that second visit, Lane offered me an unsigned Sukenobu image of a courtesan and a client under a padded bedding kimono (fig. 36). More than forty years later, in the 2013–14 exhibition "Shunga: Sex and Pleasure in Japanese Art," the British Museum exhibited two other erotic designs attributed to Sukenobu, both similar in color and size to mine, both of which are reproduced here (figs. 37 and 38). I believe all three prints came from the same folding album.

FIG. 35. Jack Hillier in the office of Yu-Ying Brown at the British Library, looking at the British Library copy of *Twelve Specimens of Celebrated Flowers* (*Meika jūnishu*) by Ōoka Shunboku (1680–1763). December 1994. Photo: Yu-Ying Brown, former Head of the Japanese Collection, the British Library

Yu-Ying Brown writes that "The book is very rare, probably a unique surviving copy. Jack saw it for the first time when the photo was taken in 1994."

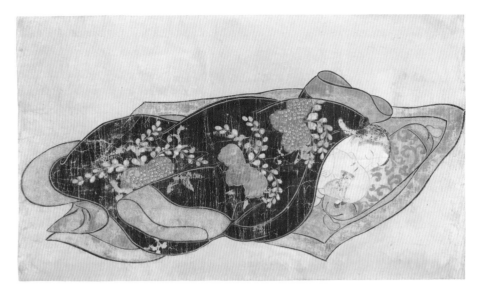

FIG. 36. Attributed to Nishikawa Sukenobu. *Couple Entwined in a Bedding Kimono* (*yogi*). Japan. Edo period, c. 1711–16. Woodblock print with hand coloring. 26.1 x 42 cm. The Mann Collection, acquired November 15, 1971

FIG. 37. Attributed to Nishikawa Sukenobu. Untitled erotic print. Japan. Edo period, c. 1711–16. Color woodblock print. 26.1 x 37.7 cm. The British Museum, Asia, 1985, 1022,0.1

The British Museum catalogue *Shunga: Sex and Pleasure in Japanese Art* (2013) includes the following observation on page 144: "Sukenobu's particular strength was the power of his delicately flowing drapery lines. While the drapery lines drawn by Edo artists of *shunga* in the same period are simple and forceful, Sukenobu draws much softer lines that flow in a more complicated manner. While they may not have the sense of dynamic action and power seen in Edo *shunga*, they instead show a fine delicacy that suggests more nuanced actions of the couple in the bedroom."

FIG. 38. Attributed to Nishikawa Sukenobu. Untitled erotic print. Japan. Edo period, c. 1711–16. Color woodblock print. 26 x 37.6 cm. Michael Fornitz Collection, Copenhagen

Organized by Donald Jenkins, who wrote an erudite accompanying catalogue, "Ukiyo-e Prints and Paintings: The Primitive Period 1680–1745: An Exhibition in Memory of Margaret O. Gentles" opened on November 6, 1971. Lenders included The Art Institute of Chicago, the Tokyo National Museum, The Metropolitan Museum of Art, New York, the Honolulu Academy of Arts, Walter Amstutz (1902–1992), Theodore Scheiwe (1897–1983), Huguette Berès, Richard P. Gale, Hans Popper (1904–1971) and others. I loaned my "altered" Sugimura and a Masanobu actor print (fig. 39). Donald Jenkins selected the Masanobu because it is an earlier state of two other impressions in The Art Institute of Chicago (figs. 40 and 41). An impression of yet another state, from the Huguette Berès Collection, was sold at Sotheby's, Paris on November 25, 2003 (lot 112) (fig. 42). For me, it is fascinating to examine the prints side by side to posit the order in which they were issued.

After the symposium and exhibition closed, I became increasingly committed to ukiyo-e. I felt secure in my position at my law firm and in the community. In tandem with my intent to achieve optimum results for my clients in a variety of financial transactions, I wanted to move to a different and more rewarding level as a collector. Earlier in 1971, at the Gerli sale, I had participated "live" for the first time in an auction, not through an agent. I felt a rush of satisfaction each time the hammer came down

OPPOSITE: FIG. 39. Okumura Masanobu. *The Actors Sanjō Kantarō II as Osome and Ichikawa Monnosuke I as Hisamatsu* in the kabuki play *Double-suicide of the Lovers Osome and Hisamatsu in White Tie-dyed Sleeves* (*Osome Hisamatsu shinjū tamoto no shirashibori*), performed at the Morita-za theater in 1720. Japan. Edo period, c. 1720. Woodblock print with hand coloring and metallic embellishment. 34 x 16.1 cm. The Mann Collection, acquired June 13, 1968

FIG. 40. Okumura Masanobu. *The Actors Segawa Kikunojō I as Osome and Sodesaki Kikutarō as Hisamatsu* in the kabuki play *Double-suicide of the Lovers Osome and Hisamatsu* (*Osome Hisamatsu shinjū*), performed at the Nakamura-za theater in the sixth lunar month in 1731. Japan. Edo period, c. 1731. Woodblock print with hand coloring and metallic and lacquerlike embellishments. 32.3 x 15.2 cm. The Art Institute of Chicago, Clarence Buckingham Collection, 1925.1837

This print is considered to have been printed from the same blocks as the Mann image in figure 39 but has substituted crests on the kimono sleeves to capture a later performance of the same play with different actors.

ABOVE: FIG. 41. Okumura Masanobu. *The Actors Sanjō Kantarō II as Osome and Ichikawa Monnosuke I as Hisamatsu* in the kabuki play *Double-suicide of the Lovers Osome and Hisamatsu in White Tie-dyed Sleeves* (*Osome Hisamatsu shinjū tamoto no shirashibori*), performed at the Morita-za theater in 1720. Japan. Edo period, c. 1720. Woodblock print with hand coloring and metallic embellishment. 33 x 16 cm. The Art Institute of Chicago, Clarence Buckingham Collection, 1925.1838

Lacking artist's signature and seals, this print, like figure 42, is considered a pirated version of the signed and sealed Mann impression in figure 39.

FIG. 42. Okumura Masanobu. *The Actors Sanjō Kantarō II as Osome and Ichikawa Monnosuke I as Hisamatsu* in the kabuki play *Double-suicide of the Lovers Osome and Hisamatsu in White Tie-dyed Sleeves* (*Osome Hisamatsu shinjū tamoto no shirashibori*), performed at the Morita-za theater in 1720. Japan. Edo period, c. 1720. Woodblock print with hand coloring and lacquerlike and metallic embellishments. 30 x 15.6 cm. Ex coll. Huguette Berès. From the catalogue *Collection Huguette Berès: Estampes, Dessins et Livres Illustrés*, Sotheby's, Paris, November 25, 2003, lot 112

FIG. 43. Otto Riese. From Rose Hempel, *Meisterwerke des Japanische Farbholzschnitte: Die Sammlung Otto Riese* (Munich; New York: Prestel, 1993), 8

on my purchases, but in an instant the euphoria could be tempered: *"Why did I bid so high?"* *"Why did no dealer or collector outbid me?"* *"What do they know that I don't?"*

Visiting Collectors in Switzerland: Riese, Schindler and Tikotin

Intent on learning about important international collections and collectors, in August 1972, I flew to London for a few days, then on to Switzerland to visit three prominent connoisseurs. I had never met any of them, but they were all well-known in the ukiyo-e world and regularly bought important prints at auctions at high prices. Bob Sawers contacted each of them on my behalf and made appointments for me over a two-day period.

The trip is mostly a blur, because so much was compressed into such a short time. After landing in Zurich, I took a train to Lausanne to see Otto Riese, a distinguished German judge (fig. 43). Apparently, we had a misunderstanding about when I was expected, because I arrived quite late. The visit was rushed, and I have a recollection of only one print: *The Actor Sakata Hangorō III as Kaminari Shōkurō*, by Katsukawa Shun'ei, as powerful in my memory as when I saw it (fig. 44). I learned recently that it was included in the trove of Riese prints sold to the Museum Angewandte Kunst in Frankfurt around 2011, after being on loan there for several years.

FIG. 44. Katsukawa Shun'ei (c. 1762–1819). *The Actor Sakata Hangorō III as Kaminari Shōkurō.* Japan. Edo period, 1794. Color woodblock print with pinkish white mica ground. 31.9 x 22.5 cm. Ex Otto Riese Collection © Museum Angewandte Kunst, Frankfurt am Main. Photo: Uwe Dettmar.

Sakata Hangorō is playing an *otokodate*, a street tough with a chivalrous heart who defends beleaguered commoners against the Edo authorities. Schedules of kabuki performances show that this print was released two months before the "large-head" actor portraits by Sharaku in figures 47–50.

The next morning, I left for Biel. Meeting the Swiss architect Werner Schindler (1905–1986) at the train station was like a scene from a spy movie: Schindler had told me to meet him near the platform, where I would find him carrying a red rose. Then we spent a few hours looking at staggering prints at his home, but I still have no recollection of specifics.

Riese and Schindler were on an elevated plane of collecting from where I was. Looking at their published prints, I recognize, with hindsight, how great their holdings were: Sharaku, Utamaro, Harunobu, "primitives." Having assembled in a scant ten years about forty-five examples, many of them minor, I was overwhelmed by the riches I saw and questioned whether I could hope to build a collection near the depth, breadth and quality of theirs.

Tikotin's gallery of Japanese art opened in 1927 in a courtyard beyond the partially obscured sign reading "Tikotin," which can be seen above his right shoulder. To Tikotin's right, partially blocking the sign, stands Wilfrid Israel, owner of the largest department store in Berlin at the time, and to his left, William Cohn, an art historian specializing in Asian art and editor of *Ostasiatische Zeitschrift*. On the sidewalk beyond them is a Tikotin showcase that probably featured Japanese art objects, meant to draw visitors to the gallery. Tikotin left Germany in 1933. Later, Wilfred Israel was instrumental in organizing the Kindertransport that permitted ten thousand Jewish children to escape Germany after the Kristallnacht pogroms of 1938.

My last visit, to Felix Tikotin (1893–1986), was memorable in a different way. Both Riese and Schindler were pure collectors, confident in their tastes and delighted to share their pleasure with a new, young collector from America. They were very gracious hosts. Tikotin, on the other hand, was primarily a dealer, and a very shrewd and successful one at that (figs. 45 and 46). He sold Riese the Shun'ei in figure 44. In 1933, after exhibiting his collection as "Berlin representative" at the Danish Royal Palace, a well-placed friend advised him not to return his property to Berlin. He immediately settled in Amsterdam and later opened a gallery in The Hague. Patriots hid the Tikotin family when the Germans invaded the Netherlands in May 1940. He had managed to secure most of his goods and the border police later apprehended smugglers with lacquer and ceramics stolen from his shop. In 1960, Tikotin moved to Switzerland to a fine old house he named Kintoki, located in Vevey, high above Lake Geneva on Mont Pèlerin. I took a funicular up the mountain and was met at the terminus by Tikotin. After taking in the scenery, we spent the next three hours viewing small Japanese calendar prints (*egoyomi*). Tiko, as he was widely known, tried his best to sell those to me, but I did not know what they were, did not really like them and did not bite. Finally, I screwed up my courage to ask if I could see anything from his private collection. Reluctantly, after "no sale," Tiko did show me several portfolios of magnificent images by Utamaro and other artists. After a pleasant lunch, it was back down the mountain, onto a train to Zurich and by plane to Chicago the next day.

One detail from that whirlwind trip that has stayed with me is one of those little exchanges that only seem to happen when traveling alone. It was at dinner one evening when I had a desire for raspberries. I do not speak any foreign language, but somehow, I do succeed in communicating in Europe. When my waiter did not understand "raspberries," and I didn't know the German or the French word, *framboises*, I managed to summon *comme fraises*, "like strawberries," and there was a flicker of understanding. I got my raspberries and I learned *framboises*, bringing my French vocabulary to about ten words.

When I returned to Chicago from that August journey, I sent each of my hosts a small pewter dish with a miniature squirrel poised on its hind legs in the center, examining a nut. I felt the model mimicked a collector and his prize, and the gifts were very well received.

I never saw Riese or Schindler after that, but I did run into Tikotin two months later at the Popper sale in New York. Otto Riese died six years after my 1972 visit; Schindler and Tikotin fourteen years later.

Looking back at my Switzerland trip, I regret how it went. Why didn't I space out those visits to the three collectors? Why didn't I ask each of them to select five or ten prints and tell me how they came to own them; what their most memorable collecting experiences were? I wish I had taken notes! I wish I had taken photographs!

The Popper Sale: *The* Ukiyo-e Event of 1972

The next major ukiyo-e event was the great Popper sale at Sotheby's, New York, in 1972, just seventeen months after the Gerli sale. Hans Popper, the president of Western Steel and Metal Corporation, was an Austrian émigré who did business in Japan, where he purchased most of his Japanese woodblock prints starting in the 1950s, when extraordinary art was coming on the postwar market. In his introduction to the auction catalogue, Jack Hillier, an ukiyo-e specialist who consulted for Sotheby's, describes him as a "man of refined taste with a wide range of cultural activities." He was a serious violinist and friend and patron of classical musicians (just like my great friend and mentor, Maurice Cottle). At his death at sixty-six, Popper owned one of the finest ukiyo-e collections outside of Japan. "International Exhibition of Ukiyo-e Masterpieces Depicting the Manners and Customs of Old Japan," a 1964 Tokyo exhibition at the time of the Tokyo Olympics, included four hundred and thirty treasures from eighteen foreign and thirty-six Japanese collections. Seventy-one were loaned by Popper.[14]

The sale was held on October 5 and 6. The auction room was crowded, and bidding was spirited. Major collectors and dealers from the United States, Europe and Japan were in the room (and, I suspect, on the telephone), including Harry Packard, Huguette Berès, Walter Amstutz, Bob Sawers, Roger Keyes, Ray Lewis, David Caplan, Nishi Saijū, Giuseppe Eskenazi, Edith Ehrman (1932–1974), Dick Gale, John Gaines and the venerable Felix Tikotin. Over a drink with Tiko, I sought his counsel on several lots. In particular, I was interested in an enchanting Utamaro of two women preparing sushi (lot 163 in the Popper catalogue) that had been shown in the 1964 Tokyo exhibition.

The condition of the sushi scene was spectacular. I was speechless when Tiko told me that he had bought *that very impression* in the 1928 Straus-Negbaur sale in Berlin for 400 DM (about $1,680 at the 1928 exchange rate). "You must remember," he added, that in 1928, 400 DM "would pay the rent on the finest house on the finest street in Berlin for a whole year." That was the last time I saw Tiko; he died in 1986. The Utamaro sold for $9,000 (hammer), far above its estimate. On June 18, 1975, it was resold at Sotheby's, New York (lot 546) for $28,000 (hammer), but not to me.

Unfortunately, I did not buy any of the thirty-nine early prints at Popper, or any of the magnificent Utamaro, Eishi or Eishō images of beautiful women. I did come

away with two Harunobu prints—the allusive picture of a young man composing a poem under maple leaves (see figure 30) and *Evening Snow on the Floss Shaper,* from the series *The Eight Parlor Views* (Mann catalogue no. 30); a Hokusai (Mann catalogue no. 108); and a Toyokuni that I later sold, as described on pages 29–30 (figure 16).[15]

I was so new to the auction world that I still felt overwhelmed by the process; I observed at Gerli and Popper, and later at Vever, Le Véel and other sales, that in order to get the best, one must set very high limits—and then be ready to exceed them. At Popper, John Gaines paid the then unheard-of price of $18,000 for an exquisite Harunobu of *Lovers Standing in the Snow under an Umbrella* (Popper lot 53), formerly in the Ledoux Collection. The hammer price was more than three times the winning bid for the next most expensive of the twenty-four Harunobu. That set the pace for the rest of the sale; the major buyers of ukiyo-e sped up. Dick Gale bought a great impression of an iconic Masanobu (Popper lot 20), formerly in the Shibui Collection, and Hiroshige's *Naruto Whirlpool* triptych (Popper lot 310).

First Sharaku Purchase

At the conclusion of the Popper auction, I approached Ray Lewis about a print of Ichikawa Ebizō as Takamura Sadanoshin, by Tōshūsai Sharaku, number 30 in Ray's *Twentieth Anniversary Catalogue* of September 1972 (fig. 47). (Although Ray and I had not yet done any business, I had been receiving his catalogues since I first contacted him in 1964.) Ray had purchased the Sharaku at the June 28, 1972 Sotheby's, London sale, the same sale at which Bob Sawers bought the Toyokuni that I rejected of a young woman emerging from her bath (see figure 27). The Sharaku first came to the market in the Tuke sale at Sotheby's on April 4, 1911. Like all aficionados of ukiyo-e, I was familiar with the Sharaku—one of the boldest and most famous of the actor bust portraits, or "large heads" (*okubi-e*). Although I read the entry in Ray's catalogue with appetite, I held off in advance of the Popper sale, as there were twenty or so lots in which I was interested. Being somewhat disappointed by my limited success at Popper, I immediately decided to buy the Ebizō "large head" from Ray, who seemed genuinely excited that I wanted it.

The print had a heavy lacquerlike black coating on Ebizō's hair, particularly on his left sideburn and above his left ear. The lacquering had caused the paper to pucker (fig. 48). Roger Keyes (then working for Ray in San Francisco) suggested that his wife, Keiko Mizushima Keyes (1939–1989), a highly respected paper conservator, could flatten the image. A few weeks later, Ray and Roger let me know that in the

OPPOSITE: FIG. 47. Tōshūsai Sharaku (act. 1794–95). *The Actor Ichikawa Ebizō as Takamura Sadanoshin,* a father driven to suicide by the disgrace of his daughter, in the kabuki play *The Beloved Wife's Particolored Leading Rope* (*Koi nyōbō somewake tazuna*), performed at the Kawarazaki-za theater in the fifth lunar month, 1794. Japan. Edo Period, 1794. Color woodblock print with lacquerlike embellishment and mica ground. 38.4 x 25.4 cm. The Mann Collection, acquired October 18, 1972

FIG. 48. Tōshūsai Sharaku. *The Actor Ichikawa Ebizō as Takamura Sadanoshin,* with puckered lacquering on the hair, before restoration. Sold Sotheby's, London, June 28, 1972, *Fine Japanese Colour Prints, Chinese and Japanese Paintings, Including the Property of Various Owners,* lot 111, pl. XI. Ex coll. Samuel Tuke. Photo from Sotheby's catalogue

FIG. 49. Tōshūsai Sharaku. *The Actor Sakata Hangorō III as the Villain Fujikawa Mizuemon* in the kabuki play *The Iris Soga of the Bunroku Era* (*Hana-ayame Bunroku Soga*), performed at the Miyako-za theater in the fifth lunar month, 1794. Japan. Edo Period, 1794. Color woodblock print with mica ground. 38.9 x 25.3 cm. The Mann Collection, acquired December 3, 1982

flattening process, dirt under the mica applied to the paper had congealed into a latticework pattern, but that the mica ground was still entirely intact. Did I still want the print? If not, Ray was prepared to fully refund my payment. I don't think I hesitated for a moment and, to this day, I am grateful that I kept it. The Sharaku has been widely exhibited since I bought it and remains one of my favorites in the collection.

I'm not sure when Sharaku first fascinated me—perhaps when Mary Diamond gave me her extra Mellor sale catalogue. Four Sharaku portraits in that 1963 sale fetched high prices. The most expensive went to Otto Riese for £1700 ($4,760, lot 290): Ichikawa Omezō as Ippei in *The Beloved Wife's Particolored Leading Rope* (*Koi nyōbō somewake tazuna*). From my earliest days as a collector, I was aware of the lure of that preeminent artist. As first expressed in *Ukiyo-e ruikō* (Various thoughts on ukiyo-e) in the late eighteenth or early nineteenth century, in an attempt to capture the true character of kabuki actors, Sharaku portrayed them as caricatures, and not in accordance with standard modes. The conventional wisdom is that this aspect of Sharaku's portraits offended collectors and is the reason why Sharaku's career seems to have lasted less than a year. In my view, however, had that been the case, we would not have so many Sharaku prints surviving to this day. If, as some suggest, only fifty or so of each of the twenty-eight mica-ground early masterpieces were made, why have as many as thirty-five of them survived? I choose to believe that they survived because they were *always* treasured and protected, not because they were rejected and hidden away.

Sharaku is one of the great and enduring mysteries of ukiyo-e. No one has determined his real name, where he came from, or where he went after his nine-month burst of activity ended in the spring of 1795 with more than one hundred forty known designs. We own four of his mica-ground actor portraits (figs. 47, 49 and 50 and see figure 108, which comes later).

Coincident with the Popper auction in October 1972, an exhibition commemorating the twenty-fifth anniversary of the death of Louis V. Ledoux was mounted at Japan House Gallery in New York, with a catalogue by Donald Jenkins (see figure 26). Most lenders of the sixty-two prints were identified, including me. I was in illustrious

FIG. 50. Tōshūsai Sharaku. *The Actor Matsumoto Kōshirō IV as the Fishmonger Gorobei* in the ballad-drama *The Iris Hair-ornament of Remembrance* (*Hana-ayame omoi no kanzashi*), an interlude in the kabuki play *A Medley of Tales of Revenge* (*Katakiuchi noriai-banashi*), performed at the Kiri-za theater in the fifth lunar month, 1794. Japan. Edo period, 1794. Color woodblock print with mica ground. 37.3 x 24.8 cm. The Mann Collection, acquired December 15, 1979

company: The Metropolitan Museum of Art, New York; Richard Gale; The Art Institute of Chicago; Roland Koscherak; John Gaines; the New York Public Library; and Edith Ehrman. Ruth Stephan Franklin (1910–1974) loaned an elegant Harunobu of a woman on a veranda, as well as a very rare portrait of the writer Santō Kyōden (1761–1816), by Chōkyōsai Eiri (active 1790s to early 1800s). Three years later, after the Louis Black sale in 1976, I wrote to Mrs. Franklin to inquire whether she would consider parting with "Woman on a Veranda." Her son, John J. Stephan, replied, saying his mother had died in 1974 and that the family planned to place her prints on loan to the Hono-lulu Academy of Arts. I have not pursued that beauty further.

Underbidder Limbo:
Henri Vever Sale, 1974

In 1974, Sotheby's announced that the ukiyo-e collection formed by the French designer of art nouveau jewelry, Henri Vever (1854–1943), would be sold at auction in London, with the first tranche of about four hundred lots to be offered on March 26. The highly detailed catalogue, compiled by Jack Hillier, arrived well before the sale date and I immediately started planning. I studied the cata-logue entries and the estimates endlessly, arriving at an extensive prioritized "wish list," made credit arrangements and booked travel. Roberta and I, married less than a year, planned to stay about a week in London. I asked Bob Sawers and Mia McCauley, Bob's future wife, to help organize a dinner party on March 22 at the White House Restaurant in Regents Park. About fifteen people joined us, including Bob and Mia; Jane McAusland, Bob's good friend, who did substantially all of Bob's conservation work when not working on the Queen's prints and drawings; Neil Davey (b. 1941) of the Japanese department, Sotheby's, London and a firm director and auctioneer; Jack Hillier and his wife, Mary; Giuseppe Eskenazi and his wife, Laura; Heinz Kaempfer (1904–1986) the former chairman of the Dutch Society for Japanese Arts and a *suri-mono* collector of renown and his wife, Eva; Ray Lewis; and Roger Keyes and his wife, Keiko. The dinner was an opportunity to introduce Roberta to many of my "ukiyo-e friends." Roberta and I will never forget that Heinz arrived at the restaurant carrying a bouquet of yellow tulips for her (fig. 51).

FIG. 51. Heinz Kaempfer, celebrating his seventy-fifth birthday in April of 1979, in the woods of the Hoge Veluwe National Park in central Holland. Photo: Raymond Kaempfer

FIG. 52. Irma Grabhorn with the ukiyo-e scholar Yamaguchi Keizaburō, around 1995. Courtesy of Yamaguchi Keizaburō and Yamaguchi Katsura

On March 20, two days before our dinner, Sotheby's held a gala reception in their galleries on New Bond Street. Connoisseurs of ukiyo-e realized the Vever Collection was one of the greatest still in private hands and that the viewing was the final opportunity to see the prints before they went into museums and private collections, perhaps never to be seen publicly again. In attendance that evening was Irma Grabhorn (1910–2003), the widow of the American publisher Edwin Grabhorn (1889–1968), many of whose superb Japanese prints were exhibited and published by the Asian Art Museum of San Francisco as *The Printer's Eye* (2013), following their acquisition by the museum (fig. 52). Irma and I walked slowly through the display and, while she admired the Vever prints, she often remarked that "her" impression of a particular design was better than the Vever example.

Not unlike my experiences at the Gerli and Popper sales just a few years earlier, I was completely unprepared for the competition at Vever. Having concluded that the presale estimates were unrealistically low, I expected to bid above the high estimates for each lot I wanted, and as much as three times the high estimate, in some cases. The first lot that grabbed me was number 30, a hand-colored Ishikawa Toyonobu (1711–1785) of a courtesan carrying a bucket of flowers in her right hand and a poem in her left. It sold for almost four times its high estimate, the first of many lots for which I was the underbidder. That set the tone for the rest of the sale. When the gavel came down on the final lot, I had bought nothing. After the sale, intent on not coming home empty-handed, I bought several fine prints that Ray Lewis had purchased in the sale, all rare images in fine condition (Mann catalogue nos. 13, 41, 43).[16]

Among the offerings on which I underbid was a slightly trimmed but otherwise alluring impression of Utamaro's *Reflective Love*, lot 175 in the Vever catalogue, a pink mica-ground picture of a dreamy woman with half-closed eyes resting her head on the back of her hand. Huguette Berès bought it and another lot I wanted, number 139, *The Actor Bandō Hikosaburō III as Sugawara no Michizane*, by Katsukawa Shun'ei. Days after the sale, I contacted Huguette to ask which Vever prints she was prepared to sell. In a letter dated April 26, 1974, she listed more than thirty, assuring me that whatever she didn't disperse would go into her "collection privée." Her asking prices were between 20 percent and 165 percent over the auction hammer prices. Most of those pearls became available only when Huguette's collection was sold at Sotheby's in 2003 and 2004, where the prices (or at least the estimates) soared even further above those in the Vever sale. Sebastian Izzard bought *Reflective Love* at the 2003 sale; it is now in a private American collection. I don't know where the Shun'ei is.

One particularly noteworthy Vever print I bought from Ray Lewis after the sale is a tableau of a monkey trainer and three young women in a boat on the Sumida River, by Okumura Masanobu (fig. 53).[17] The print was shown in the great 1909 exhibit organized by Charles Vignier (1863–1934) and Inada Hogitarō at the Grand Palais in Paris, and was published by von Seidlitz in German and French editions in 1910 and 1911. Then it disappeared from public view until 1974, when it reappeared in the Vever sale. To my knowledge, it had not been publicly displayed for over sixty years. When the Japanese print scholar Narazaki Muneshige came to our home in July 1978, he gazed at this design for what seemed like twenty or thirty minutes, never having seen it before. He had been told that the print was "in Chicago" and assumed The Art Institute of Chicago had it. When he visited the museum and asked to see the print, he learned it was in our collection and he asked to pay us a visit. For Narazaki-sensei to come to our home was a singular honor. He was one of the leading ukiyo-e scholars of his day, authoring countless books on the subject, published in multiple editions and translations. Narazaki had come to Chicago seven years earlier, in 1971, as a participant in the "Primitives" symposium at the Art Institute, but I did not meet him on that occasion. I wrote Roger Keyes, telling him of Narazaki's visit, and Roger replied. "I can just see Narazaki looking at your Masanobu and hear him saying 'Haaaaa!' from deep in his throat."[18]

It took a while for me to recover from the Vever sale. The week or so in London went from high to low and back again. The first viewing of the prints at Sotheby's was exhilarating. I enjoyed wandering the gallery with Irma Grabhorn, Bob Sawers, David Caplan, Huguette Berès and other dealers and collectors. We were delighted by our discussions with Heinz Kaempfer, with Ray Lewis and Roger Keyes, with various representatives of Sotheby's, and others. But entering the famed auction room with the venerable green felt-covered horseshoe-shaped table where the leading dealers and collectors sat during the auction and where, for many years, objects were passed from person to person during the sale, was a new high. I believe there is still a plaque on the wall dedicated to the "underbidder," the unsung hero of every auction of every object who drives the price up to its winning bid.

As intense as the action was, the Vever sale itself was a low. It was crushing to be left out of every transaction after so much anticipation, forethought and planning. My post-sale purchases mollified my disappointment to some extent, but my failure to buy Utamaro's *Reflective Love*, Shun'ei's portrait of Bandō Hikosaburō III and several other iconic designs hurts to this day.

PAGES 60–61

FIG. 53. Okumura Masanobu. *A Monkey Trainer of the Floating World on the Sumida River* (*Sumidagawa ukiyo sarumawashi*). Japan. Edo period, c. 1750. Color woodblock print. 32.1 x 44.6 cm. The Mann Collection, acquired March 26, 1974

隅田川浮世揲ばい

Reluctance to Step Up

Taking a broad view of my collecting, I must admit that I often held back in auctions, and in other purchase opportunities. I feared making a mistake, of spending more than I could afford, or of paying what I considered at the time more than a print was worth. I did not want to appear to be profligate—an undisciplined buyer willing to pay any price asked. As the underbidder, I was always "safe" in a sense, because there was another person willing to pay more. Yes, it could appear that *both* the "winner" and the underbidder were fools, but at least I would have company.

My fears and concerns manifested in too many situations, several of which are described in this memoir. These situations include: 1. My unwillingness to pay Nagatani $500 for Hokusai's *Shower below the Summit* in 1961; 2. My refusal to buy the Toyokuni large head from the Mellor sale that Janette Ostier offered for $800 in 1964; 3. My hesitation, starting in 1972, to pay $4,000 for a Red Fuji that went to Gaines at the Gerli sale or $25,000 for the one at the Black sale bought by Nishi; 4. Declining Utamaro's *Reflective Love* from Vever that Berès offered in 1974; 5. Passing on Hokusai's "Ghost prints" offered by Kondo Sentarō in 1985, discussed below; and 6. Failing to bid on the Kaigetsudō Dohan *Courtesan Playing with a Cat* at Vever I in 1974 or at Christie's in 2013, also remarked on later.

And again: Just a few months after the purchase of the Yamamoto Collection, described below, David Caplan offered me a twelve-sheet erotic album by Hishikawa Moronobu from the Yamamoto Collection for $100,000. The price for the entire set was not negotiable. But he did offer the first two sheets of the album, neither of which is "explicit," for $75,000. The first sheet is the same as the Ledoux version in the Metropolitan Museum (fig. 54). I considered this opportunity very carefully, but decided against it—yet another reluctance to "step up" that I still regret.

FIG. 54. Hishikawa Moronobu (1630/31?–1694). *Lovers beside Autumn Grasses*. Japan. Edo period, 1680s. Woodblock print. 23.5 x 33.7 cm. The Metropolitan Museum of Art, New York, Harris Brisbane Dick and Rogers Fund, 1949, JP3069

Sometime later (I cannot recall the year), I thought I had the option on another choice Moronobu sheet from an erotic album. While at lunch with Bob Sawers at a restaurant off New Bond Street in London, Bob casually showed me a snapshot. I immediately *did* "step up" and said I would buy it, but Bob did not have control of the print and, when he tried to get it, it was gone.

Louis Black Sale, 1976

I *did* recover from the disappointments at Vever and made several important purchases during the next two years, including an intimate scene of lovers on the private second floor of a teahouse from Utamaro's *The Poem of the Pillow* (fig. 55); and the majestic, but controversial, image of Hanamurasaki of the Tamaya, by Chōbunsai Eishi (1756–1829), previously owned by Ledoux (Mann catalogue no. 75).[19]

I also bought two very good impressions of *Fireworks, Ryōgoku Bridge* from Hiroshige's *One Hundred Views of Famous Places in Edo* (figs. 56 and 57). I find it continuously rewarding to compare them to each other and to the impression in the Mary Ainsworth Collection at the Allen Memorial Art Museum, Oberlin College, Oberlin, Ohio (fig. 58).

On March 4, 1976, some of the ukiyo-e collected by Louis W. Black (1905–1958), a Harvard-educated Boston lawyer, was sold at Sotheby's, New York. The first gem that

FIG. 55. Kitagawa Utamaro (1753?–1806). *Lovers in the Private Second-floor Room of a Teahouse*, from the album *The Poem of the Pillow* (*Utamakura*). Japan. Edo period, 1788. Color woodblock print. 26.5 x 37.8 cm. The Mann Collection, acquired April 23, 1974

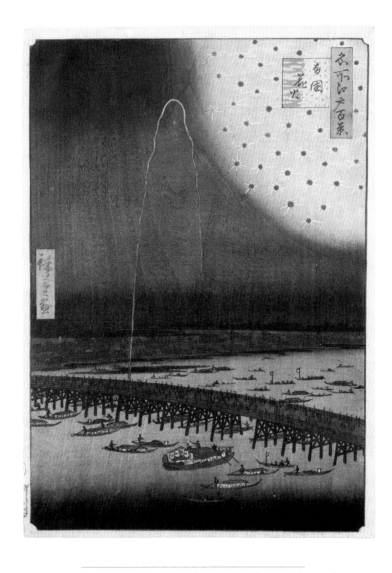

FIG. 56. Utagawa Hiroshige. *Fireworks, Ryōgoku Bridge* (*Ryōgoku hanabi*), from the series *One Hundred Views of Famous Places in Edo* (*Meisho Edo hyakkei*). Japan. Edo period, 1858. Color woodblock print. 35 x 23.2 cm. The Mann Collection, acquired October 4, 1974

FIG. 57. Utagawa Hiroshige. *Fireworks, Ryōgoku Bridge* (*Ryōgoku hanabi*), from the series *One Hundred Views of Famous Places in Edo* (*Meisho Edo hyakkei*). Japan. Edo period, 1858. Color woodblock print. 36 x 24.4 cm. The Mann Collection, acquired October 4, 1974

OPPOSITE: FIG. 58. Utagawa Hiroshige. *Fireworks, Ryōgoku Bridge* (*Ryōgoku hanabi*), from the series *One Hundred Views of Famous Places in Edo* (*Meisho Edo hyakkei*). Japan. Edo period, 1858. Color woodblock print. 36.6 x 23.9 cm. Allen Memorial Art Museum, Oberlin, OH, Mary A. Ainsworth Bequest, 1950.1442

The three impressions of fireworks demonstrate the printer's skills in creating different atmospheric and visual effects. In figure 56, the bursting fireworks obscure the surrounding details as one experiences from a sudden flash of bright light. In figure 57, the fireworks have faded, so the travelers on the bridge and the buildings on the far bank are distinct. In figure 58, the fireworks have extinguished, and the details are no longer clear because the glow is gone.

caught my eye was a Sugimura Jihei (fig. 59). The extensive inscription can be summed up with the paraphrase that even white-haired old men and old ladies are excited by the thought of love and that everyone spends the time in amorous play.[20]

The sale catalogue for the Black Collection indicated that two other designs from the twelve-print album from which the Sugimura came were reproduced in Donald Jenkins's 1971 *Ukiyo-e Prints and Paintings: The Primitive Period, 1680–1745*. At that time, the remaining nine designs had not been located and Shibui Kiyoshi, a connoisseur with a large collection of erotica (and who was one of the participants at the 1971 symposium at the Art Institute), had not recorded the series. I had never seen the design before and, as prints by Sugimura Jihei are uncommon and this one was particularly lovely, I decided to "go for it."

In the days before the Black sale, I discussed the print with Ray Lewis, who praised the design, and asked him to bid for it on my behalf. The morning of the sale, Ray reported that John Gaines had telephoned him the previous evening, asking him to bid on it for him. Ray told Gaines that he already had an interested client and declined Gaines's request. At the auction, Ray went to my limit, but Gaines, bidding

FIG. 59. Attributed to Sugimura Jihei. *Courtesan and Samurai*. Japan. Edo period, 1680s. Woodblock print with hand coloring. 26.6 x 36.2 cm. The Mann Collection, acquired May 24, 1979

66

けらはまなそくを
いろぐくあゆらを無にい
けそのぞくわぞくを
ろふうの
ふんのつえ

by telephone, won the lot. It was not until Gaines changed direction and put some of his prints into auction that I was able to buy the Sugimura, three years later.

Sidney Ward

In late March 1976, soon after the Black sale, Roberta and I and our three daughters went to Walt Disney World for a vacation. (David, less than a year old, was too young to go.) We stopped in Winter Park, about twenty miles northeast of Disney World, to visit Sidney Ward, his wife, Sarah, and their five children (fig. 60). Sid was a distinguished tax lawyer who worked closely with one of my law partners on a number of projects. He was also an avid ukiyo-e collector, active at both the Popper sale in 1972 (where we first met) and at the first Vever sale in 1974. Chronicling his collection, he privately published the carefully researched *One Hundred Japanese Prints* (1975) and *One Hundred Surimono* (1976), copies of which he gave us after viewing prints together and enjoying a warm family dinner.

In 1979, Sid retired from the practice of law and moved to Tokyo with his wife and their youngest daughter, to continue his Japanese language studies in pursuit of a graduate degree in East Asian Studies at Sophia University. On December 3, 1982, I was bidding at Christie's on Sid's Sharaku "large head" of Sakata Hangorō III against a telephone bidder, whom I later learned was calling from Mexico. Abruptly, the bidding stopped at my bid, well below the level I expected, and I bought the print. The phone line to Mexico had gone dead and couldn't be restored, another vagary of the collector's world (see figure 49).

Visiting Jacob Pins in Jerusalem

In late 1976, Roberta and I traveled to Israel for the first time; none of the children joined us. I contacted Jacob Pins (1917–2005), an ukiyo-e collector and woodcut artist who had emigrated from Germany to a new home in Palestine in 1936 (figs. 61 and 62). We arranged a visit to his grand home on Ethiopia Street, opposite the Ethiopian Church, in Jerusalem. I remember elaborately and elegantly decorated walls and

ceilings. Jacob was a genteel host and showed us a number of the pillar prints he collected and wrote about so enthusiastically. Although we communicated by letter a few times after our visit, we never met again. In 1982, Bob Sawers published Jacob's *The Japanese Pillar Print: Hashira-e*, the definitive work on the genre. The Mann Collection Kiyoshige of Ichikawa Ebizō II in a Shibaraku scene is illustrated in the volume (plate 4) and on the back cover of the slip case (see figure 64). After Pins died, his collection went to the Israel Museum in Jerusalem.

On that Israel trip, we also stopped at the Tikotin Museum of Japanese Art in Haifa that houses about eighty-five-hundred Japanese works of art, including ukiyo-e prints and paintings, textiles, ceramics and antiques. As I have already described, I first met Tiko at his home in Vevey, Switzerland, in August 1972, then saw him again that October at the Popper sale in New York.

A Curious Encounter with John Gaines, 1979

John R. Gaines (1928–2005) had been formidable at the 1972 Popper sale (fig. 63a). He was a legendary horse breeder, the owner of Gainesway Farm in Lexington, Kentucky, and the founder of the Breeders' Cup World Championships races, an annual series of Grade I Thoroughbred horse races. He was a leading collector of Western prints, but his interests expanded to ukiyo-e in the early 1970s. At the 1971 Gerli sale, he bought the Hokusai Red Fuji I wanted, as mentioned earlier, and an extremely rare print attributed to Katsukawa Shunchō (lot 53). Gaines was unpredictable competition at auctions, often jumping the increments established by the auctioneer: "$5,000!" when the auctioneer was asking for $1,000—much like the wild bidding at auctions of Chinese art today. This show of confidence (perhaps impatience) was intimidating. He bought select prints at high prices. When he sold most of his ukiyo-e in 1979, they fetched considerably higher prices than he had paid.

John Gaines marked his exit from the field of ukiyo-e by offering around twenty of his prints at Sotheby's, New York, May 23–25, 1979. This time, I was able to buy the Sugimura erotic print I had so wanted in the Louis Black sale in 1976 (see figure 59). Years after the Black/Gaines sales, Shibui Kiyoshi identified the Sugimura as a design from what he called Series D.[21] It was Shibui who, in 1926, discovered that a group of images formerly ascribed to Hishikawa Moronobu was the work of a separate artist, Sugimura Jihei. My understanding is that Shibui came to this realization when he noticed that inscriptions on certain prints attributed to Moronobu were, in fact, the signature of Sugimura Jihei, a theretofore unknown artist.

Other bonuses of the Gaines sale were the acquisition of Hokusai's *Morning Glories and Tree Frog*, from the "Large Flowers" series, which John bought at the second Vever sale in 1975 (lot 287), and the right-hand sheet of a diptych by Utamaro entitled *Diversions of the Four Seasons: The Color and Fragrance of Flowers*, which he bought at the first Vever sale in 1974 (lot 169) (figs. 63b, c). Both prints significantly enhanced my collection. After the sale, Bob Sawers and I had a drink at the Carlyle Hotel on Seventy-sixth and Madison Avenue with Gaines, who told us that he had held back from the auction an "excellent" impression of Hokusai's

FIG. 63a. John R. Gaines. Courtesy of Gloria Gaines Callen

FIG. 63b. Katsushika Hokusai. *Morning Glories (Asagao) and Tree Frog,* from the "Large Flowers" series. Japan. Edo period, early 1830s. Color woodblock print. 25 x 37.5 cm. The Mann Collection, acquired May 24, 1979

FIG. 63c. Kitagawa Utamaro. *Diversions of the Four Seasons: The Color and Fragrance of Flowers* (*Shiki asobi hana no iroka*), right panel of a diptych. Japan. Edo period, c. 1783. Color woodblock print. 36.8 x 24.2 cm. The Mann Collection, acquired May 24, 1979

Shower below the Summit. Bob said he was familiar with that work and it had no condition issues. Relying on Bob's confidence (and probably still smarting from not having bought the print when Nagatani offered me one in 1961, eighteen years earlier), I agreed that I would make the transaction directly with Gaines and pay Bob a commission when it closed.

Gaines then balked. He put off my efforts to complete the sale at the price agreed. He kept postponing delivery, and ultimately chose not to return my phone calls. Three years later, in the spring of 1982, Gaines sent the print to me—with a 50 percent price increase—with a ten-day right of first refusal. The print I received turned out to be in poor condition, with a quarter-size repair in the sky and a prominent center fold—so I returned it. On March 1, 1983, I bought a better *Shower below the Summit* from the dealer Anders Rikkardson, at a lower price than Gaines originally agreed to (see figure 5).

I've never known what to make of the Gaines *Shower below the Summit*. Where was the "excellent" impression he offered me after the auction of his other prints? Why hadn't he consigned it to Sotheby's with those? Maybe he acquired it after the catalogue was printed, but why would he send me a decidedly inferior print so long afterward? I have never known, as I had no further contact with John Gaines after returning the Hokusai he sent me.

The Kaigetsudō Saga: Impeccable Credentials

In late 1977, about fifty prints formerly owned by Yamamoto Hatsujirō, a Japanese businessman, were acquired by David Caplan, Nishi Saijū and Bob Sawers. In return for helping finance their purchase, I was allowed to participate by telephone in the division that they held in Tokyo. Nishi had been the go-between in the purchase, and I assumed he was thoroughly familiar with the prints, while Caplan and Sawers were seeing them for the first time. I had only a set of very blurry photocopies, five or six images per sheet, that gave no idea of the quality or condition of the originals.

There were nine Sharaku, seven Utamaro, a Hokusai Red Fuji, a little-known Chōki and more than fifteen early prints, including ones by Sugimura Jihei, Kiyomasu, Kiyoshige, Toyonobu, Kiyohiro, Masanobu and Kaigetsudō artists.

I was happy to get a Kiyoshige pillar print of Ichikawa Ebizō II (Danjūrō II) that had been in "Ukiyo-e Masterpieces," the exhibition held in conjunction with the Tokyo Olympics in 1964, to which Hans Popper lent so many prints (fig. 64). Jacob Pins illustrated the Kiyoshige in his book *The Japanese Pillar Print*, as noted above. It was loaned to the Musée des Arts Decoratifs, Paris, between June 1 and October 3, 1966, for "Images du Temps qui Passe: Peintures et Estampes d'Ukiyo-e," an exhibition sponsored by the *Nihon Keizai Shinbun*, joined by L'Union Centrale des Arts Decoratifs. Suzuki Jūzō was involved in organizing and cataloguing the Tokyo and Paris shows; the dealer Harry Packard contributed to the Paris one. The only other impression of the Kiyoshige I have located is in the Tokyo National Museum (fig. 65).

What I could not have known when I bought the Kiyoshige was that the traditional paper on which it was printed was very thin and weak in many places. Multiple expert repairs, which appear to be quite old, are visible on the verso of the print, each with a narrow (3 mm) strip of paper covering the original weakened by age. On the face of the print, many of the repaired/strengthened areas were in-painted. I overlooked those condition problems because of the scarcity of the image and the power of the design.

A Toyonobu print of a young man-about-town carrying a lantern in vertical, hanging-scroll format (*kakemono-e*) was also captivating (fig. 66). From Jack Hillier's three-volume 1976 book on the Vever Collection (vol. 1, no. 65), I was aware of one later image with a gap in it, where the two blocks from which the "hanging scroll" print was made were joined vertically, because the woodblocks had shrunk. On October 30, 1997, twenty years after I got my Toyonobu at the Yamamoto dispersal, the Vever example appeared in the final Vever auction. Because it was a late printing and in poor condition, it did not sell.

75

As mentioned, the Yamamoto prints included two purportedly by Kaigetsudō. I have been attracted to prints of that school since I saw them in James Michener's book, even before the day in early 1961 when I held six of them in New York at the Metropolitan Museum. I am still mesmerized by their stateliness. The opportunity to add an example to my collection was irresistible.

One of the two Yamamoto Kaigetsudō was clearly "wrong." Other spurious Kaigetsudō had come up at auction over the preceding ten years. The other one owned by Yamamoto (the "Questionable Kaigetsudō") had almost impeccable credentials. It had been in the 1964 Tokyo "Ukiyo-e Masterpieces" exhibition, as well as in "Images du Temps qui Passe" in Paris. Further, the Questionable Kaigetsudō was the same design as one of the three Kaigetsudō owned by Irma Grabhorn, the widow of Edwin Grabhorn (figs. 67 and 68).[22]

My decision to purchase the Yamamoto Questionable Kaigetsudō was influenced by the paucity of extant designs by Kaigetsudō artists—twenty-two or so, with no more than four known impressions of any given design. Most authenticated Kaigetsudō prints are in museums. At the turn of the twentieth century, the legendary connoisseur Raymond Koechlin (1860–1931) found five Kaigetsudō at a *bouquiniste* stall alongside the Seine in Paris, folded together so they would fit inside a small album. The Ledoux Collection included six—five from the Koechlin Collection, four of which went to The Metropolitan Museum of Art, New York, following Ledoux's death in 1948. I have had the pleasure of examining the four in The Art Institute of Chicago on multiple occasions.

Although the Yamamoto Questionable Kaigetsudō did not appear in any of the standard catalogues, I did not doubt its authenticity and relayed my telephone bids through Bob Sawers to the other members of the investment group.

Within months after receiving the Questionable Kaigetsudō, I started nagging myself, *"Why hadn't there been more competition from others in the investment group? Why was it not published more widely? Why was there no public record of either the Grabhorn or the Yamamoto impression earlier than the 1960s?"*

The Grabhorn Kaigetsudō

In May 1978, Roberta and I flew to San Francisco. Through the intercession of Roger Keyes, and in response to a letter I wrote to Irma Grabhorn on April 10, she invited us to "bruncheon" (as she called it) on May 7, following which we would view her Kaigetsudō courtesan. Mrs. Grabhorn lived in a mansion on Chestnut Street. The great room had very high ceilings and heavy, burgundy-colored velvet drapes; there was a musty, "old-world" feeling. (A young Sotheby's representative whom Mrs. Grabhorn knew and trusted was also present.) At first, she was rather diffident and distant, as if she suspected that Roberta and I would try to convince her to sell something to us. After lunch, we adjourned to a study where the matted Grabhorn Kaigetsudō was resting on an easel on top of a storage cabinet. Although we had not brought ours to San Francisco, I had "memorized" certain details sufficiently to know that it was printed from the same blocks as the Grabhorn print, with the same thick orange pigment and paper, the same line breaks and other flaws. Once the "study period" ended, Mrs. Grabhorn relaxed, accepting that our interest in making the comparison was genuine. Roberta and I took our leave with profuse "thank yous" all around, although we had trouble breaking away and had to decline an invitation for the next day, as we were scheduled to return to Chicago.

I wanted to see more of the Grabhorn Collection, but the Kaigetsudō was the only print Mrs. Grabhorn had in the house. She did show us a number of loose sheets from the collection catalogues published by Edwin and Marjorie Grabhorn and The Grabhorn Press in 1959, 1960, 1962 and 1965. (Marjorie was Edwin Grabhorn's second wife; Irma was his third.) I was satisfied that I had accomplished my goal of determining that the Grabhorn print and the Mann print came from the same blocks; there was still no proof they were produced in the early eighteenth century from a design by Kaigetsudō Anchi. Over the years, nothing came to light to strengthen the case for authenticity. Furthermore, in the lead-up to the exhibition of our collection at the Ōta Museum in Tokyo in 1994, the Ōta's selection committee did not choose our Kaigetsudō.

Perhaps the coup de grâce came with the publication of an article by Julia Meech in *Impressions* 25 (2003). "Edwin Grabhorn: Printer and Print Collector" dealt in some depth with ukiyo-e sold by Harry Packard, the American collector and dealer who started buying from desperate Japanese after the Pacific War. Here's what Meech had to say about the Grabhorn "Kaigetsudō":

> Packard sold Grabhorn what now appears to be a controversial Kaigetsudō Anchi image of a standing courtesan in 1958 for $2,000. It is printed on suitably worm-eaten and soiled old paper, and *only one other impression* [emphasis added] is known. . . . Packard acknowledged that, because it had been doubted by Kaneko [a knowledgeable print dealer], he had taken it to three respected authorities for authentication. These three were Nakajima at the Shōbisha, a print gallery founded in the 1920s by Matsuki Kihachirō; Fujikake Shizuya, the editor of the prestigious art journal *Kokka* and a former professor at the University of Tokyo who had specialized in ukiyo-e for over forty years; and, last but not least, the well-known Tokyo print publisher, Watanabe Shōzaburō (1885–1962), a man who had been in the business for more than fifty years and who affixed a dated certificate of authentication to the verso. Packard said he had acquired the print from a private collector, Mr. Tase in Yamagata Prefecture to the north of Tokyo. . . . James Michener had supposedly already offered Packard $3,000 for it. Watanabe certified this as an original print (*genbanga*). Unfortunately, the hand-colored orange pigment is clearly "wrong." The pigment is rather like that used in the first decades of the twentieth century by Takamizawa Enji (1870–1927), a collector who made facsimiles as a hobby. Fujikake once confessed that he couldn't tell Takamizawa's creations from original prints. The fact that only two impressions survive, both with identical hand coloring, may be more than a coincidence.[23]

Of course, the "one other impression" is the Questionable Kaigetsudō I bought in the Yamamoto transaction, and both are likely the work of Takamizawa, as suggested above.

The *Impressions* 2015 Companion Issue, published twelve years later by the Japanese Art Society of America, is titled "Rare Correspondence: Letters from Harry Packard to Edwin Grabhorn: 1950–64." The journal, edited by Julia Meech and Jane Oliver,

includes a number of letters from Harry Packard (or his wife, Carol) to Ed Grabhorn concerning ukiyo-e purchased by Packard on Grabhorn's behalf, or otherwise offered and sold to Grabhorn by Packard. Although the letters do not include any of the correspondence from Grabhorn's end, nevertheless, they present insight into both men. Packard often comes across as petulant and very demanding, especially about prompt payment (fig. 69). Several letters address the question of the authenticity of the Grabhorn Kaigetsudō, the names of the experts who vouched for it and the names of those who expressed doubts. While the correspondence details many, many prints purchased or at least considered by Grabhorn, it is only this Kaigetsudō that is questioned, often and at length. One of the experts on whom Packard relied (but who was not mentioned in the correspondence as having opined on the Grabhorn Kaigetsudō) was Nishi Saijū, the dealer I first met at the Gerli sale in 1971, seven years prior to our visit to Mrs. Grabhorn. In a 1958 letter, Packard remarks to Grabhorn that he trusted Nishi about 75 percent of the time.[24]

According to a June 5, 1958 letter from Packard to Grabhorn, an impressive cast of experts agreed that the Questionable Kaigetsudō was "right." We don't know from whom or when Yamamoto acquired his Questionable Kaigetsudō, but it had to have been prior to its inclusion in the "Masterpieces" exhibition in 1964. Grabhorn bought his Questionable Kaigetsudō courtesan in 1958, the same year Packard revealed to Grabhorn that it was not "one of a kind." When Caplan, Nishi and Sawers secured the Yamamoto cache in 1977, Nishi must have weighed the "coincidence" of two nearly identical Kaigetsudō reaching the market with no prior publication history or provenance. In the same June 5, 1958 letter to Edwin Grabhorn, Packard claims that the Grabhorn example "has passed as a genuine print in Japan for over 20 years."[25] The plausible story I have pieced together is that Nishi bought the print from the Mr. Tase quoted in the Meech extract above and sold it to Packard, who passed it on to Edwin Grabhorn. When Nishi arranged the Yamamoto division in 1977, the "impeccably credentialed" Questionable Kaigetsudō went to me for a hefty price. In my zeal to acquire it, I passed on remarkable works by Kiyomasu, Utamaro and Sharaku—and a fine Red Fuji.

Even before publication of the correspondence between Packard and Grabhorn, in light of the controversy and uncertainty I sold the Kaigetsudō to a fully informed and knowledgeable expert for a token amount in 2012, with the mutual goal of keeping it off the market. I have been assured that the Grabhorn impression now in the Asian Art Museum of San Francisco was purchased as a "curiosity" and will remain there.

Coincidently, the Grabhorn Collection also contained an impression of Kaigetsudō Dohan's *Courtesan Playing with a Cat*, now at the Asian Art Museum (2005. 100.6). Christie's, New York, offered another example of this design on September 18, 2013. The print had sold for £14,000 (about $33,000) at the first Vever auction on March 26, 1974—to Nishi Saijū, of all people. At the time of the 2013 Christie's auction, the print was owned by the late Sakamoto Gorō (1923–2016), a well-known Japanese dealer. A representative of Christie's, Katsura Yamaguchi, brought the print to Chicago before the auction so that we could enjoy the unusual opportunity to compare it to the hand-colored image owned by The Art Institute of Chicago. The print sold for $243,650 at the Christie's auction. I did not participate.

Year of the Gidwitz and the "Large Fish" Series, 1980

The decade of the 1980s was replete with new and different opportunities. Adele Gidwitz (1918–2020) and her husband, Willard (1908–1981), lived on the shore of Lake Michigan less than half a mile from the first house in Highland Park that Roberta and I bought after we married in 1973. Willard's older brother, Gerald (1907–2006), founded the cosmetics and hair-care-products giant Helene Curtis Industries, which the Gidwitz brothers, including Joseph Gidwitz (1905–1995), controlled until it was sold to Unilever in 1996. As I knew them slightly, I spoke with Adele and Willard Gidwitz at the Gerli auction in 1971 and the Popper auction in 1972, but we had no significant contact in Chicago, and they never asked to see my collection.

The Gidwitzes were a private couple with eclectic and refined tastes. In 1963, they bought Picasso's 1941 portrait *Dora Maar au Chat* from the Galerie Berggruen in Paris for $106,000. The picture had a Chicago connection, once having been owned by Leigh B. Block (1905–1987), the president, then the chairman of the board of The Art Institute of Chicago from 1970 to 1975. In 2006, after Willard's death, Adele sold the Picasso through Sotheby's, New York, for $95,200,000, including buyer's commission.

I don't know when or what prompted the Gidwitzes' interest in ukiyo-e. When Willard began to suffer the ravages of dementia and his health declined precipitously, Adele decided to sell. In early 1979, she contacted me. She had an appraisal that Roger Keyes had made sometime after the Popper sale in October 1972, when he was still associated with Ray Lewis. Adele felt the valuation was out of date and low.

In response to Adele's overture, I turned to Bob Sawers, who knew the Gidwitzes and had a sense of the collection. He suggested that we organize a consortium to buy and divide it as we had done with the Yamamoto group. Bob brought in his "friendly competitors," Huguette Berès, David Caplan and Nishi Saijū.

Bob flew over from London in the spring of 1979. Working off the Keyes appraisal, he produced an updated valuation, which was more than double the Keyes total of seven years earlier. In June, Mrs. Gidwitz agreed to the reappraisal as the purchase price, subject to adjustment when the consortium could assemble and study the prints more closely. I worked out the contract and payment terms with her attorney.

At the beginning of January 1980, a portion of the purchase price was wired to the Gidwitzes, with the balance to be paid on June 2, 1980. After the buying group signed the contracts at our house on January 19, 1980, I delivered them and collected the prints. Ten minutes later, they were on our dining-room table (figs. 70 and 71a–c).

The collection comprised important early prints; figure prints by Harunobu, Utamaro and Eishi; two Sharaku actors; twenty-three of the twenty-eight designs in the Hokusai series *One Hundred Poems by One Hundred Poets, Explained by the Nurse*; and fine nineteenth-century landscapes. We rejected a few as being of negligible commercial value or as facsimiles. In the case of one Hiroshige "bird-and-flower" offering, we determined it was a reprint by comparing the Gidwitz impression to one of mine deemed original.[26]

The division procedure was simple. After a print was passed around the table for one more examination, each of the participants wrote a "bid" on a slip of paper. We disclosed our bids, and the person placing the highest bid bought the print for that amount. When the mini-auction ended, the winning bids were totaled. As the sum exceeded the price agreed upon with Mrs. Gidwitz, we allocated the excess among ourselves in proportion to the aggregate amount each of us had "bid" in the division process. One of the real coups for me was my successful bid on a fine impression of

FIG. 70. (left to right) David Caplan, Nishi Kōzō, Bob Sawers, George Mann, Huguette Berès and Nishi Saijū at the Mann home in Highland Park, IL. January 1980

FIGS. 71 a–c. Viewing Gidwitz prints on the Mann dining-room table. January 1980

a) Bob Sawers and Huguette Berès

b) Nishi Kōzō, son-in-law/ adopted son of Nishi Saijū, Bob Sawers and Huguette Berès

c) David Caplan, Nishi Kōzō, Nishi Saijū and Bob Sawers with calculators, after the division of prints

FIG. 72. Utagawa Hiroshige. *Sudden Shower over Ōhashi Bridge, Atake* (*Ōhashi Atake no yūdachi*), from the series *One Hundred Views of Famous Places in Edo* (*Meisho Edo hyakkei*). Japan. Edo period, 1857. Color woodblock print. 36.9 x 24.7 cm. The Mann Collection, acquired January 19, 1980

PAGES 84–85: FIG. 73. Utagawa Hiroshige. *Gray Mullet, Camellia and Spikenard Shoots* (*Bora, Tsubaki, Udo*), from the untitled series known as "Every Variety of Fish" (*Uo tsukushi*). Japan. Edo period, 1830s. Color woodblock print with mica embellishment. 25.6 x 37 cm. The Mann Collection, acquired January 19, 1980

Hiroshige's *Ōhashi Bridge* (fig. 72). It was a mere $100 above Nishi's bid, and I still recollect our mutual surprise at the narrow margin of my "victory."

After the auction, dealing continued. Bob Sawers had won the Hiroshige prints popularly called "Large Fish" that I fancied. I knew little about the set when I first saw it in the Gidwitz Collection. Clearly, the prints were very fine, with astounding, subtle coloring and flashes of mica that simulated the glint of fish scales. There was neither a publisher's mark nor a censor's seal on any of them, indicating a private printing. Bob accepted my offer to buy the set for a small profit (fig. 73). (See Mann catalogue nos. 118.1–14.) All in all, I bought over twenty Gidwitz prints that day.

Later that evening, we reconvened at our home for a relaxed dinner with great wines. It was the only occasion on which I drank three premier burgundies, all of which I had bought a year earlier in an "end of bin" sale: Richebourg, La Tâche and Echezeaux. Exhausted, we ended our celebration about 11 p.m. Huguette Berès stayed the night with us, and the others stayed at a local hotel. Our daughters, all teenagers, probably slept at friends' homes that Saturday night, but our son, David, just five years old, went to bed before the festivities concluded. All of our guests left for their respective home countries on Sunday, packages of prints in hand.

After the transaction, I ran into Adele Gidwitz only occasionally and only at the Art Institute. I don't know how she felt about selling the prints. In July 2019, Roberta and I spotted Adele in a wheelchair listening intently to a string recital in Ravinia Park. She looked well, at age one hundred and one.

Over the months following the Gidwitz adventure, I tried to learn more of the history of the Hiroshige "Large Fish" album. I concluded that Gidwitz had purchased it from Kondo Sentarō, the owner and proprietor of the famous Red Lantern Shop at 236 Shinmonzen Street in Kyoto. Bob Sawers confirmed that provenance, although I never learned when or how Kondo-san acquired the album (nor when the Gidwitzes bought it from him). It is likely that Kondo owned the set before 1970, because Suzuki Jūzō published it in his monumental *Utagawa Hiroshige* (1970). From Suzuki's book, I realized that the complete album included the original four sheets of poetry that the fish prints were commissioned to illustrate. After some thought, and discussions with Bob Sawers, I decided that a personal visit to Kondo (rather than a letter) was the only way to find out. More about that later.

On that single day in January of 1980, the Mann Collection grew from 72 to 98 prints, and by year's end, to 111. I was now approaching a "critical mass" that soon might be *large* enough if *good* enough to justify a "single owner" exhibition at a venue in Japan—my long-held desire. At the same time, I started to become more selective. Over the next twenty-four years, until 2004, when I made what I believe was my final purchase, 71 prints came into my collection, no more than 7 in any given year (and, in two years, none).

The Reaction of Others

Even after the Gidwitz success, I was still rather circumspect. While my friends, law partners and associates knew I was very active in Japanese art, I doubt if many of them knew how serious that interest was. Our children acknowledged my "hobby," but probably did not realize how important it was *to me*, until they reached their late teens. Usually, they were away at school or with friends when visitors came to see the

葛花加二　栗穂加二

神わつまれ
明るのほらき
釣り針の
桅壽あを
こそ橋やちそく
年廻川
春喜

一 鯔 無穂賀二

田子れうまや
不このゝ掬椅
性乃とよを
とりまをの
ままくくつの
魚

桧垣
之魚

左音
廣重画

collection, but I believe they would say they appreciate my pride and pleasure in what I have put together.

However, none of my aunts, uncles or cousins knew I collected Japanese art. Roberta's parents had little, if any, knowledge of what I was doing—or why. My parents continued to think it a waste of attention and money. (After all, it was my father who, after visiting the New York offices of Ben Heller [1925–2019], the textile merchant turned powerhouse in abstract art, reported he had seen "goofy pictures" on the walls.) The Cottle family knew my interests were serious, but I had less contact with them after I married. Both Roberta's parents and mine, as well as the Cottles, did attend our exhibition at the Art Institute in 1982, described below, so they knew our collection had some status. I also was gratified to learn that Adolph Herseth (1921–2013), the principal trumpeter of the Chicago Symphony Orchestra for fifty-three years, was a lover of ukiyo-e and had come to see the show. His son, Steven, an associate in a Chicago law firm, and the rest of the Herseth family, came to the museum for a private tour.

Roberta always has understood that ukiyo-e is central to my life, but has had concerns about the cost, recognizing that prints are not a very liquid asset. She often helped me "apply the brakes," but never stood in the way of growing the collection. Roberta does not suffer from the "buy, buy, buy" addiction I have. She can appreciate a work of art without a need to own it. The only print she ever coveted was the Shun'ei of Bandō Hikosaburō III as Sugawara no Michizane in the Vever I sale in 1974, which went to Huguette Berès. Of course, I was the underbidder.

1980 Continued: Sharaku and Hokusai and Another Le Véel Sale in Paris

Although 1980 was the "Year of the Gidwitz," there was more to come. The Centre Culturel du Marais sponsored "Le Fou de Peinture: Hokusai et son Temps," opening on October 6. The show included over four hundred Hokusai prints, paintings, drawings and illustrated books, as well as textiles, bronzes and other objects of the period. Many prints were displayed in waist-high cases with chairs close by for convenient and comfortable viewing.

FIG. 74. George Mann on Quai Voltaire, Paris, beneath poster advertising the Galerie Berès Sharaku exhibition. October 1980

FIG. 75. Roberta Mann at the window of Galerie Berès with a photograph of a Mann Sharaku. October 1980

OPPOSITE:

FIG. 76. Galerie Berès

FIG. 77. Roberta Mann and Roger Keyes at a bar in Paris. October 1980

FIG. 78. George and Roberta Mann with two of their Sharaku prints at Galerie Berès. November 1980

FIG. 79. Bob Sawers and Huguette Berès at Galerie Berès. October 1980

That same fall, Huguette Berès presented an exhibition of sixty-four Sharaku actor portraits, including two of ours, in her gallery on Quai Voltaire. (At that time, we did not yet own the Vever impression of Sharaku's *Sanogawa Ichimatsu as Onayo*, which was also in Huguette's show; see figure 108.) Large posters advertising her exhibition hung on lampposts throughout Paris, and it was thrilling to come upon an image of a Mann Collection Sharaku while strolling through a square. We stayed at the Hotel Voltaire along the Quai from Huguette's gallery. A huge image of our Matsumoto Kōshirō as Gorobei looked back at us from a lamppost just outside our window (figs. 74–79).

The Hokusai exhibit in the Marais and the Sharaku show at Galerie Berès ("Sharaku: Portraits d'Acteurs 1794–1795") coincided with the sale of the second part of the collection of Ernest Le Véel (1874–1951), on October 24, 1980 through Ader, Picard, Tajan, auctioneers, at Nouveau Drouot. Stimulated by these exhibitions, I was a strong buyer at Le Véel II, not having been a buyer at Le Véel I a year earlier. Our eight new acquisitions were crisp impressions, in fine condition, with well-preserved color. Toyokuni's print of Kataoka Nizaemon VII was in much better condition and had fresher color than the one we owned. Buying the Le Véel example encouraged Roberta and me to donate the one we already had to The Art Institute of Chicago (1981.368). The sale garnered a lot of publicity, not all of it accurate: Souren Melikian, in the November 1–2, 1980 *International Herald Tribune*, wrote, "Sotheby's experts who advise the British Rail Pension Fund could be seen acquiring . . . Hokusai's marvelous print of hunters making a fire in the snow."

山里は冬ぞさびしさまさりける人目も草もかれぬと思へば

源宗于朝臣

百人一首 うばがゑとき

前北斎 卍

FIG. 80. Katsushika Hokusai. *The Poem of Minamoto Muneyuki*, from the series *One Hundred Poems by One Hundred Poets, Explained by the Nurse* (*Hyakunin isshu uba ga etoki*). Japan. Edo Period, 1830s. Color woodblock print. 25.9 x 37.7 cm. The Mann Collection, acquired October 24, 1980

FIG. 81. Ader, Picard, Tajan catalogue photograph of a woodblock print by Eishōsai Chōki (act. c. 1790s–early 1800s) of a young woman applying lip rouge while gazing at her image in a mirror. Ex coll. Ernest Le Véel, sold November 5, 1981, current location unknown

It was I who purchased that Hokusai, but I never did ask Souren who gave him the wrong information (fig. 80).[27]

Third Sale of the Le Véel Collection in Paris

In the late fall of 1981, I received a catalogue from Ader, Picard, Tajan for the third dispersal of prints from the Le Véel Collection on November 5. The catalogue promised a number of opportunities, none more exciting than a portrait by Eishōsai Chōki of a young woman applying lip rouge while gazing at her image in a mirror. The print had a yellow mica ground and, although a bit pale and soiled, the color was mostly well preserved. This was absolutely the most riveting print I had ever seen (fig. 81).

The morning after Roberta and I arrived in Paris, I was even more captivated by the Chōki when I saw it at the Nouveau Drouot. That afternoon, we visited Huguette Berès at her gallery. As we entered, I caught sight of a four-panel folding screen on display in one corner. I recognized it from catalogues I had glanced at over the years as a set of five-color lithographs by Pierre Bonnard of a parade of nursemaids leading their charges in front of a line of horse-drawn cabs (*Promenade des Nourrices, Frise des Fiacres,* 1897) (fig. 82). The screen is evocative of ukiyo-e because of its flat planes, odd perspective and silhouetted figures. I told Huguette that it knocked me out. After visiting with her for a while, Roberta and I returned to our hotel to prepare for the evening. Huguette had invited us, along with a few other friends in town for the Le Véel sale, for an informal supper at her home in Paris.

When we arrived at Huguette's elegant apartment, the first thing that caught my eye was the Bonnard screen. "Why Huguette," I exclaimed, "how kind of you to bring the screen home for us to enjoy this evening!" Nonchalantly, Huguette replied, "Oh no, I did not bring it home. I have *two* of these screens." I was speechless. One of her two Bonnard screens sold at Christie's, Paris, on March 22, 2018 for €25,000 ($30,815; sale 15723, lot 58). I think that had I known Huguette's Bonnard screen was coming up for sale, I might have bid on it. It could have moved to our home in Highland Park as an enduring reminder of Huguette, of Paris and of the early days of my enchantment with ukiyo-e.

There were eight or nine of us at supper that evening: Souren Melikian, then covering the art scene in a weekly column for the *International Herald Tribune*; the Gidwitz Gang: Caplan, Nishi and Sawers; Huguette's son, Pierre, and her daughter, Anisabelle, who runs the Berès gallery now. Nishi's son-in-law, Kōzō, may have been there, as well, but my recollection is hazy. Dinner conversation quickly turned to the Le Véel sale the next day. Melikian, playing the role of "*provocateur*," tried to get us to reveal our specific interests, but none of us would disclose anything for fear of giving an edge to our competition. I do recall that Melikian asked specifically about the Chōki and I replied, casually (but guardedly), that I thought it was a stunning print.

The auction started the next afternoon around 2:30 and proceeded at a comfortable pace. I was attracted to a Kiyonaga scene (lot 9) of the actor Ichikawa Danjūrō V (1741–1806) strolling with his young son, Ebizō IV, riding on the shoulders of the actor Ichikawa Masugorō, and two women (Mann catalogue no. 63). Ebizō, about six years old, wears a kimono bearing the formal Ichikawa family crest, three nested, square rice-measure cups, while his father wears a transparent coat bearing the family's informal crest (*kaemon*) of a carp swimming upstream. This print *might* show the family on the way to the theater for the young actor's debut in 1782. It sang to me (and I bought it), perhaps because of its relation to my Ebizō, my first Sharaku, that I bought from Ray Lewis in 1972.

I waited tensely for the Chōki. It seemed like an eternity before lot 38 came up, although it was probably only twenty or thirty minutes. Her unaffected beauty, her freshness, her aura hypnotized me—I had to have that print!

As bidding on the Chōki began, there was a murmur in the room. I was seated in the second or third row, to the auctioneer's right. Roberta sat to my right and watched the auctioneer (and the electronic board that records the progress of the auction in multiple currencies). She knew my "longing" and she knew my "limit." The bidding was rapid, and my maximum was soon eclipsed, whereupon Roberta relaxed. But

FIG. 82. Pierre Bonnard (1867–1947). *Promenade des Nourrices, Frise des Fiacres* (Promenade of nursemaids, line of carriage cabs). France. 1897. Color lithographs printed in five colors mounted as a four-panel folding screen. Published by Molines, Paris in an edition of 110. 146.5 x 45 cm each panel. Private collection, ex coll. Huguette Berès. Photo © Christie's Images / Bridgeman Images

we all know that passion often displaces reason. I did not know against whom I was bidding and, because my bidding was discreet—I raised a pencil before my chest or face until the auctioneer noticed me, and thereafter held steady to stay in—Roberta did not know I was still in the fight. My shins were perspiring! That's what it feels like when you are in a contest for a work of art you want that much. When the hammer came down at ten times its high estimate, the crowd applauded the billionaire Japanese real estate magnate Rinji Shino (1909–1996) on his victory. I slumped in my chair. As the session ended, the buyer was surrounded by adoring crowds, bright lights, press representatives and cameramen from Japanese TV.

In the November 7–8 edition of the *International Herald Tribune*, Melikian included the following description of the sale:

> Several prints in the sale suffered from faded colors. This did not prevent an exquisite study of a young woman painting her lips by Momokawa Choki from establishing the world-record high for a Japanese print . . . The optimistic cataloguer had described it as being in "an excellent state of preservation and coloring." The colors were in fact rather palish and slightly soiled, the background coming nowhere near the delicate golden hue suggested by the reproduction in the catalogue plate. However, the composition is a masterpiece by unanimous consent among the French, American and Japanese dealers and collectors with whom this reporter spoke. It is perhaps Choki's supreme achievement—and no one could remember seeing another impression in the market.
>
> Bidding went briskly up to [a level] at which point David Caplan, the Tokyo-based U.S. dealer, gave up. The contest was then fought between George Mann, a collector from Chicago, and Rinji Shino, a descendant of the 13th century imperial family and a tycoon from Shirahama, near Osaka, who made the final winning bid.

Later in the article, Melikian noted, "An admirable print by Torii Kiyonaga, included in the traveling exhibition 'Toulouse-Lautrec–Utamaro' held in Japan last year [1980], went to Mann."

Years later, Rinji Shino, having suffered business reverses, sold the Chōki at auction. It was a ghost of the brilliant print it was in 1981, apparently having been bleached by sunlight for many years, and fetched a much lower sum. I stayed away.

The only laugh resulting from the Chōki debacle was that the January 1982 issue of *Art + Auction* reported that the competition for the Chōki "between the two major collectors, the American Thomas [sic] Mann and the Japanese Francophile Rinji Shino, was ferocious." After reading the article, the late Harry A. Russell (d. c. 2000), a noted New York collector and friend, asked me to autograph his copy of *The Magic Mountain*.

Oceans of Wisdom, 1983

Throughout the sixty years in which I have been active in the Japanese print world, great works kept appearing as if out of a magic hat. In the September 22, 1983 sale at Christie's, New York, a complete set of the ten prints comprising Hokusai's *One Thousand Pictures of the Ocean*, also known as *Oceans of Wisdom*, was offered in ten separate lots (fig. 83). The set had sterling provenance, having gone from the Spaulding

FIG. 83. Katsushika Hokusai. *Fishing Boats at Chōshi in Shimōsa Province (Sōshū Chōshi)*, from the series *One Thousand Pictures of the Ocean (Chie no umi)*. Japan. Edo period, 1833–34. Color woodblock print. 18.9 x 25.8 cm. The Art Institute of Chicago, Kate S. Buckingham Endowment, 1983.583

Collection to the Gookin, Colonna and Garland Collections, successively. They had been sold as a lot in the Garland Sale at Parke Bernet in New York on April 12, 1945 and, to my knowledge, were off the market until they came up at Christie's in 1983. At the time, The Art Institute of Chicago had none of the *Oceans of Wisdom* designs. When I learned that the set was to be sold, I approached Osamu Ueda, the keeper of the Buckingham Collection, and suggested that the museum bid on one or more of them. Surprisingly, Ueda-san was only vaguely familiar with the series and, at first, had little interest in pursuing them. I urged him to review the catalogue and look for references to the series in other publications. That research got him going, and he took the purchase proposal up through the museum hierarchy for approval. I would have gone after one or two of the prints myself but, because of my associations with the Art Institute, museum ethics required that I step aside. (I had recently completed my term as president of the Auxiliary Board of the Art Institute, and I was also a member of the Asian Art Advisory Committee.)

Recognizing the rarity of the designs, as well as their significance to the museum's overall collection of Hokusai works, James Wood (1941–2010), the director and president of the Art Institute, authorized Ray Lewis, as agent, to bid on the three best designs in the set: *Fishing by Torchlight, Kai Province (Kōshū hiburi)*, lot 112; *Whaling off Gotō Island (Gotō kujira tsugi)*, lot 113; and *Chōshi in Shimōsa Province*, lot 117. Ray and I sat together at the sale. The first two prints were knocked down to Ray—in each case, the bidding quickly went beyond the catalogue estimate, but remained within the limits set by the museum. When the third came up, the bidding moved rapidly beyond the estimate and up to the museum's limit. The bid was against us. Ray paused, "What do I do?" "Keep bidding," I whispered, "I will cover the extra cost." The lot was knocked down to Ray at the next increment. The Art Institute of Chicago had acquired the three finest prints of the series. Some museum trustees raised a fuss over my unauthorized decision to exceed my authority (by some $5,000), but that issue quickly faded, and, in the end, the museum was delighted to pay the entire cost of all purchases.

Japan 1985 and the Ongoing Story of the "Large Fish"

In October 1985, Roberta and I went to Japan for the first time. We stayed at the "new" Imperial Hotel in Tokyo, just opposite the Imperial Palace and close to the Ginza district downtown. We went on classic sightseeing tours—Tsukiji fish market at 5 a.m., the Imperial Palace grounds, the Tokyo National Museum, shopping, dining—leaving us exhausted. Tokyo was bright, modern, noisy, bustling and easy to navigate if you weren't traveling to out-of-the-way places. I loved the push-button illuminated routing maps in the subway. Unusual for me, we did not visit any galleries to look for ukiyo-e. But on one occasion, a middle-aged Japanese man asked *me* for directions—and I understood his question! More amazing, I knew the answer and was able to communicate that information, with a few hand signals and a mishmash of Japanese.

Before we left Chicago on that trip, we arranged to meet Yutaka Mino in Tokyo for dinner one evening, and the hour-long trip to Kamakura the next day to meet his parents. Mino was the associate curator of Japanese art at The Art Institute of Chicago, a position he held until 1994. He was in Japan to visit his parents, who lived in a three-hundred-year-old house they had discovered in the north of Japan and moved to Kamakura.

The night before the journey, Mino treated Roberta and me to dinner at a restaurant owned by Watahira Kameo, an old friend of the Mino family whose hobby was collecting original score cards from golf courses around the world. The delicacy served at his restaurant was raw chicken, which we endured politely. The next day, visiting Yutaka's parents, we enjoyed seeing an array of their precious antique tea implements (mostly Oribe ware) (fig. 84). We then began our journey from Kamakura to Hakone, where we were to spend a few nights before going on to Kyoto. After making two train changes to Hakone, we took a local bus up a long, treacherous road to the Ryūguden inn, perched high on a hill, with a commanding view of Lake Ashi and Mount Fuji. It was raining so heavily that when we got off the bus, we could not see the inn, although it was less than fifty meters away. After welcoming tea and steeping hot baths, we

FIG. 84. Yutaka Mino (far right) and his parents. Kamakura. October 6, 1985

FIG. 85. Red Lantern Shop, Kyoto According to the print dealer Anders Rikardson (d. 2020), the Red Lantern Shop was owned and run by Kondo Sentarō. After his death in 1985, his mother took over for a few years before passing on the management to Kondo's son, who closed the business several more years later. While the Red Lantern Shop did sell ukiyo-e, its concentration was on contemporary prints, most from the 1960s and 1970s.

settled in for an elaborate meal brought to our room before retiring on the thick futons rolled out for the night. The rain continued, but I awakened about 4 a.m. to a clear sky and a full moon. And there was Mount Fuji, in all its glory, across Lake Ashi, without its usual veil of clouds. I sat at the window until sunrise. I never saw Fuji like that again. Even in the dawn, the mountain was not as brilliantly colored as the many images of Red Fuji I have seen, but I felt privileged to see glorious Mount Fuji in clear weather, a serenity many visitors to Japan never experience.

A few days later, we took the Shinkansen "bullet" train to Kyoto and checked into Hiiragiya, a traditional inn founded in 1818 and located across the street from the more famous (and even older) Tawaraya. Intent on tracking down the missing sheets of poetry from Hiroshige's "Large Fish" series purchased from the Gidwitzes in 1980, I telephoned the Red Lantern Shop only to learn that Kondo Sentarō was in Tokyo, and that he would return "maybe tomorrow." I called the next day, but he was still away. He returned to Kyoto two days before we were to leave for Chicago.

On our last full day in Japan, we were invited to the shop, an old, simple wooden building at a corner location on Shinmonzen Street in the heart of the art and antiques section of Kyoto (fig. 85). Entering, we found a relatively large, "stage-like" elevation that was mostly enclosed by a curtain. With absolutely no formalities, Kondo (a slight man who appeared a little befuddled) ushered us upstairs to a sitting room. Kondo's wife served tea and we chatted briefly. Without any prompting on my part, and without any hesitation on his, Kondo took the sheets of poetry and the album covers from a dusty bookcase behind him (fig. 86). Although I had expected that Kondo had the four sheets of poetry, my heart beat faster when he nonchalantly placed them on the table before us. I forced myself to look casually at the sheets and ask calmly if he had anything else to show me. He flattered us by saying that, for a collection at the level of ours (how did he know?), he had very little.

But, then he showed us a Toshinobu of a young man riding an ox while playing the flute; a Hiroshige of a peacock and peonies (figs. 87 and 88); and the five prints comprising the *One Hundred Ghost Stories* series (*Hyaku monogatari*) by Hokusai.

FIG. 86. Utagawa Hiroshige. Sheet 1, Spring, of four sheets of thirty-one-syllable light verse (*kyōka*) in the untitled album of poetry and prints known as "Every Variety of Fish" (*Uo tsukushi*). Japan. Edo period, early 1830s. Color woodblock print. 25.6 x 37 cm. The Mann Collection, gift of Kondo Sentarō, October 9, 1985

The four sheets are printed with light verse about various seasonal fish and shellfish. The vertical poems are arranged under topical headings, here "sea bream" and "black sea bream / small sea bream" (*tai, kurodai / kodai*). The names of the two compilers, Komogaki (Suzugaki?) Makuzu and Toshigaki Maharu, are to the right. Each poem is followed at the bottom of the sheet with the poet's name and, in some cases in smaller characters, his location.

This was the only time in my collecting experience that I have wanted to buy each and every print a dealer presented for consideration. I asked the price of each, but when we came to the poetry from the "Large Fish" series, Kondo said, "Oh, that's my 'compliment' to you." I was absolutely stunned by the gift and, to this day, speculate on why Kondo did such a generous thing. Perhaps he felt that he had already sold those sheets when he sold the balance of the album to the Gidwitzes. Perhaps he felt that they should not be separated from the other images and that the set should be completed. Perhaps he felt they had no commercial value when separated from the rest of the album. I'll never know.

When I caught my breath after Kondo's magnanimous present, Roberta and I decided to buy the Toshinobu and the Hiroshige but, much as we loved and admired the Ghost prints, declined them as being beyond our budget. As we prepared to go, Kondo asked us to leave behind the sheets of poetry and the Toshinobu and Hiroshige we bought—he would deliver them to us at our inn the next day, before we were to depart for the airport. He graciously invited us to dine with him that evening—our last in Japan—but we declined, with regrets. The next day, when delivering our package, Kondo said, with a smile and a twinkle, that he might have a fine Chōki for us in the near future; he would be in touch.

On our return to Chicago, I could not get the image of the Ghost prints out of my mind. I wrote to Kondo-san on November 7, 1985, offering to purchase them. But, alas, Kondo had died shortly after we saw him in Kyoto. In an undated reply, signed "Mrs. Kondo, S.," a price was suggested, but I demurred. On each of three subsequent visits to Kyoto, we have gone by The Red Lantern Shop and found it shuttered.

Tōdai-ji at The Art Institute of Chicago

"The Great Eastern Temple: Treasures of Japanese Buddhist Art from Tōdai-ji" opened at The Art Institute of Chicago on June 28 and ran through September 7, 1986. Holdings from this eighth-century temple, located in Nara south of Kyoto, were displayed in the United States for the only time in their history. The eponymous catalogue was edited by Yutaka Mino. The exhibition was a huge success for Mino and for the Art Institute. Opening and closing ceremonies conducted by Buddhist priests were fascinating, the objects (many of which had never before left Japan), compelling. We learned that most of the loans to Chicago were on view at the temple in Nara only once a year.

The dinner at the museum commemorating the opening included a number of dignitaries, such as Chicago Mayor Richard M. Daley and his wife, Maggie, with whom we sat. Hiroshi Sugimoto (b. 1948), some of whose arresting photographs from the *Seascapes* series we were to acquire ten years later, was also at our table.

New Year's Celebration in Kyoto, 1986

In November 1986, just two months after the Tōdai-ji exhibition closed, Roberta and I were pleased to host a dinner at our home for four honored guests: Kobayashi Yosōji (1913–2000), the president of the *Yomiuri Shinbun* newspaper/media group from 1981 to 1991 and the president and later chairman of Nippon Television Network (NTV); his wife (the daughter of the former *Yomiuri Shinbun* president Shōriki Matsutarō); Kurata Katsuhiro, general manager of International Operations for NTV; and Osamu Ueda (fig. 89). Dinner was arranged at the request of James Wood, the director of the Art Institute, and Yutaka Mino—Kobayashi-san had requested a visit to a local private home. I believe the Yomiuri group came to Chicago to negotiate a loan of important works from the museum's collection. The home-cooked dinner was rather formal, but some of our children joined us. (Strangely, none claims memory of that dinner, beyond their vivid imitation of Kurata-san's repeated "Mr. Kobayashi says . . ." in providing translations.) During the course of the evening, I mentioned that our family planned to be in Japan in December. The Kobayashis invited us to join them for dinner at the Yomiuri headquarters in Tokyo, and we gladly accepted.

OPPOSITE: FIG. 87. Okumura Toshinobu (act. 1717–50). *A Young Man-about-town Astride an Ox and Playing the Flute*, alluding to Hakoōmaru, the hero Soga no Gorō in his youth. Japan. Edo period, 1720s–30s. Woodblock print with hand coloring and metallic embellishment. 33.6 x 16.1 cm. The Mann Collection, acquired October 9, 1985

FIG. 88. Utagawa Hiroshige. *Peacock and Peonies*. Japan. Edo period, 1830s. Color woodblock print. 38.3 x 17.4 cm. The Mann Collection, acquired October 9, 1985

FIG. 89. Osamu Ueda, George Mann, Kobayashi Yosōji and Roberta Mann at the Mann home, Highland Park, IL. November 1986

FIG. 90. Left to right: David Mann, Roberta and George Mann, Elizabeth Malkin Lund, Julie Malkin Sacks, Debra Malkin Dockser, Brad Dockser and Randi Malkin Steinberger, visiting the Great Buddha in Kamakura. December 1986

The next month, Roberta and I, our four children, a niece and Brad Dockser, then our eldest daughter's boyfriend and now our son-in-law, embarked on the most enriching journey we ever have undertaken. In Tokyo, we made an early-morning tour of Tsukiji fish market, strolled around Meiji Shrine, walked the Ginza and went to fun restaurants for *teppanyaki*. We had lunch at a *gyōza* (dumpling) restaurant on a side street in the Harajuku district, where we thought the "pot stickers" would be U.S. appetizer-size (5 cm/2 inches long). Each of the eight of us ordered a dish of six of those delicacies, but when they arrived, we were shocked to see they were about four times as large as we expected! Our table was almost too small to hold all the platters of food and the young people crowding the shop laughed uproariously.

We traveled to Kamakura to see the outdoor bronze Buddha that we had missed on our visit in 1985 (fig. 90). Again, we called on Yutaka Mino's parents and were privileged to see more of their eight hundred fine, tea-related objects. Mrs. Mino presented a brief and modified demonstration of the Way of Tea. Yutaka then treated our family to a simple *shōjin ryōri*, a classic Buddhist vegetarian luncheon. That evening, back in Tokyo, we were the guests of the dealer Tajima Mitsuru of London Gallery. Taj wanted to keep the meal simple for the children, so he, too, invited us for a *shōjin ryōri* meal! The "day of the vegetable" was a wonderful exercise in discipline for the whole family.

On December 23, a few days later, we were met at the Prince Hotel by two limousines with American and Japanese flags fluttering on the fenders. Whisked off to Yomiuri headquarters, we joined Mr. and Mrs. Kobayashi and Mr. Kurata. We admired the company's impressive collection of Western art, including more than one Renoir, and the teahouse on the premises (figs. 91 and 92). Perhaps the highlight of the visit was when Kurata-san presented our eleven-year-old son, David, with an

FIG. 91. Mann family at Yomiuri Group teahouse in Tokyo. December 1986.

Left to right: George Mann, Randi Malkin Steinberger, Brad Dockser, Elizabeth Malkin Lund, Julie Malkin Sacks (blue dress), Debra Malkin Dockser, Roberta Mann, David Mann, our hosts (Mrs. and Mr. Kobayashi Yosōji) and Kurata Katsuhiro

FIG. 92. Enjoying a bowl of tea at Yomiuri Group teahouse in Tokyo. December 1986. Left to right: George Mann, Debra Malkin Dockser, David Mann, Randi Malkin Steinberger

FIG. 93. David Mann in Yomiuri Giants baseball jacket. December 1986

FIG. 94. George and Roberta Mann at the Hiiragiya inn, Kyoto. December 1986

FIG. 95. Roberta Mann, crawling through the pillar in the Great Buddha Hall at Tōdai-ji, Nara. December 1986

Legend has it that crawling through the narrow square at the base of the pillar is a symbolic gesture of entering the nostril of the Buddha, thereby gaining greater chance at enlightenment in a future life.

FIG. 96. David Mann (far left) with Kawashima Eiji and Kawashima Hiroaki. In the back: the abbot Shinkai with Jeffrey Gilbert. Kyoto, January 1, 1987

authentic Yomiuri Giants baseball team jacket, which he still has (fig. 93). Then back to our hotel in the shiny black limousines.

It was snowing when we left Tokyo on the high-speed Shinkansen to Nagoya, changing to an express train for a few days in the traditional old towns of Takayama, in the Japan Alps, and north to Kanazawa. We then went south on the Thunderbird Express to Kyoto, where we stayed at the venerable Hiiragiya inn, once again. There, we enjoyed deep tub soaks, sleeping on futons, strolls in the garden (with a dusting of snow on the ground) and *kaiseki* dining (fig. 94). We also made a day trip to Tōdai-ji, the Great Eastern Temple, in Nara, having just admired its riches only three months earlier at the Art Institute. Roberta and two of our children crawled through the slot in the lucky pillar in the Great Buddha Hall (fig. 95).

On New Year's Eve, we followed the throngs to the shrines, marveling at the fine kimonos worn by so many in observance of the New Year. Our family did not finish the elaborate meal served us that evening, so it was all left for breakfast the next morning, along with our American staples of juice, cereal and toast. The most unforgettable adventure of all, though, was a visit to Myōshin-ji Temple on New Year's Day.

Our son, David, met Kawashima Eiji at a boy's camp in Minnesota the previous summer, and they became good friends. Eiji's father, Shinkai, was the abbot of a sub-temple at Myōshin-ji, a complex of fifty sub-temples and the head temple of the Rinzai Zen sect. Eiji's first visit to the United States was to attend that boy's camp, and David was the first (perhaps the only) person he met who was familiar with Japanese culture. The boys were the same age. In advance of our trip to Japan, I suggested that David write to Eiji to tell him we were coming over.

When we arrived in Kyoto, Eiji, his father and his younger brother, Hiroaki, met us at Hiiragiya and welcomed us to their city. They invited us to spend part of New Year's Day at their residence at the temple. We arrived at the complex late in the afternoon on New Year's Day and were ushered into a formal reception room, where we were served frothy, bright-green tea as we sat on the floor. The other guests were Jeffrey and Emiko Gilbert, an American couple, coincidentally from the Chicago area, and their children.[28] The Gilberts were friends of the Kawashimas and had been invited (I believe) to translate and to explain customs, as needed. They were living in Kyoto in connection with Jeffrey's contribution to *The Complete History of Japanese*

Photography, a twelve-volume study published by Shōgakukan, beginning in 1986. Eiji's father entered, wearing simple robes, greeted us warmly and promptly excused himself to perform New Year's duties. While we were chatting with the Gilberts, Eiji entered with a shout of *"Dinner!"* and led us to the family's living quarters. We felt as if we were leaving the fourteenth century and entering the twentieth (figs. 96 and 97). Loud Western music was blaring, furnishings were modern, there was a Christmas tree and a Menorah. Eiji's mother, Yuriko, was dressed in an American-style skirt and sweater, and when Shinkai finished with his parishioners, he returned and changed into Western clothes, as well. Dinner was relaxed and informal, television blasting and conversation lively. Shortly after we finished, a group of dour-faced young monks in gray robes filed in. Once the residence door closed, they became quite raucous (fig. 98). One started playing the piano and singing rock songs, asking if he reminded us of Jimi Hendrix. After an hour or so of animated fun, Jeff Gilbert suggested that we should leave, as the spirits were, by that time, flowing quite freely. And we did, following much mutual bowing and "thank yous" in English and Japanese.

We returned to Chicago a few days later, already hungry to go back to Japan.

Over the next few years, between our return from Japan in January 1987 and the very important Scheiwe sales of March and October 1989, I bought six prints out of the hundreds (thousands?) that came to market, including my first mica-ground Utamaro (fig. 99). During the same period, I also placed the nine prints for sale at Christie's on April 22, 1987; six sold and three were "bought in," as I mentioned earlier. The prints I sold included the image of Sawamura Sōjūrō III, by Toyokuni, now in the van Biema Collection at the Sackler Gallery at the Smithsonian, referred to above (see figure 16).

Theodor Scheiwe Collection

Theodor Scheiwe, a German who made his fortune in the timber business, discovered prints on a trip to the United States in the 1920s, and became one of the most prominent European ukiyo-e collectors. His name appears often on price lists for sales at Sotheby's and Christie's in the 1960s and 1970s (Scheiwe is listed twenty-nine times on the price list for the Mellor sale at Sotheby's in July 1963). The prints he bought were always fine examples of distinctive and rare designs. In the spring and fall of 1989,

FIG. 97. The Gilbert sisters, from Flossmoor, IL, and the Kawashima brothers. Kyoto, January 1, 1987
FIG. 98. Raucous monks at Kawashima home

PAGE 102: FIG. 99. Kitagawa Utamaro. *The Courtesan Hanaōgi of the Gomeirō,* from the series *Comparison of the Charms of Beauties* (*Bijin kiryō kurabe*). Japan. Edo period. 1790s. Color woodblock print with mica ground. 37.8 x 25.1 cm. The Mann Collection, acquired December 8, 1987

PAGE 103: FIG. 100. Chōkyōsai Eiri (act. 1790s–early 1800s). *The Flowers of Edo: The Master of Yanagibashi* (*Edo no hana Yanagibashi natori*). Japan. Edo period, c. 1795. Color woodblock print with mica ground. 36.8 x 25.2 cm. The Mann Collection, acquired March 21, 1989

OPPOSITE: FIG. 101. Suzuki Harunobu. *Young Woman Visiting a Shrine on a Stormy Night,* alluding to the Noh play *Aridōshi.* Japan. Edo period, late 1760s. Color woodblock print. 28.6 x 21.1 cm. The Mann Collection, acquired April 15, 1991

472 lots of Scheiwe prints were sold in two installments at Christie's, New York. They had been published for various exhibitions by Dr. Rose Hempel (1920–2009), who had also written on the collection of Otto Riese, whom I visited in 1972, as noted earlier.

The Scheiwe catalogues include extraordinary prints by Kunimasa (c. 1773–1810), Utamaro, Sharaku and Hokusai—as well as several rare images from the Osaka region. As was always the case, I could not possibly go for everything I wanted. In the first sale, on March 21, I concentrated on and acquired the Eiri portrait of the singer Tomimoto Buzendayū, the cover lot (fig. 100). The impressions at the Musée Guimet in Paris and at The Metropolitan Museum of Art are the only others known to me. The hammer price was extremely high, and I did not consider any other major print in the sale. I also bought a first state, "deluxe" impression of Hokushū's *Nakamura Utaemon III as Kanawa Gorō Imakuni and Arashi Koroku IV as Omiwa* (lot 162 in the Christie's, New York sale *Japanese Prints, Paintings, Illustrated Books and Drawings from the Collection of the Late Theodor Scheiwe, Part I,* Mann catalogue no. 162). A Ryūkōsai Jokei of the actor Ichikawa Danzō (lot 160) in the same Scheiwe auction sold for $70,000 (hammer price), almost nine times its high estimate. I had dropped out of the bidding early. When it came up again at Christie's about ten years later, on March 26, 1998, I bought it for less than half the price for which it was sold in the Scheiwe auction (lot 262 in the Christie's, New York sale of Japanese art on March 26, 1998; Mann catalogue no. 159). Sometimes, you get lucky.

I did not attend nor bid in Scheiwe, Part II, on October 16 of that year.

Walter Amstutz Collection

Dr. Walter Amstutz, another preeminent collector living in Switzerland (along with Riese, Schindler, and "Tiko") traveled across the United States with Roger Keyes in the fall of 1972, stopping at museum and private collections. When they visited our home in October to look at my forty-five prints, Walter remarked on the orderly way in which I kept them in acid-free mounts, sharing that he kept his prints in folders in file cabinets. That was one of the reasons he gave for declining my request to visit him in Zurich earlier that year. That evening, we dined at Café de Paris, an elegant Chicago restaurant, since closed. Later, Roger wrote to say that Amstutz had "a very pleasant trip back to San Francisco and a whirlwind visit to Yosemite before he left for Hawai'i and Japan."

Walter Amstutz was a well-mannered man whose profession was publishing, but whose proclivity was skiing and climbing. In 1924, he founded the Swiss Academic Ski Club in Bern and became one of the outstanding leaders and administrators of the sport. From his early years, he also collected ukiyo-e and formed an important collection, which was sold by Sotheby's in Tokyo on April 15, 1991.[29]

I only learned of the range of the Amstutz Collection when it came up for sale in Tokyo. The catalogue of 233 lots of prints was almost entirely in color, which was still unusual then. Bidding by telephone from Chicago, very early in the morning, I was able to get six lots, including two brilliant designs by Harunobu: *Women Collecting Salt at Tagonoura with Mount Fuji in the Distance* (Mann catalogue no. 37) and *Young Woman Visiting a Shrine on a Stormy Night* (fig. 101). In general, the prices realized at that sale look unusually high, when viewed against the past fifty years or so.

Buying (1994) and Selling (2012) an Ukiyo-e Painting

Sebastian Izzard, then the head of Christie's Japanese department in New York and now a longtime dealer with his own gallery in Manhattan, told me that an exceptional Toyokuni painting would be offered in Christie's April 2, 1994 sale. Although I owned only one painting (a work signed "Eishi," purchased from Sotheby's in 1971, described in note 11), Sebastian suggested I consider the Toyokuni because of its sublime composition, superb condition and impeccable provenance (fig. 102). The hanging scroll was being offered by the estate of Blanchette Rockefeller (1909–1992), the widow of John D. Rockefeller III (1906–1978), and had previously been owned by the Tokyo dealer Kumita Shōhei and by the New York dealer Nathan V. Hammer. Also included in the auction were about one hundred ukiyo-e prints, the principal reason why I attended the presale exhibition. But when I looked at the Toyokuni painting, I concentrated my energy and resources on it. Perhaps because I regretted passing on the Kanbun-era painting David Newman sold to the Art Institute in 1989, I decided to bid on the Toyokuni.

The painting was a great addition to the collection and hung for most of the time in the living room or foyer of our home. However, in 2012, Sebastian Izzard, then, as now, the principal adviser to Roger Weston (b. 1943) on the formation of his esteemed collection of ukiyo-e beauty paintings, asked if I would be willing to sell the painting to Roger. Examples from Roger's paintings toured major cities in Japan in 2015 and were exhibited at The Art Institute of Chicago in 2018, accompanied by a gorgeous catalogue, *Painting the Floating World: Ukiyo-e Masterpieces from the Weston Collection*, edited by Roger L. Weston Associate Curator of Japanese Art Janice Katz, at the Art Institute, and Mami Hatayama, the curator of the Weston Collection. (The catalogue won the 2019 annual Museum Publications Design Competition first prize for exhibition catalogues, awarded by the American Alliance of Museums.) A few of Roger's pieces usually are displayed in one of the galleries comprising the Roger L. and Pamela Weston Wing, and Japanese Art Galleries at the Art Institute. Roger and Pam are active members of the Asian art-collecting community in Chicago, and we have known them for years. He has a terrific eye, is very patient and has been more than generous in sharing his collection with others. When Sebastian suggested a "migration" of the Mann Toyokuni to the Westons, I hesitated only slightly. I had stopped buying ukiyo-e and liked the idea of having a hand in determining where the painting ended up. While I loved (and still love) the Toyokuni, I thought of it as slightly alone in a collection of prints. We settled the exchange in April 2012, all parties delighted that this beauty, having lived for almost twenty years in Highland Park, had a new home in the Chicago area. It was moving to see it alongside other choice Japanese paintings in the Weston Collection exhibition at the Art Institute, in 2018.

Anguish and Relief: Adding a Chōki

I had been "silent" for about a year until the Christie's catalogue arrived for the November 2, 1996 auction in New York. The sale promised jewels from the 1790s: beauty prints by Kiyomasu, Eishō, Eisui, Utamaro and Chōki; actor portraits by Sharaku; and a few first-rate landscapes from the 1830s and 1840s.

When I flipped through the Christie's catalogue, I was "blown away" by a double portrait by Chōki of Moto, a maidservant of the Yoshidaya, and the geisha Mizue. Sebastian Izzard recommended I look carefully at the print, much as he had drawn

FIG. 102. Utagawa Toyokuni. *Woman Wearing a Summer Kimono*. c. 1795. Hanging scroll; ink and color on silk. 93.4 x 34 cm. WESTON COLLECTION, no. 109. Photo: Steven Tucker. Photo used with permission. All rights reserved

The young woman is looking at herself in a folding hand mirror. The verse, as translated in *Painting the Floating World: Ukiyo-e Masterpieces from the Weston Collection* (The Art Institute of Chicago, 2018), reads:

taoyame no	Graceful looks
kehai utsuseru	fading in
asa kagami	the fickle mirror of morning.
haka naki yo o ba	Do you know so little
kage to shirazu ya	of life's fleeting images?

Akihide

Akihide (Miwa Akihide, 1737–1809)

Translation by Jennifer Preston, with the assistance of Mami Hatayama

107

婦女人相十品

相觀 歌麿考画

FIG. 103. Kitagawa Utamaro. *Woman Exhaling Smoke from a Pipe*, from the series *Ten Types in the Physiognomic Study of Women* (*Fujo ninsō juppon*). Japan. Edo period, c. 1792–93. Color woodblock print with mica ground. 39.1 x 26 cm. The Mann Collection, acquired November 2, 1996

OPPOSITE: FIG. 104. Eishōsai Chōki (act. c. 1790s–early 1800s). *Mizue, a Geisha, and Moto, a Waitress at Yoshidaya [in Shinmachi, Osaka]* (*Geiko Mizue Yoshidaya nakai Moto*) Japan. Edo period, c. 1794. Color woodblock print with mica ground. 37.3 x 24.9 cm. The Mann Collection, acquired November 2, 1996

my attention to the Toyokuni painting I bought in 1994, described just above. An Utamaro of a woman smoking, from the series of ten types of female physiognomy, although somewhat faded, was also fetching, as the collection had few of the more major images by Utamaro (fig. 103).

But the Chōki had me. Until then, I had not encountered such pristine color and condition in a Japanese print (fig. 104).

Oddly, I do not remember my emotions during the auction. My heart probably was thudding with anxiety. Would I win this Chōki or be rejected as I was in 1981? With David Caplan of Mita Arts acting as my agent, both the Chōki and the Utamaro became mine.

Over the years, I asked David and and others to bid for me. I wanted professional, independent advice on my own assessments of the quality, rarity and value of the prints. While I had confidence in my own assessments, I felt more comfortable

with independent advice. With their decades of involvement in the print market, these dealers knew whether there were other impressions and where they were; if they had been sold in recent years, publicly or privately; and often, the prices realized. At other auctions, my agent might suggest I increase my limit. On rare occasions, I was told I would not have to pay as much as I'd planned. Another consideration was my desire to hide my participation in auctions until after the sales. As I got better known in the ukiyo-e community, I had a concern, probably unfounded, that my bidding might spur someone else to pay more attention to the lot. And if a dealer bought a print on my behalf, it was *always* easier to arrange delivery of the print to my home.

After David collected the Chōki and Utamaro from Christie's and delivered them to me, I asked Bernd Jesse, then an assistant curator of Japanese Art at The Art Institute of Chicago, if I could bring my new Chōki to the museum. (Bernd was at the museum from 1995 until 2001, when he returned to Germany; he is now lecturer in Japanology at his alma mater, Goethe University in Frankfurt.) Assuming our new purchase was unique, as Christie's catalogue stated, I asked Bernd to determine if *similar* Chōki images were in the museum collection. A few days later, to my surprise, Bernd brought out an impression of the *same design*, albeit dirty and faded and with damage and repair (fig. 105). The museum bought the print at the Mellor sale at Sotheby's, London (July 10, 1963, lot 282), with Jack Hillier bidding as agent.

My heart sank when we immediately noticed differences in the cup Moto is holding and in the crest on her left sleeve. Had I inadvertently purchased *another* reproduction? By the grace of the lightbox, we were able to see that a skilled restorer had managed to mask paper losses in the cup and the crest by teasing the surrounding paper fibers to patch the holes in the Art Institute print. In doing so, the restorer had to sacrifice tiny parts of the original design.

Anguish turned to relief. This Chōki masterpiece is one of my favorites. Acquiring it made up for the Chōki beauty I couldn't catch at Le Véel, fifteen years earlier. But not completely—I still wish I had both.

Truth be told, I have several favorites in my collection, although the Chōki image of Moto and Mizue might be the "first among equals." Masanobu's *Monkey Trainer of the Floating World on the Sumida River* (see figure 53); Toyonobu's *Courtesan Parading with Her Girl Attendant* (Mann catalogue no. 24); Harunobu's *Young Woman Visiting a Shrine on a Stormy Night* (see figure 101); Sharaku's portraits of Ebizō (see figure 47)

FIG. 105. Eishōsai Chōki. *Mizue, a Geisha, and Moto, a Waitress at Yoshidaya [in Shinmachi, Osaka]*. Japan. Edo period, c. 1794. Color woodblock print with mica ground. 37.4 x 24.8 cm. The Art Institute of Chicago, Clarence Buckingham Collection, 1963.1152

and Onayo (see figure 108 below); and Tomi-moto Buzendayū, by Eiri (see figure 100), which I purchased in the Scheiwe sale, all belong to this special group.

Final Henri Vever Sale: London, 1997

The remaining ukiyo-e from Henri Vever were offered at Sotheby's, London, on October 30, 1997 (fig. 106). Before the initial three sales in 1974, 1975 and 1977, about two hundred prints had been selected by Jack Hillier and the Vever family, purportedly to be held back for posterity. I never knew what caused a change of heart and the family's decision to sell.

This final Vever auction included quite a number of exceptional prints, including Kaigetsudō Dohan's image of a courtesan striding to the left; the *Awabi Fishers* triptych by Utamaro; eleven (!) Sharaku prints; and Hokusai's fine Great Wave and Red Fuji. By then, I already had a very good Great Wave purchased in the April 27, 1993 Christie's, New York sale (lot 164) (see figure 137 below). Although I was still pining for a Red Fuji, I settled on two other prints in Vever IV, both rarer than the Hokusai: a Sharaku "large head" and a domestic scene by Torii Kiyohiro of two young women trimming their toenails and washing their feet on a veranda (fig. 107).

The impression of the Sharaku *Sanogawa Ichimatsu III as Onayo* is near flawless, and the condition is superb (fig. 108). As much as I wanted it, I chose not to bid on the *Onayo* when the lot came up, hoping it would be "passed"—then I could buy it below the reserve. Indeed, no one bid. David Caplan and I approached Neil Davey, the auctioneer, and agreed to a purchase at the reserve price.

The auction catalogue, compiled by Jack Hillier, stated that there was "another impression" of *Onayo* in the 1911 Vignier and Inada catalogue, no. 280, plate LXXXIII. Only months later did I compare our new *Onayo* to the one in Vignier and Inada—and discovered that they were the *same print*, evidenced by the crease in the upper right corner. In the 1911 catalogue, the owner is listed as "Swet" (most assuredly, "Swettenham"). I presume that Vever acquired the print directly from Sir Frank Swettenham (1850–1946) after the Vignier and Inada catalogue was published and before the Swettenham Collection was sold at Sotheby's in 1912, because the *Onayo* was not listed in the catalogue of that sale.

I have not found a better version of the *Onayo* in any of the standard Sharaku catalogues. The print has since been exhibited in Tokyo and New York.

Berès "Collection Privée" Goes Public

In 1999, the grand doyenne of ukiyo-e, Huguette Berès, died in Paris. I first met Huguette in the mid-1960s, but never bought any significant prints from her. Unlike Bob Sawers and Ray Lewis, Berès—like Nishi Saijū and David Caplan—was a collector as well as a dealer. Berès, Nishi, Caplan and I had similar tastes, so it hardly ever occurred that any of them would be willing to part with something that I wanted, at a price I was willing to pay. At Vever I, as I described earlier, Huguette bought at least

FIG. 106. George and Roberta Mann at Sotheby's, London for the final Vever sale in October 1997

PAGE 112: FIG. 107. Torii Kiyohiro (act. 1737–76). *Two Young Women on a Veranda Trimming Their Toenails and Washing Their Feet.* Japan. Edo period, c. 1760. Color woodblock print. 42.5 x 30.2 cm. The Mann Collection, acquired October 30, 1997
The print is apparently unique and is in choice condition.

PAGE 113: FIG. 108. Tōshūsai Sharaku. *The Actor Sanogawa Ichimatsu III as Onayo, a Courtesan of the Gion District, Kyoto* in the kabuki play *The Iris Soga of the Bunroku Era* (*Hana-ayame Bunroku Soga*), performed at the Miyako-za theater in the fifth lunar month, 1794. Japan. Edo period, 1794. Color woodblock print with mica ground. 38.9 x 25.9 cm. The Mann Collection, acquired October 30, 1997

a half dozen lots on which I was the underbidder. She offered them to me afterward at sharply higher prices. Nevertheless, we remained, as Huguette herself always put it, "friendly competitors" at auctions. The Huguette Berès "collection privée" of Japanese prints was offered at Sotheby's, Paris, in two installments: November 27, 2002, and November 23, 2003.

As I stated earlier, there was one print that nagged at Roberta in the manner that Hokusai's Red Fuji has haunted me: Shun'ei's bust portrait of Bandō Hikosaburō III as Sugawara no Michizane, sold in the first Vever auction in March 1974 (lot 139). I also loved it. The blacks are luminous, the condition stellar. Huguette outbid me and offered to sell it to me after the Vever sale at an exorbitant markup. She joked that I would get it only if our son, David, married Florence, her granddaughter! I wonder whether Huguette's daughter, Anisabelle, considered Roberta's and my hankering for the Shun'ei when she and Sotheby's agreed on the estimate (and the reserve) for the print in the 2002 sale of her mother's estate. The estimate was so high that the print failed to elicit a bid. The pink mica-ground *Reflective Love* by Utamaro, which Huguette bought at Vever I and offered to me after that sale, was another on my "wish list," but it went to Sebastian Izzard (presumably for a client). In the end, I was shut out at the 2002 Berès sale.

While disappointing for me, the 2002 Berès sale was fortuitous for The Art Institute of Chicago. For about two decades prior to her death, the irrepressible Dorothy Braude Edinburg (1920–2015), who grew up in Michigan, but lived in Brookline, a suburb of Boston, had a deep commitment to the Art Institute, thanks to strong relationships with the curators of Western prints and Chinese art. Between 1998 and 2014, the museum mounted at least six exhibitions of some fifteen hundred works, primarily Chinese ceramics and Western prints and drawings, donated by Dorothy over the years. She had a delightful penchant for smaller objects, perhaps because she was petite herself, but more likely because they fit in her breakfront.

It was important to the Art Institute that the relationship with Dorothy be nurtured, and I was seen as a secondary source of support in that effort. Primary support was provided by Suzanne Folds McCullough, who retired as the chair and curator of prints and drawings at the Art Institute in 2016, after forty years at the museum; Elinor Pearlstein, associate curator of Chinese art until 2017; and David C. Hilliard, a prominent, highly respected member of the museum's board of trustees. Hilliard is also a collector of important Old Master prints and drawings, and an intellectual-property attorney in Chicago with important contacts in Boston, having come from that area.

I first met Dorothy in April 1996, when she and other members of the Friends of Asiatic Art from the Museum of Fine Arts, Boston, came to see prints at our home (figs. 109a, b and 110). We became good friends, communicating by then-novel e-mail, often concerning one of her interests—Japanese illustrated books.[30] From time to time, when Dorothy found a Japanese illustrated book that appealed to her, she asked my opinion. And each time, I protested that I had no knowledge of illustrated books nor of the complexities of that medium, but it did not put her off. So, I was not surprised when she contacted me in the fall of 2002 about lot 193 in the upcoming Berès sale at Sotheby's in Paris: the 1767 woodblock-printed album by Itō Jakuchū titled *Stone-printed Sketches*, in a style (*ishizuri-e*) that imitates black-and-white stone rubbings (fig. 111). Once again, I emphasized that I was not knowledgeable, but Dorothy was determined to get some input from me.

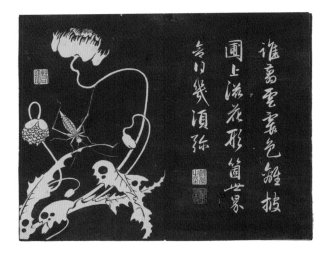

FIG. 109a. Dorothy Braude Edinburg (third from left) at the Mann home in Highland Park, IL, with Friends of Asian Art group from Boston, viewing Japanese prints. 1996

FIG. 109b. George Mann showing prints to the Friends of Asian Art from Boston. 1996

A painting by Toyokuni, now in the Weston Collection, hangs on the wall at right.

FIG. 110. Dorothy Edinburg, viewing portraits of Henrietta Herz, by Anton Graff (1736–1813), left, and Amalie Beer, by Johann Karl Kretschmar (1769–1847), right, at the opening of "The Power of Conversation: Jewish Women and Their Salons," McMullen Museum of Art, Boston College. August 2005. Courtesy of Jo-Ann Pinkowitz

FIG. 111. Itō Jakuchū (1716–1800). *Poppies*, from *Stone-printed Sketches* (*Soken sekisatsu*). Japan. Edo period, 1767. Woodblock-printed book. 17.7 x 28.5 cm each page. The Art Institute of Chicago, Gift of Dorothy Braude Edinburg to the Harry B. and Bessie K. Braude Memorial Collection, 2013.316

Selections from the Berès sale, including the Jakuchū book, were displayed at Sotheby's, London, before returning to Paris for the sale. As I was in London at the time, I went to the viewing, where I noticed discoloration in certain places in the Jakuchū book. I contacted Timothy Clark, then head of the Japanese section in the Department of Asia at the British Museum and asked if I could examine the museum's impression of the same book. The Jakuchū book for sale was slightly better than the one at the British Museum (which, coincidentally, came to that museum from

FIG. 112. Tōshūsai Sharaku. *The Actors Ōtani Hiroji III as Hata no Taizan Taketora; Segawa Tomisaburō II as Prince Koretaka Disguised as the Ōtomo Family Maid Wakakusa; and Bandō Hikosaburō III as Godai Saburō Chikatada* in the kabuki play *Intercalary Year Praise of a Famous Poem* (*Urūo yoshi meika no homare*), performed at the Miyako-za theater in the eleventh lunar month, 1794. Japan. Edo period, 1794. Color woodblock prints. 31.1 x 14.1 cm, left panel; 30.4 x 14.1 cm, center panel; 30 x 14 cm, right panel. The Art Institute of Chicago, Kate S. Buckingham Endowment, 2003.337 (left); Clarence Buckingham Collection, 1928.1062 (center); Clarence Buckingham Collection, 1928.1061 (right)

Jack Hillier in 1979), but the discoloration still bothered me. I called Pamela de Tristan, a highly respected British conservator, active in the field since 1981 and a friend of Bob Sawers and asked her to examine the Berès Jakuchū. When she pronounced it "fine," I gave Dorothy the "thumbs up," and she went after the book at the Paris auction. Her successful bid was almost three times Sotheby's high estimate, but she was pleased to have bought it. The volume came to The Art Institute of Chicago after Dorothy's death in 2013, as part of a large donation; she also bequeathed $35 million to the museum.

The 2003 Berès sale was similar in variety and emphasis to the 2002 sale. I was able to buy one print: an unsigned Kunimasa portrait of Nakamura Noshio II that Huguette had bought at Vever II (Mann catalogue no. 96).[31]

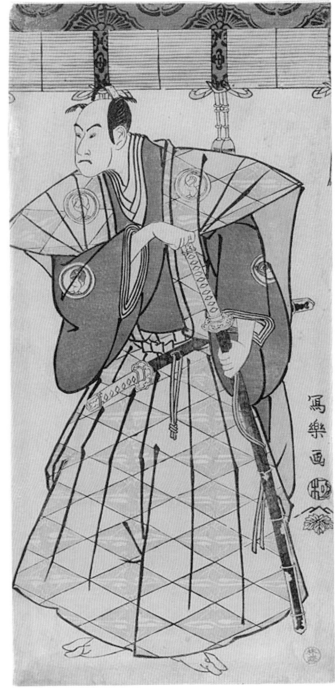

Also included in the 2003 Berès sale was an *aizuri-e* version of Hokusai's *Fuji in Clear Weather*. A number of all-blue states of this design exist, and they are controversial. Those issues notwithstanding, the bidding was vigorous, and the price went to twice the high estimate. When the hammer fell, a gentleman in the audience rose, announced he was a representative of the Republic of France and exercised the pre-emption rights (*Droit de Préemption*) of the State to purchase the print. Although I was vaguely aware of this right, I had never seen it in action. The crowd, mostly French, erupted in applause knowing that this Hokusai, controversial as it is, would remain in France. Not too many years later, Roberta and I saw an exhibition of Hokusai gems at the Musée Guimet in Paris that included the "Blue Fuji" from Berès.

Like the 2002 sale, the 2003 Berès auction was also fortuitous for The Art Institute of Chicago. Included in the sale was Sharaku's portrait of Ōtani Hiroji III as Hata no Daizen Taketora in *Intercalary Year Praise of a Famous Poem*, performed at the Miyako-za theater in Edo (Tokyo) in 1794. That print is the left-hand sheet of a triptych (fig. 112). Huguette Berès bought it for 680,000 FF (about $125,000 at the conversion rate then in effect) on June 3, 1992, at the Drouot Richelieu in Paris (H. Chayette and L. Calmels, Commissaires Priseurs). I knew that the Art Institute owned the other two panels, depicting Bandō Hikosaburō as Godai Saburō Chikatada and Segawa Tomisaburō as a maid who turns out to be Prince Koretaka. All three panels bear the seal of the connoisseur/dealer Hayashi Tadamasa (1853–1906) and were sold to separate buyers in the stupendous Hayashi sale in Paris in 1902. The two sheets of the triptych already owned by the Art Institute were acquired in 1928 from the German businessman Alexander G. Moslé (1862–1949). I do not know the ownership history of the third panel between its sale in the 1902 Hayashi auction and the Berès purchase in 1992.

While other collections have one or two of the three panels in the Sharaku triptych, I am not aware of any that includes all three.[32] The opportunity to reunite the Hayashi triptych after being separated for one hundred years *and* to enhance the Art Institute's already stellar Sharaku holdings with the only extant complete triptych was compelling. The director of the Art Institute, Jim Wood, agreed. I was authorized to bid for the print on the museum's behalf, without engaging the services of a professional agent. I am certain no other participant at the auction realized the history that was unfolding—the panel would complete the triptych for The Art Institute of Chicago. I was excited and nervous, but my bidding limit was generous, and I had no trouble getting the lot—at considerably less than Huguette paid for it in 1992.[33] It was quite an experience, bringing the print back to the museum and laying it alongside the other two panels.

Wrestling with an Elephant

Adolphe Stoclet (1871–1949) was a Belgian financier trained as an engineer and noted for his extensive art collections. He commissioned the Palais Stoclet, a Secessionist masterpiece in Brussels designed by Josef Hoffman, with interiors by Gustav Klimt, Kolomon Moser and others. His wife, Suzanne Stevens (1874–1959), came from a Parisian family of art collectors, including her uncle, the painter Alfred Stevens. Husband and wife complemented each other perfectly, and their family connections gave them entrée to the avant-garde throughout Europe. In addition to contemporary art and classical Chinese, Tibetan and African art, the Stoclets began acquiring ukiyo-e avidly in the early twentieth century.

Although about two hundred seventy-five prints from the collection were sold by Philippe R. Stoclet (b. 1931), a nephew of Adolphe and Suzanne, at Sotheby's, London in 1965, the balance of the collection remained largely unknown until the 2004 sale. The catalogue was a revelation, including many images either never seen before, or otherwise known in only one or two impressions.

Roberta and I flew to London for the June 8 sale. I spent hours studying the prints placed on long tables around which crowds of collectors, dealers and other curious individuals milled, jostling for seats. As with most auctions, groups of ten or twenty prints were stacked into folders. I located three of the four prints in which

I was interested, confirmed they were as fine as they looked in the catalogue, and moved on to a fourth: a Kiyomasu of two actors wrestling with an elephant in a scene from a complicated kabuki drama (fig. 113). When I opened the folder, the "real life" print was so vivid it just about took my breath away. Here I was, face-to-face with an image known in only two other impressions: one, also hand-colored, but differently, at the Nelson-Atkins Museum of Art in Kansas City; and one (of which I was then unaware) uncolored, at the Museum of Fine Arts, Boston (figs. 114 and 115).[34] I had admired illustrations of the Nelson-Atkins impression in catalogues and assumed that it and the Stoclet example were both published at the beginning of the eighteenth century, when Kiyomasu was active and when the kabuki drama was performed. I had no difficulty acquiring not only the Kiyomasu, but also prints by Toyonobu, Kiyohiro and Ryūkōsai Jokei.

However, I soon learned that there was uncertainty about when the Nelson-Atkins Kiyomasu was published.[35] And two days after the sale, on June 10, I excitedly wrote Roger Keyes to tell him I had purchased the Stoclet Kiyomasu, and received the following reply, dated June 16:

> Dear George,
> I remember the moment Mr. Suzuki and I opened the portfolio at Kansas City and saw the wonderful Kiyomasu print with the elephant! [Their discovery occurred in 1971, several months prior to the "Primitives" Symposium at the Art Institute, described elsewhere herein.] We both knew the Kiyomine copy. Neither of us had ever seen an original. How thrilled we both were! And now it turns out that Mr. Stoclet owned another impression, and you have purchased it!! . . . [T]he print captures a unique moment of historical excitement. Murataya, the fifth-generation descendant of the original publisher, rediscovered the *block* [emphasis added] for this print around 1812. He showed it to Tatekawa Emba [Enba], the novelist and kabuki historian. Emba identified the performance and dated the print. This was the period when the first history of ukiyo-e was still in manuscript, when writers like Kyoden and Bakin collected any printed fragments of the early ukiyo-e they could find and saved them in scrapbooks. And here was an actual *block* [emphasis added] that had survived from the earliest days of the actor portrait tradition! More people got involved. Ichikawa Danjūrō VII composed a verse, and Kiyomine, the fifth-generation head of the Torii school, copied the print. The thing that makes your print the more special of the two, however, is that the writer Tatekawa Emba actually owned it!! That is his handwriting at the top of the print. He signed and sealed it at the left. (His signature reads Tatekawa Danshuro. Danshuro because that sounds like Danjūrō, I think. He was very close to the Ichikawa family. You find his poems and comments on Kunisada surimono of Danjūrō VII. And, of course the Ichikawa family was central to his classic theater chronology, Kabuki nendaiki. His seal reads Emba.)

Some impressions of the Kiyomine "copy" mentioned by Roger, including the Honolulu Museum impression, have an extensive printed inscription (fig. 116). It reads in part: "This design is from an old *block* [emphasis added] in the possession of [the publisher] . . .", a statement consistent with Roger's conclusion that it was the Kiyomasu block that had survived for over one hundred years. Further, the inscription

FIG. 113. Torii Kiyomasu I (act. c. 1704–18?). *Wrestling with an Elephant* (*Zōbiki*): *The Actors Ichikawa Danjūrō I as Yamanoue Gennaisaemon and Yamanaka Heikurō I as Prince Suzuka* (*Suzuka no Ōji*) in the kabuki play *The Courtesan Wang Zhaojun* (*Keisei Ōshōkun*), performed at the Nakamura-za theater, first lunar month, 1701. Japan. Edo period, early 18th century. Woodblock print with hand coloring. 63.1 x 32.2 cm. The Mann Collection, acquired June 8, 2004

FIG. 114. Torii Kiyomasu I. *Wrestling with an Elephant* (*Zōbiki*): *The Actors Ichikawa Danjūrō I as Yamanoue Gennaisaemon and Yamanaka Heikurō I as Prince Suzuka* (*Suzuka no Ōji*) in *The Courtesan Wang Zhaojun*. Japan. Edo period, early 18th century. Woodblock print with hand coloring. 59 x 32.4 cm. The Nelson-Atkins Museum of Art, William Rockhill Nelson Trust, 32-143/9

FIG. 115. After Torii Kiyomasu I. *Wrestling with an Elephant (Zōbiki): The Actors Ichikawa Danjūrō I as Yamanoue Gennaisaemon and Yamanaka Heikurō I as Prince Susuka (Suzuka no Ōji)* in *The Courtesan Wang Zhaojun.* Japan. Meiji–Taishō-period (first quarter 20th century) impression from an Edo-period woodblock. Woodblock print. 73.5 x 34.5 cm. Museum of Fine Arts, Boston, William S. and John T. Spaulding Collection, RES.21.312. Photograph © 2021 Museum of Fine Arts, Boston

FIG. 116. Torii Kiyomine (1787–1868). *The Actors Ichikawa Danjūrō I as Yamanoue Gennaisaemon and Yamanaka Heikurō I as Prince Suzuka (Suzuka no Ōji).* Japan. Edo period, 1812. Woodblock print with hand coloring. 49.2 x 22.9 cm. Honolulu Museum of Art, Gift of James A. Michener, 1972 (16268)

is signed "Tatekawa Enba at the age of seventy," which corresponds to the year 1812.[36] Because Enba's signature is on my Kiyomasu impression and on the Kiyomine, as well, it is reasonable to conclude that Enba conferred with the publisher in determining how the Kiyomine should be colored, and that my Kiyomasu, then owned by Enba, was considered in the process.

I sent a copy of Roger's reply to Ken Caplan (David's son and now the director of their firm, Mita Arts Gallery, in Tokyo), asking for his reaction. Ken confirmed his and David's opinion that the Kiyomasu was issued in the early eighteenth century, and reminded me about something that occurred at the viewing before the sale:

> [My] young dealer friend, Mr. Takashima of the gallery Beniya, who has an eagle eye (and whom you met in London while inspecting the print) . . . believes that your print was made far earlier than the 19th century. He also thinks that the example in the Nelson-Atkins was made later and your example is the earlier, original version.[37]

I remembered meeting Takashima Masao at the viewing, and discussing when the Kiyomasu was printed, but I did not grasp the significance of his comments. Now, with Roger's letter and Ken's report, I had inconsistent views on the date the Kiyomasu was printed: the catalogue implied it was issued in the early *eighteenth* century, when the drama depicted was presented; Roger thought the print was made in the *nineteenth* century from an old block; Caplan and Takashima proposed that it was made in the *eighteenth* century, perhaps early in that century. And furthermore, the inscription on the Kiyomine and the Enba signature on both Kiyomasu prints indicate an early *nineteenth*-century date.

The print depicts Ichikawa Danjūrō I as Yamanoue Gennaisaemon and Yamanaka Heikurō as Suzuka no Ōji wrestling with an elephant in the kabuki drama *The Courtesan Wang Zhaojun,* performed at the Nakamura-za theater in the spring of 1701. There are two handwritten inscriptions on the Stoclet impression, both by Tatekawa (Utei) Enba (1743–1822). It is believed these inscriptions (which do not appear on the Nelson-Atkins and Boston examples) were added by Enba in the early nineteenth century. The Stoclet sale catalogue states that the Kiyomasu bears a "seal and manuscript text written by an unidentified contemporary collector giving details of the play and the actors." I bought the print not realizing that there was any mystery to it at all or that Roger Keyes would determine that the "contemporary" collector was none other than Tatekawa Enba.

I loaned the Kiyomasu to an exhibition at the University of Chicago in 2012. David Waterhouse, Professor Emeritus in East Asian Studies at the University of Toronto, commented on our Kiyomasu in the exhibition catalogue, *Awash in Color: French and Japanese Prints*, Smart Museum of Art, University of Chicago (2012), 94:

> In his handwritten inscription on the Kiyomasu I print, Enba describes it as *denrai no kohan,* "an old block which has been handed down." *Kohan* could be interpreted as referring to either the block or the print itself, but is more likely to refer to the block. . . . Roger Keyes has . . . suggested that both surviving impressions of the Kiyomasu [the Nelson-Atkins print and the Stoclet print] were made from the original block at the same time . . . and that Enba himself owned the [Stoclet] print. However, this remains speculative. . . . It is not clear

when Emiya [the publisher] made his prints from the "old block"; it could have been much earlier, perhaps as early as 1701, even if the block too survived into the nineteenth century. The hand-coloring on the [Stoclet] print, with mineral pigments that include green, yellow, gray and orange-red, appears to be original.

Alfred Haft, of the Sainsbury Institute and British Museum who has translated inscriptions on many prints in our collection, wrote to me on July 10, 2019 concerning *kohan*:

> In regard to *kohan*, from what I can tell, the Edo-period examples given in *Nihon kokugo daijiten* (Dictionary of the Japanese language) may point toward something more like "old publication" than "old woodblock," and the dictionary seems to imply that the meaning "old woodblock" may be more recent.

Roger Keyes and Suzuki Jūzō brought the Nelson-Atkins impression of the print to the attention of Howard Link, at the then-named Honolulu Academy of Arts, in 1971.[38] Suzuki-sensei also introduced the Nelson-Atkins print to the scholarly world later the same year at the ukiyo-e "Primitives" symposium at The Art Institute of Chicago.[39] The two scholars identified the actors, the roles and the production. They also noted that in 1812, Torii Kiyomine produced a "copy" of this design in reduced format, as an homage to his forebear.

The Nelson-Atkins Kiyomasu bears the seal of Ōta Nanpo (1749–1823), the poet and scholar who often collaborated with ukiyo-e artists (such as Hokusai) during the early part of the nineteenth century.[40] It is ironic that two of the three known impressions of this great design are inscribed or sealed by two of the most important chroniclers of the early history of kabuki, and that they died but a year apart: Tatekawa Enba in 1822 and Ōta Nanpo in 1823. The solution to the conundrum over when the prints were released—in the early eighteenth century when Kiyomasu was working, or later—is yet to come, but my hunch is the three impressions I have located were all printed from the same block, but well after the block was carved in the early eighteenth century. I suspect my Kiyomasu was hand colored in the middle-to-late eighteenth century, and the Nelson- Atkins print was hand colored "later."

What I Look For in a Japanese Print

I estimate that twenty or so of the prints I bought in the 1960s I donated to The Art Institute of Chicago. I sold around ten others because I felt, at the time, they were of lesser quality than the rest of my collection. When I started to attend auctions in New York and London in the 1970s, I was forming my standards for quality, condition, state, rarity and provenance. Perhaps the most subjective of the criteria is that of "quality." One develops a personal sense of quality after spending countless hours examining works at museums and auctions, in other collections and in publications. No doubt, I am influenced by what others have chosen to collect and by the views of scholars.

One also must take into account that the ukiyo-e artist was commissioned by a publisher for a given design and did not control the printing process. That fell to a team of wood-block cutters and printers hired by the publisher, with variant results. During the printing stage, the publisher might send a proof copy of the print to the artist, asking for direction on coloration. Blocks might shrink or wear out after multiple editions, compromising clarity and coloration. Prints portraying actors in kabuki dramas were sometimes recut to insert the crests (*mon*) of actors who performed in subsequent presentations of the same drama. This practice is evident if one compares my Masanobu print of Hisamatsu and Osome (see figure 39) with one of the two Masanobu designs of those lovers in the Art Institute collection (see figures 40 and 41). Images printed from such recut blocks often show more wear than earlier editions. With multiple printings of a design over a considerable period (months, sometimes years), later editions show block degradation in predictable areas. For example, the double line border of the title cartouches from Hokusai's series *Thirty-six Views of Mount Fuji* shows line breaks in later printings that are not seen in early ones.

Condition is an important factor and includes such matters as fading, staining or other discoloration, and physical damage, such as trimming, tearing, rubbing, creasing or paper loss. Few prints made before the 1750s are pristine. For me, if the design "sings," some condition problems can be overlooked. (I never have been bothered by collector "notations" or seals on art—they give me information and a feeling of continuity and kinship with former collectors.) When I find an early work in outstanding condition—Masanobu's *A Monkey Trainer of the Floating World on the Sumida River*, figure 53, or Toyonobu's *A Courtesan Parading with Her Girl Attendant* (Mann catalogue no. 24)—it is very exciting.

Many prints were produced in multiple states. Usually, but not always, the preferred state is the earliest. Blocks were often recut and then reused, sometimes by a different publisher hoping to capitalize on the successful rerelease of a given design or series. Suzuki Harunobu, the first artist to use multiple printed colors (in the 1760s), each requiring a separate block, generally issued designs without a signature. Later editions—in which the colors were sometimes changed—often have a signature. When I made my first purchase (see figure 6), I did not know that it was a later impression. I would likely "pass" on that print today, because I now know that early impressions are available.

Rarity has always attracted my attention. Some condition problems can be overlooked if the example is the only one, or one of very few impressions known to survive, *and* it is otherwise compelling.

Provenance is always a consideration. Many of my prints were once in distinguished collections in Europe, Japan or the United States: Barboutau, Hayashi, Vever, Ledoux, Amstutz, Gerli, Le Véel, Ehrman, Berès, Gidwitz, Garland, Schraubstadter, Stoclet, Maroni, Fuller, Mellor, Popper, Haviland, Gaines, Takano, Schindler, Scheiwe, Tuke, among others. Why? Because each of those collectors is respected as having had refined taste. I enjoy tracing provenance through catalogues and other books published since the early twentieth century. Ledoux's policies of limiting his collection to two hundred prints and focusing on very rare early prints have influenced me strongly. Returning often to the five-volume Ledoux catalogue, I always conclude that there is hardly a print in it that I would not want to own, in addition to the four already in my collection. Because of Ledoux's high standards, I determined to try to buy what I considered to be the better designs in a series, and to reach for those in preferred condition. Complete series generally have not interested me, except for the "Large Fish" set by Hiroshige (see figure 73 and Mann catalogue nos. 118.1–14). Unlike Ledoux, I never set a limit on the *number* of prints to include in my collection, so I never disposed of prints because they exceeded an arbitrary limit.

On a handful of occasions, I purchased an inferior impression (or a later state) of a particular image because I felt I "needed" the print to keep the collection balanced, but had not yet found a more acceptable example at a reasonable price.

At times, I postponed the purchase of a widely available image, such as a Hiroshige landscape, until I found a superior one. The result has been that I lack "key" designs. I always felt a better Hokusai Red Fuji would become available, and the price would be more favorable. A Hokusai boom had been building for some time. In 2019, a Red Fuji sold at Christie's, New York for $507,000, and I suspect private transactions have been even higher.

Because of my desire to have the "better" or "best" impression of any particular design, I have considered replacing a print when I found that elusive superior one. I bought Toyokuni's *Kataoka Nizaemon VII as Bantarō* at the second Le Véel auction in 1980 (fig. 117). Actually I already owned one (fig. 118). The one I owned was "down" in color: the blue-striped leg coverings worn by the actor, for example, were a buff color, having faded from the pale blue visible in the print which is now in my collection. We donated it to The Art Institute of Chicago for others to study the differences (fig. 118).

To give another example of "weeding," in April 1987, as described above, I sold six prints at auction at Christie's, New York. Included was a rather toned Eishō of the courtesan Kasugano after a bath, from the series *A Comparison of Beauties of the Pleasure Quarters* (*Kakuchū bijin kurabe*). Looking back on that sale, I believe it was a mistake. I wanted to improve the average quality of my collection by selling some (but not all) prints that were not up to the general standard of the majority. I do feel I have sold or donated several pieces prematurely by culling the collection from time to time.

My tastes and interests have not changed significantly over the years. While I did buy Hiroshige and Hokusai to start, I very soon turned to eighteenth-century prints, some black-and-white designs (*sumizuri-e*), and others hand-colored. I also became fascinated by the inventive and intricate patterns on the dress of young beauties in the work of Harunobu. And actor prints from the middle to third quarter of the eighteenth century are so different and arresting: dramatic costuming, a crest (*mon*) on a kimono identifying the actor, elaborate face and body makeup, and impossibly complicated kabuki story lines. The progression of my collecting interests did not follow any identifiable course.

Conservation and Caring

From my first visit to the print study room at the Metropolitan Museum in New York in 1961, I have been attentive to the care and preservation of ukiyo-e. I was shocked by the shoddy matting at the Met (a problem long-since rectified), and a few years later found that acid-free mats were also not the norm at The Art Institute of Chicago. Thanks largely to the efforts of Osamu Ueda, that changed. As a result, I have always been scrupulous about the mounting, storage and conservation of prints. I only display them at home when we have interested visitors. All prints are mounted in acid-free matting (a practice I have followed since the early 1960s), and all interleaving is inert. When we lend to museums, we require assurance that the lighting is at safe and proper levels. Prints are rarely on display at such venues for more than six weeks.

I want my prints to show to their best advantage. From time to time, I have had skilled paper conservators repair tears, remove stains, fill in worm holes and other paper losses—plus perform other steps to accomplish that goal. But not every effort was entirely successful. The first conservator to whom I turned was Harold Tribolet (1911–1993), the manager of the Department of Graphic Conservation at R. R. Donnelley & Sons Co. in Chicago until 1993. As a consultant in Florence, Italy after the great floods of 1966–67, Harold gained renown as a "magician" with paper conservation. Through friends at Donnelley, I engaged his services to clean Toyokuni's image of Segawa Kikunojō III (Mann catalogue no. 87). The print had embedded dirt along the bottom edge. Unfortunately, Mr. Tribolet chose to clean the dirt by removing the dirty fibers, leaving the paper thinned in that area.

In the 1960s, Bob Sawers introduced me to Jane McAusland in London, and she provided expert advice and care on a number of our prints (as well as a Lautrec poster).

In the 1970s and into the 1980s, I turned to Keiko Mizushima Keyes, who provided exceptional treatment of woodblock prints to museums and collectors around the world. She applied her skills to two, among others, of my most prized prints, the Ichikawa Ebizō by Sharaku and Matsumoto Kōshirō IV by Shunkō, (figures 48 and 119). Keiko was strict about doing as little as necessary to a print, intent on stabilizing

春好画

but not enhancing it. She issued detailed condition reports and proposals before doing any work. Once I signed off, she always did what she said she had planned, and the results were always great—except for the mishap with the Sharaku portrait of Ebizō in 1972, as detailed earlier.

Keiko Keyes exuded warmth and confidence. She and her husband, Roger, loved classical music and devoted themselves to their daughter, Aenea Mizushima Keyes, a gifted violinist from a very early age. I remember the Keyes family visiting Chicago with the primary task of finding a new violin for Aenea, although I don't recall if they were successful. On a trip one summer, Keiko and Roger joined Roberta and me for dinner and a concert on the lawn of the Ravinia Park Summer Festival near our home in Highland Park.

Anne Rosenthal, in San Francisco, subtly and deftly repaired a number of our prints over the years, particularly in anticipation of the 1994 exhibition of the Mann Collection at the Ōta Memorial Museum in Tokyo. Anne trained with Keiko and is a worthy and talented successor to her prominence. One of her most delicate and poignant tasks was replacing a repair originally done by Keiko on the Shunkō in figure 119 that became discolored over the years. When I consulted with Roger Keyes about the work Anne was to do, he asked me to preserve the repair Keiko had done and Anne was to replace. I gave Keiko's repair to Roger shortly after the project was completed.

Sharing the Collection

From the beginning, I wanted to share my love for, and fascination with, ukiyo-e by showing my prints to friends and colleagues; speaking to groups of interested viewers; permitting items from the collection to be reproduced in catalogues; and lending to exhibitions at important institutions (figs. 120a–c and 121a–c).

Generally speaking, "show and tell" experiences with friends and associates during the early years failed. I encountered few people with any knowledge or appreciation of ukiyo-e until many years later, after the collection had become better known and our friends had become aware of the significance of ukiyo-e in the development of modern Western art. But for the better part of my first twenty years of collecting, my interest was very solitary and confined to occasional interactions with others in the field. Except for the Cottle family, curators at the Art Institute and Mary Diamond at the Mori Gallery, there was no one else who could satisfy my craving for "ukiyo-e culture" in Chicago. Visits by Bob Sawers from London, David Caplan from Tokyo or Matthi Forrer from Leiden were always major events, and occasional trips by Roberta and me to New York or London were essential (figs. 122 and 123).

Over the years, speaking invitations have come from diverse groups: the Harvard Club of Chicago; the Asian Art Council at The Art Institute of Chicago; The Japan America Society of Chicago; the Japanese Art Society of America; the New England East Asian Art History Seminar; the Asian Art Society at the Indianapolis Museum of Art; and the Friends of Asian Art at the Museum of Fine Arts, Houston. Perhaps the first opportunity came when Robin Stern, a family friend who taught a course on ukiyo-e at the School of The Art Institute, asked me to speak to her class about connoisseurship. The students were young and distracted. When I completed my carefully prepared talk, focusing on scholarship and connoisseurship and comparing multiple states of various prints, I noticed that about 10 percent of the class was

FIGS. 120a–c. The Japanese Art Society of America visits the Mann home in Highland Park, IL to view prints. September 26, 2010. Photos: Julia Meech

FIG. 121a, below. George Mann describing a print for his Japanese Art Society of America visitors. November 17, 2018. Photo: Julia Meech

FIGS. 121b, c. George Mann with Japanese
Art Society of America visitors.
November 17, 2018. Photos: Julia Meech

nodding off. Then a student raised his hand and asked: "What do these prints cost?" I
was a bit crestfallen, as *that* was the only question posed.

Notwithstanding Robin's class, the questions are usually the best part of the
speaking experience. Following a talk at the Art Institute in 2004 on the museum's
exhibition of Tōshūsai Sharaku (for which I had selected the prints and prepared the
didactic material), I was asked who owned the elaborate, often voluminous robes
worn by actors onstage. I had no idea, but I was rescued by Sato Shōzō (b. 1933), who
happened to be in the audience. Sato-sensei, a professor emeritus of the College of
Art and Design at the University of Illinois, is the author of a number of books on
Japanese art and culture and is widely known for adapting Western classics (for example, "Medea," "Macbeth" and "Madame Butterfly") to kabuki theater. He informed
all of us that the robes were the property of the theatrical family, such as the Ichikawa
family, and are passed down from generation to generation.

The Art Institute of Chicago

Around the time of my first ukiyo-e purchase in 1961—Hiroshige's *Drum Bridge,
Meguro* (see figure 6)—that my close relationship with The Art Institute of Chicago's
Department of Oriental Art (now known as the Department of Asian Art) began.
Within a few years after starting law practice at McDermott in 1961, I asked Peggie
Gentles, the keeper of the Buckingham Collection of Japanese Prints, if I might view
prints in storage. To my great delight, Miss Gentles (as I always addressed her) agreed
and, from time to time over the years, I walked the few blocks from my office to the

museum and made my way through portfolio after portfolio of woodcuts by Sharaku, Utamaro, early figure prints or landscapes.

Peggie Gentles was very generous with her time in showing prints to interested collectors and scholars. She removed the matted works from the portfolios or boxes in which they were stored, slipped out the protective glassine paper, and, if asked, raised the window mats. She would also lift prints to show the versos. Visitors were not permitted to touch prints, boxes or portfolios, and she always wore white cotton gloves when handling them. Formal and polite, she appreciated visits from people with a genuine interest in ukiyo-e because she liked to tutor us. Also, she often had a few prints (usually duplicates) that the Art Institute received as gifts that were not accessioned into the collection. Those were sold, and the proceeds used for acquisition of more important examples. At the end of November 1967, she offered to sell me *Sudden Shower at Mount Tenpō in Osaka* by the Osaka artist Yashima Gakutei (fig. 124). I bought it for a modest $100. That dubious practice was discontinued by the museum a number of years ago.

As my interest in ukiyo-e grew, I had increasing contact with the department. As already mentioned, Donald Jenkins joined the Art Institute as the associate curator of Oriental Art in 1969, following Margaret Gentles's death earlier in the year. I felt an instant bonding with Donald. He was always available and receptive, helping with issues of authenticity and providing opinions on quality. Donald is one of the most gracious people I have ever met, and that characteristic made every meeting a pleasure. In early 1970, Jack V. Sewell (1923–2010), the curator of Oriental and Classical Art from 1950 until he retired in 1988, invited me to join The Orientals, a group of individuals interested in the arts of Asia. Dues were $25 annually. The organization had no more than one meeting a year, and it was primarily a social event. I was appointed to the Oriental Art (now "Asian Art") Advisory Committee in December 1975, and I remain a member. In 1978, I was invited to join the Auxiliary Board of the Art Institute (founded in 1973). I was elected a vice president in 1979 and became the president in 1980. Upon completing my term as president in 1982, I continued on the Auxiliary Board until 1987. From 1986 until the fall of 2017, I was a member of the museum's Board of Trustees.

FIG. 122. Viewing prints at the Mann home in Highland Park. Left to right: Robert Sawers, Suzuki Jūzō, Roger Keyes, George Mann and Matthi Forrer. David Mann in the foreground. March 18, 1979

FIG. 123. Roberta and George Mann inspecting prints offered by Robert Sawers in his room at the Carlyle Hotel, New York City. July 1980. Photo: Robert Sawers

FIG. 124. Yashima Gakutei (1786?–1868). *Sudden Shower at Mount Tenpō in Osaka (Ōsaka Tenpōzan yūdachi no kei)*, from the series *Famous Places of Naniwa [Osaka]: Fine Views of Mount Tenpō at a Glance (Naniwa meisho Tenpōzan shōkei ichiran)*. Japan. Edo period, 1830s. Color woodblock print. 25.4 x 36.8 cm. The Mann Collection, acquired November 30, 1967

During my term as president, the Auxiliary Board organized eighteen lectures under the leadership of department curators. Heads of various disciplines in the museum selected the speakers, vetted their topics and made certain their papers were completed, presented, proofed and submitted for publication. The lectures, given in 1979, included "Hokusai's Illustrations for the One Hundred Poems," by Roger Keyes. *The Art Institute of Chicago Centennial Lectures* (Chicago: Contemporary Books, Inc.) was published in 1983.

In 2004, Jay Xu, then the recently appointed curator of Asian Art at the Art Institute (now the director of the Asian Art Museum of San Francisco), enjoined me and Mack Trapp, with whom we traveled to Kyoto in 2005, to revive The Orientals, established in 1926. The group was renamed the Asian Art Council, and I served as its president until 2007 and on its board until 2019. In June, 2020, the Asian Art Council was merged into the fundraising-focused Sustaining Fellows, a move deeply disappointing to me and other members.

Throughout his career in Chicago, I consulted with Osamu Ueda, the keeper of the Buckingham Collection of Japanese Prints from 1972 to 1994, whenever I considered a new acquisition or had questions about prints already in my collection. I received important advice from other knowledgeable curators at the Art Institute over the years, including, to reiterate, Donald Jenkins before he left in 1974 to join the Portland Art Museum (he retired as the director of that museum in 2004), and now, Janice Katz (figs. 125 and 126a, b).

It must have been in the middle to late 1990s that I became a volunteer in the Department of Asian Art. As I was still practicing law, my time at the museum was generally unscheduled and involved projects without deadlines. I started (but never completed) a detailed catalogue of the museum's more than eighty Sharaku prints, trying to find where the Art Institute's or a comparable image is reproduced. On a more organized and time-sensitive basis, I helped select prints for Buckingham Gallery exhibitions, with a new rotation about every six weeks.

Following retirement from the practice of law in 2001, I began volunteering with the conservation team in the Department of Prints and Drawings at the Art Institute. Although I was already helping in the Department of Asian Art, I wanted to do hands-on conservation, hoping I could help out on ukiyo-e. (All conservation of ukiyo-e was and is performed in the conservation lab of the Department of Prints and Drawings.) Of course, I had no training and no relevant skill. Therefore, I was entrusted with projects that required neither. For example, the Department of Prints and Drawings had a large collection of insignificant nineteenth-century English prints with surface dirt in the margins. I concentrated on removing that dirt, using granulated erasers. (There was virtually no chance of doing any damage in that task, so the museum was not taking a risk in humoring me.) After finishing that project, I moved on to the museum's collection of important architectural drawings by David Adler (1882–1949), the noted Chicago architect. The drawings had been improperly stored for years, resulting in creases that required "easing." By misting the very brittle paper with distilled water and applying the weight of large rag-paper blotters for three or four weeks, the creases gradually "relaxed." When the drawings finally flattened, I repaired cracks and splits with narrow strips of inert, conservation-quality tape. Here, the works were more important than the English prints on which I had apprenticed, and the risk of damage was greater. One afternoon, the department chair entered the conservation lab to find me hard at work, wearing my green eye shade with magnifying lenses, but with no supervising staff present. She was appalled, and I decided, then and there, that I would abandon my conservation career.

I then returned to the Department of Asian Art and, for several years, starting about 2007, resumed assisting in organizing exhibitions—about six per year. I conferred with Janice Katz on the theme of each show, helped select prints to be displayed and wrote drafts of didactic materials. I often composed the didactics at home, relying primarily on photocopies of the museum's card index. Brief labels were the norm, as elaborate information generally was glossed over by visitors. Because much of the information in the Art Institute card index was decades old, I verified what I could from reference books in my own library or, later, from internet sources. After "resting" in storage for about five years (the museum norm), a number of those rotations have been reinstalled. Themes were often seasonal or devoted to a particular artist, such as Sharaku or Utamaro. We also did shows spotlighting the Art Institute's exemplary collections of early ukiyo-e; Hokusai; bird-and-flower images; and actor portraits, among others. A particularly successful rotation focuses on connoisseurship, using two, three or four impressions of a single image.

As a trustee (from 1986 until 2017), I participated in several board meetings a year at the museum. When the meetings were switched from midday to late afternoons, and I was no longer at my office downtown (after I retired in 2001), I attended very rarely, because it was so inconvenient. (The museum is twenty-five miles from our home, and late-day, rush-hour traffic is often unbearable.) I always went to twice-yearly meetings of the African and Amerindian Advisory Committee and the Photography Advisory Committee. I left those advisory committees (Photography in the 1990s, African/Amerindian in 2019), as my interest in those departments diminished. While a member of those committees, I looked forward to our get-togethers, because they were stimulating and educational and gave me the sense of participating in decisions (primarily, acquisitions) important to the museum. Asian Art Advisory Committee meetings, also held about twice yearly, always offer something different and I rarely miss them.

Exhibitions of the Mann Collection
The Art Institute of Chicago

The first exhibition of sixty-eight Mann prints (substantially the entire collection at that time) was presented at The Art Institute of Chicago from April 15 to May 30, 1982. (There was no catalogue.) The show, comprising the work of some twenty-five artists, was mounted in the space usually dedicated to the museum's own Japanese print holdings (totaling some twelve- to fourteen-thousand examples). It was an exhilarating experience and I was sorry to see the show come down (figs. 127–30). I was proud to have formed a collection worthy of exhibition at the Art Institute, and determined to "grow" it by making more significant acquisitions. I was already thinking about the chance of an exhibition in Japan, and I knew that at least one hundred more examples were required to encourage any Japanese institution to consider that possibility.

OPPOSITE: FIG. 127. Opening night of the Mann exhibition at The Art Institute of Chicago. April 1982. Left to right: James Wood and his wife, Emese Forizs; Roberta and George Mann; Osamu Ueda and his wife, Fuji; and Jack V. Sewell, Curator of Oriental and Classical Art

FIG. 128. View of the Mann exhibition at The Art Institute of Chicago. April 1982

FIG. 129. George Mann, speaking with the collector David C. Ruttenberg at the opening of the Mann exhibition at The Art Institute of Chicago. April 1982

FIG. 130. George Mann speaking with the collectors Paula and Herb Molner at the opening of the Mann exhibition at The Art Institute of Chicago. April 1982

We probably have over fifty catalogues of exhibitions mounted through the years at the Chiba, MOA, Ōta, Riccar and other museums in Japan; at Mitsukoshi and other department-store galleries; and at venues commemorating events, such as the tenth anniversary of the founding of the Japan Ukiyo-e Society. I still riffle through those catalogues on occasion, wistful about the rarities I never saw. And in almost every single catalogue I find paragons I will never own.

Ōta Museum, Tokyo

The first opportunity for an exhibition of Mann prints abroad occurred some twelve years later. In October 1994, thirty-three years after I bought my first Japanese print and twelve years after the show at The Art Institute of Chicago, an exhibition of the "Mann Collection of Ukiyo-e" opened at the Ukiyo-e Ōta Memorial Museum of Art in Tokyo. The museum produced a handsome catalogue, partially in color, and I have distributed all but a few copies to friends. About one hundred forty of our prints (the collection had doubled in size) were displayed in two installments over a nine-week period. The museum is housed in a two-story structure on a quiet street near Ueno Park. The display was carefully planned, and the prints were stylishly presented. David Caplan and his son Ken were the main forces behind the realization of this dream of mine, and I shall be thankful to them always for their efforts.

The show opened at the Ōta on October 1, 1994, ran through the 26th, and then closed for a few days while about seventy prints were rotated. Part II ran from November 1 through 26. The opening was the subject of an article in the evening edition of the *Asahi Shinbun* newspaper on October 3, 1994. Nagata Seiji (1951–2018), then the eminent vice director and curator-in-chief of the Ōta Memorial Museum of Art, selected the prints after viewing the entire collection at our home earlier in the year. I understood and accepted Nagata's decisions, except for one, described below.

Of course, the Questionable Kaigetsudō acquired from Yamamoto was not considered. The Eishi *Picture of the Courtesan Hanamurasaki of the Tamaya out Walking*

FIG. 131. David Caplan (left) and Ken Caplan with Roberta Mann, by the poster advertising the Mann exhibition at the entrance to the Ōta Memorial Museum. Tokyo, September 26, 1994

FIG. 132. Nagata Seiji with Roberta and George Mann. Tokyo, September 26, 1994

from Ledoux (Mann catalogue no. 74) is not universally accepted (Ledoux called his a "third state"). Several other examples of lesser quality or condition were also excluded. However, the rejection of the Ichikawa Ebizō II by Kiyoshige in figure 64 disappointed me, as I knew only one other in the Tokyo National Museum. Based on my examination of a high-resolution photo of that print (see figure 65), it is identical to ours, although the condition and hand coloring are superior, by a long shot.

Roberta and I arrived in Tokyo about a week before the opening (figs. 131–35). The Ōta family was very generous, hosting two preopening dinners: one included Ōta family members (and was quite formal); the other consisted of museum personnel (and was more relaxed). Of course, David and Ken Caplan were at both parties. Seeing our prints at a prestigious museum in Tokyo was a joy and an honor. The trip was enhanced by a visit to kabuki theater, casual and festive meals at Edogin and Inakaya (among others) and a trip to Kyoto, where we stopped again at the Hiiragiya inn and toured more temples and shrines of that treasure-house city.

FIGS. 133a–c. Visitors enjoying the Mann exhibition at the Ōta Memorial Museum, Tokyo. September, 1994

FIGS. 134a, b. Ōta family hosts a formal dinner before the Mann exhibition at the Ōta Memorial Museum opening in Tokyo. October 1994

FIG. 135. Informal dinner with staff of the Ōta Memorial Museum. Tokyo, October 1994

One of our more adventurous outings on our own in Tokyo was an excursion to the Hiroshige Restaurant near Nakano Station on the Chūō Line, about forty-five minutes from the Hotel Okura, where we were staying. We chose it because the description in Zagat's restaurant guide promised a nineteenth-century rural dining experience—akin to stopping for a meal on the Tōkaidō Road. The journey was complicated and required rides on two trains on different lines. When we arrived at our second stop, we found no street signs in English, a heavy rainstorm and no idea of the direction in which to walk. A friendly local, noticing our bewilderment, led us toward the restaurant on his bicycle; I recognized the Hiroshige signature on the illuminated restaurant sign from about a block away.

The dinner was memorable. The restaurant served food in the style it would have been prepared for travelers at a roadside inn in the nineteenth century. The *sake* was milky white. The hostess wore a *haori* jacket of coarse brown fabric. The shelf behind the bar had a display of folk objects (*mingei*) from the nineteenth century, including an *uma-no-me zara* ("horse-eye" plate): a heavily potted, glazed stoneware plate with seven oval-shaped decorations freely executed in underglaze-iron pigment on a crackled ground. There is a similar plate in our own collection (fig. 136).

Roberta and I sat at the bar and savored the dishes recommended. Although the menu was entirely in Japanese, our hostess (whom I took to be the owner) spoke some English and was able to tell us what we were served. More unexpected, three young men dressed in suits and ties sat at the bar with us and conversed in fluent English throughout the meal. All had attended college in the United States (in one

FIG. 136. Horse-eye Dish. Japan. Edo period, late 18th or early 19th century. Diam. 28 cm. Stoneware with iron-oxide design. The Mann Collection

case, Vanderbilt University) and worked in the Ministry of Foreign Affairs. When the evening ended, they took us back to our hotel by taxi.

We visited the Ōta Museum every day for the next several days. There were always visitors, and I was prepared to reply to any questions. Naturally, the only person who spoke to us was a Japanese-American who lived in Winnetka, about ten miles from our home in Highland Park.

Loans to American Institutions
In the spring of 2006, in honor of the centennial of the gift of cherry trees near the basin in Washington, DC, given by the Japanese government to the people of the United States, the Freer|Sackler Gallery mounted a landmark exhibition of works by Japan's most famous artist, Katsushika Hokusai. Attendance topped all records—a quarter million people in ten weeks. Ann Yonemura, the senior associate curator of Japanese art, asked us to lend Hokusai's Great Wave (fig. 137); *The Poem of Minamoto Muneyuki* (see figure 80); our blue *Ushibori* (see figure 12) and *Kirifuri Waterfall* (Mann catalogue no. 109). Roberta and I attended the opening on March 3, 2006. The dinner at the Freer was sumptuous. Supreme Court Justice Ruth Bader Ginsburg, dressed in an elegant black sheath dress with a faintly Japanese motif, was at a table nearby.[41]

We bought the Great Wave, as I mentioned above, at a Christie's, New York, sale on April 27, 1993. The impression is strong, the cartouche clear, the print untrimmed, with no centerfold. The color is a little pale—the pink cloud now more of a buff tone. Although I liked the print, and always wanted this quintessential image, I felt the catalogue estimate was too high, and decided not to bid against the seller's reserve price. That strategy worked, and the print was bought in. After the sale, I called Sebastian Izzard to make a post-sale purchase at the vendor's reserve price. It flabbergasts me to see impressions of the Great Wave selling at auction in New York in the past two years for anywhere from $500,000 to $1,000,000.

Our Great Wave was the single print displayed in a small room near the entrance to the Freer|Sackler exhibition (fig. 137). Roberta and I stood nearby for a bit of the evening, just to hear comments from visitors. While eavesdropping, Norman Mineta, then United States Secretary of Transportation, walked in, looked at the print and, in a voice appropriate to a highly placed governmental official, announced that his parents were born in the town with this particular view of Fuji. James Ulak, then the senior curator of Japanese art at the Freer|Sackler and an old friend from his days at The Art Institute of Chicago, where he was the associate curator of Japanese Art, accompanied Secretary Mineta on his tour of the exhibition and introduced him to Roberta and me, a gratifying moment for us.

In 2008, the Asia Society in New York mounted "Designed for Pleasure: The World of Edo Japan in Prints and Paintings, 1680–1860," organized by the Japanese Art Society of America (JASA). Julia Meech and Jane Oliver edited the spectacular catalogue and selected the prints, paintings and illustrated books included in the exhibition. They enlisted me to help organize the catalogue and to comment on its drafts and didactic texts for the exhibition. I was credited as a co-curator, along with Julia, Jane, Sebastian Izzard and Allison Tolman, then president of JASA, and our colleagues at Asia Society, Adriana Proser, in-house curator, and Marion Kocut. Roberta and I loaned to the show sixteen prints, as well as our Toyokuni painting (now in the Weston Collection) (figs. 138a–e). I willingly collaborated with Adriana Proser on a short YouTube feature on the exhibition that is still accessible online.[42]

Return to Japan and Other Interests

Roberta and I traveled to Japan once again in November 2005. We flew directly to Kansai International Airport near Osaka and spent a week in Kyoto with Mack Trapp, my former law partner of forty years, his wife, Carol, and Mac Plant and his wife, Wickie. The two "Macks" (or "Macs") were prominent trusts-and-estates lawyers, both having been active in the American College of Trust and Estate Counsel (ACTEC). The Trapps wanted to show the Plants their favorite places in Japan, having traveled there more than a dozen times in the previous fifty years or so out of a deep and abiding love of the country, its people and its culture. The week in Kyoto was filled with visits to Ginkaku-ji, Kinkaku-ji, Fushimi Inari, Kiyomizu-dera, Katsura Imperial Villa, Sanjūsangendō, Tenryū-ji and many other sights.

We explored the antique shops and bought a few examples of Japanese folk art. When we wandered into the exclusive gallery of Yanagi Takashi on Nawate Street, we found an exhibit of ceramics by Hosokawa Morihiro (b. 1938), the former prime minister of Japan. The shop was crowded with buyers, many Westerners, competing to buy pieces. Affected by the frenzy, we bought a shallow platter that struck us for its flowing lines and colors.

The Trapps and the Plants then went on to Tokyo, while Roberta and I took the Shinkansen to Kurashiki to explore the old willow-lined canals and the Ōhara Museum of Art. Then to Naoshima, the art island in the Inland Sea with stunning small museums designed by Ando Tadao (b. 1941). We stayed at Benesse House, in which one is free to wander through the collections of important modern and contemporary art after the day tourists have taken the ferry back to the mainland.

We were especially drawn to photos from the series *Seascapes*, by Hiroshi Sugimoto, on the courtyard walls visible from the Benesse House dining room.

FIG. 137. Katsushika Hokusai. *Under the Well of the Great Wave off Kanagawa* (*Kanagawa oki nami ura*), from the series *Thirty-six Views of Mount Fuji* (*Fugaku sanjūrokkei*). Japan. Edo period, 1830s. Color woodblock print, 26.1 x 38.4 cm. The Mann Collection, acquired April 27, 1993

FIGS. 138a–e. Opening night of "Designed for Pleasure: The World of Edo Japan in Prints and Paintings, 1680–1860," Asia Society Museum, New York City, organized by Asia Society and the Japanese Art Society of America. February 25, 2008. Photos: Elsa Ruiz/Asia Society

a. George Mann (far left) with Mary Wallach, Jean Entwisle, David Solo, unidentifed woman, and Joan Cohen

b. George Mann with one of his prints, Hiroshige's *Ōhashi*

c. David Waterhouse and his wife, the woodblock-print artist Naoko Matsubara, speaking with Joan Cohen

d. Guests enjoying the display of prints

e. Left to right: Geoffrey Oliver, George Mann, Merlin Dailey, Roberta Mann and Angela Burgger

To take in the *Seascapes* and the sea simultaneously is sublime (fig. 139). From Naoshima we traveled to Okayama, where we saw a plate by Yamamoto Yūichi (b. 1935) in a shop window and added it to our "new-ish" and fast-growing collection of contemporary ceramics (fig. 140). Then on to Mishima by train to visit Robert Yellin in Kyoto, the transplanted American and dealer in contemporary pottery and ceramics.

Perhaps the most enduring memory of that sublime journey to Japan is the sight of majestic Mount Fuji poking grandly through the clouds as we left Japan to fly home (fig. 141).

We still love to travel, although we do so less and less. Before COVID-19 precautions in 2020 precluded most cultural activities, we subscribed to the Lyric Opera of Chicago, the Shakespeare Theater in Chicago, Writer's Theater in Glencoe and Ravinia Festival, the summer residence of the Chicago Symphony Orchestra and where Gitta Gradova Cottle used to perform. We skied at Snowmass Mountain, near Aspen, Colorado, until 2015. We like to read, and in December 2018 completed another course at the University of Chicago Adult Education Center on James Joyce's *Ulysses*—Roberta for the third time and I for the fourth. We traveled to Ireland in August 2018 and, among other activities, visited the Joyce Museum at the Martello Tower in Sandy Mount, the location of the first chapter of *Ulysses*.

I think studying literature at the Adult Education Center provides the best continuing satisfaction for me, something I've been doing for about eight years. I've read

FIG. 139. Benesse House, Naoshima, showing Sugimoto *Seascapes* series and view of Inland Sea. November 2019. Photo: Allan Reich

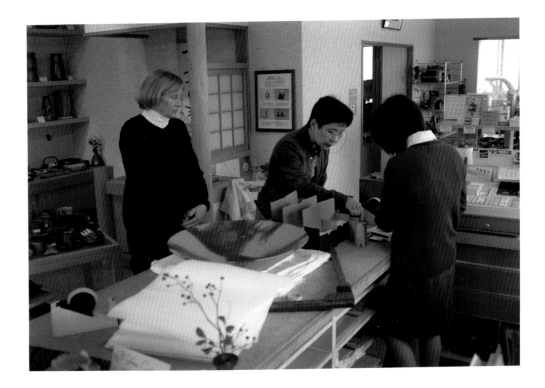

FIG. 140. Roberta Mann, purchasing a large, Bizen-style stoneware platter by Yamamoto Yūichi (b. 1935). Inbe, Okayama Prefecture. November 2005

Yamamoto Yūichi is the eldest son of the Living National Treasure Yamamoto Tōshū.

Cervantes and Plato and Proust and Tolstoy and Joyce and Dostoyevsky and Shakespeare, and on and on. I retain precious little from these readings, but feel good about trying to replace the opportunities squandered at Harvard College.

But the greatest joy comes from our large family of four children, all married, and the twelve grandchildren they are raising. Roberta has been the gentle and patient partner in both my life and collecting. She has indulged my enthusiasms and assuaged my regrets over a print missed or a mistake made. Her encouragement of my sitting down to write this memoir has much to do with its completion after so many years.

Postscript

Over the past sixty years or so of studying and collecting, I have met and come to know many fascinating, bizarre, diverse, deep, sensitive characters. Memories include coffee with "Tiko" (Felix Tikotin) in New York at the time of the Popper sale in 1972, describing the prints he bought at the Straus-Negbaur sale in Berlin in 1928; Maurie Cottle waxing eloquent about a monumental Tang-dynasty figure of a horse in 1959; Werner Schindler, meeting me at the train in Biel, Switzerland, in 1972, carrying a red rose so I would recognize him; Richard Lane, at my apartment in Chicago in 1971, viewing my prints and saying that I had "twenty years of good purchases but only ten years of mistakes" (I never understood what that meant—I had only been collecting for ten years at that point—but I took it as a compliment); Dick Gale, sitting alongside me at the Gerli sale in 1971 expressing his indifference about the fantastic Masanobu perspective print I was about to buy; Roger Keyes and Suzuki Jūzō, on a visit to our home in 1979, animatedly discussing the fact that our impression of Shunshō's *Sumo Wrestlers of the Eastern Group* was "early," as evidenced by the block carver's failure to remove excess wood carving from the seal at the bottom; David Caplan at the Popper auction in 1972, expressing his dismay at failing, yet again, to win the bid on Utamaro's half-length portrait of Ohisa (lot 154); Heinz Kaempfer, bringing yellow tulips to Roberta at the dinner we hosted in London at the time of Vever I in 1974; David Caplan, recounting how much his Jewish mother liked Hiroshige's *Ōi*, from the *Sixty-nine Stages of the Kisokaidō*, because it had a "Yiddish name"—and on and on and on.

I bought very few prints in Japan. I never felt I had integrated into "the world" of Japanese art in Japan. I interacted for decades with David Caplan, who has lived in Tokyo for almost sixty years, and have participated indirectly in one or more "dealer auctions" in Japan, but these activities did not permit me to become one of that close-knit community. When I joined David Caplan, Nishi Saijū and Bob Sawers in purchasing the Yamamoto Collection in 1978, I did so by telephone and as a "passive" member of that group. There were other transactions with those three (along with Huguette Berès), notably the Gidwitz private auction, or with members of the group, but I never felt more than a respected "outsider," someone allowed to see and to buy "better" prints, from time to time, because I was polite, deferential, honest, some-what knowledgeable and able to help finance purchases. I think it took many years to develop that standing. I admire all of those dealers because of their knowledge and experience and they all became friends, to one degree or another. Nishi Saijū, particularly, had a vast understanding of the history of ukiyo-e. He handled innumerable prints, and with his death in 1995, that knowledge and experience was lost to the rest of us.

Notwithstanding the recent purchase of a twentieth-century painting of a kabuki actor and two twenty-first-century Japanese pots, I have retired from collecting. I bought my last ukiyo-e prints at the Stoclet sale in London in 2004. Whenever the prints I still "want" *do* become available, from time to time, they cost more than I am willing to pay.

Is there a declining emphasis on the approach I have taken in pursuit of ukiyo-e? I doubt it. I know that other contemporary collectors of Edo-period Japanese prints possess similar tastes: Henry Steiner in Hong Kong, who recently sold his collection, Harlow Higginbotham in Chicago, and Edmond Freis in Las Vegas come to mind.

FIG. 141. Mount Fuji from airplane as the Manns started their return flight to Chicago. November 2005. Photo: George Mann

There are others, some of whom guard their privacy and anonymity assiduously, and I apologize to those I have overlooked. Lee Dirks of Jupiter, Florida, has assembled a collection that toured five venues in Japan in 2018–19 in the exhibition "Popular Impressions: Japanese Prints from the Lee E. Dirks Collection," curated by the late Nagata Seiji. Among many masterpieces and great rarities, Dirks owns a Kaigetsudō from the Ficke and Grabhorn Collections, a breathtaking impression of Utamaro's *Reflective Love* (I was the underbidder on the Vever impression of that design in 1974), and one of what I believe to be only three known impressions of Hokusai's print of two young women under an umbrella, one looking through a telescope, from the series *Seven Fashionable Habits* (*Fūryū nakute nanakuse*) acquired from the former Grabhorn Collection. (The others are in the Hagi Uragami Museum, donated to the museum by Uragami Toshirō in 1996, and the Kobe City Museum)

I think it is still possible to build a wonderful Edo-period ukiyo-e collection, as Lee Dirks has done, but one must have the wherewithal, plenty of patience and discipline. Seek and rely on the expertise of respected dealers, curators, scholars and other collectors. To the extent possible, buy prints from early, often deluxe, editions in the best condition. Go for quality, buy selectively, share your enjoyment with others. Reach for what you love.

The intersection of family, work and ukiyo-e has been complicated and challenging. I look back with astonishment at the energy and devotion required to build a collection, and with wistful longing for that excitement. I plan to keep the collection together as long as I am able, but eventually, it will pass to my family, to be held or disposed of as they determine. One of the most rewarding aspects of collecting ukiyo-e has been the introduction to the culture, history, traditions, customs, foods and wonder of Japan. Most of all, meeting the people of Japan is rewarding. I have a continuing fantasy that at least some of our grandchildren will travel there with us, some day. Scheduling is impossible.

NOTES

1. An earlier version of these recollections was published in H. George Mann, "Passionate Pursuit: My Adventures in Ukiyo-e," *Impressions,* The Journal of the Ukiyo-e Society of America, 25 (2003): 77–91.

2. E. Caswell Perry, "Lilla S. Perry; A Retrospect," *Impressions,* The Official Publication of the Ukiyo-e Society of America, 14 (Spring 1988): 12.

3. For the complete story, see Yuriko Kuchiki, "The Enemy Trader," *Impressions*, The Journal of the Japanese Art Society of America, 34 (2013): 33–53.

4. We have kept our prints stored in Solander-type storage boxes almost from the first acquisition. At first, I bought storage boxes from Spink and Gaborc in New York, but in the 1970s, I ordered archival boxes from the bookbinding team at the Newberry Library in Chicago. Still later, I shifted the prints to lighter-weight, commercially manufactured archival storage boxes. All the prints are matted professionally, on acid-free paper, with acid-free hinging and interleaving.

5. I sold some prints at auction in the 1970s and donated nineteen to The Art Institute of Chicago in 1974. I also bought several wonderful *surimono*, including work by Totoya Hokkei (1780–1850), some for as little as $15, which I gave to friends as holiday gifts.

6. Both are reproduced in Julia Meech, *Frank Lloyd Wright and the Art of Japan: The Architect's Other Passion* (New York: Japan Society and Harry N. Abrams, 2001), plates 100 and 101, pp. 124–25.

7. See H. George Mann, "Osamu Ueda (1928–2011)," *Impressions*, The Journal of the Japanese Art Society of America, 33 (2012): 113. Ueda traveled to Chicago in 1971 to work on the "Primitives" symposium, and Donald Jenkins suggested he be hired as Keeper of the Buckingham Japanese Prints and as Assistant Curator. When Jenkins retired and left Chicago for Portland in 1974, Ueda was promoted to Associate Curator, and continued as Keeper, the two positions from which Ueda retired in 1990.

8. Stephen Little, "The Richard Lane Collection," *Orientations* 36 (2): 93; Julia Meech,

"Richard Lane (1926–2002): Scholar and Collector," *Impressions*, The Journal of the Japanese Art Society of America, 26 (2004): 107–13.

9. The Sugimura was reproduced later by Horioka Chimyo, "An Essay on Sugimura Jihei," *Ukiyoe geijutsu / Ukiyo-e Art* 40 (1973): 17, fig. 30.

10. Louis V. Ledoux, *Japanese Prints of the Primitive Period in the Collection of Louis V. Ledoux* (New York: E. Weyhe, 1942), no. 5 (ex coll. Jaekel).

11. At the time, I owned only one painting, a standing beauty signed *Chōbunsai Eishi zu*, which I bought for about $1,000 at Sotheby's, London in 1971. In 1972, I sent the painting to Harold (Phil) Stern (1922–1977) at the Freer Gallery for his assessment. Stern was the first curator of Japanese art at the museum and its director from 1971 until his death. After keeping the painting for many months, Phil wrote to me on January 12, 1973: "I have studied this work a number of times and remain on the fence about it. It is a fine painting, and yet there are certain questions that remain in my mind as to whether or not it is by Eishi's hand. At the present point I remain willing to accept it unless some other scholar can prove it wrong. I have also shown it again to Professor Narazaki and he feels much as I do about it—that we cannot prove anything wrong about it and yet there is some slight intangible quality that makes us a little wary." The painting remains in our collection.

12. Julia Meech, "Who Was Harry Packard?," *Impressions*, The Journal of the Japanese Art Society of America, 32 (2011): 83–113.

13. See Roger S. Keyes on the "Pink Fuji" in the Smith College Museum of Art. Roger S. Keyes, "*Pink Fuji:* The Print Hokusai Saw," *Impressions*, The Journal of the Japanese Art Society of America, 29 (2007–2008): 69–75.

14. That exhibition, held at the Shirokiya Nihonbashi Tokyo department store from October 9 to 21, was sponsored by the *Nihon Keizai Shinbun* newspaper and the Ukiyo-e Society of Japan, which published a sumptuous exhibition catalogue in 1969.

15. Eventually, I did acquire one of Popper's several Utamaro: the mica-ground *Hanaogi of the Gomeirō* from *Comparison of the Charms of Beauties* (*Bijin kiryō kurabe*) (see fig. 99). The Utamaro had been acquired by the British Rail Pension Fund as part of a highly unusual investment strategy, but was sold at auction (to me) when the fund changed direction in 1987.

16. Roger Keyes describes the nail-biting exercise of advising and bidding on behalf of clients in the 1974 Vever sale in an interview published in *Impressions*, The Journal of the Japanese Art Society of America, 41 (2020): 83.

17. Three other prints from Vever I came into our collection, all through Ray Lewis: Mann Collection catalogue numbers 41, 43 and 54.

18. Letter from Roger Keyes to the author, July 25, 1978.

19. This print, which Ledoux describes as "the only recorded impression of what may be the third state of the subject," is unique in its coloration. See Ledoux, *Sharaku to Toyokuni*, no. 42, Eishi.

20. The inscription is transcribed, transliterated and translated by Alfred Haft for Mann Collection number 3 on pages 160–61 of this volume. The paraphrased version in the text derives from Julia Meech and Jane Oliver, eds., *Designed for Pleasure*, fig. 18, p. 39.

21. Nine other images from Series D are illustrated in Sebastian Izzard, *Early Images from the Floating World: Japanese Paintings, Prints, and Illustrated Books, 1660–1720* (New York: Sebastian Izzard LLC Asian Art, 2008), the catalogue accompanying the sale of the former Shibui Collection. Sotheby's, London, May 3, 1965 catalogue for the sale of prints from the Adolphe Stoclet Collection includes another image (lot 45), which is apparently from the same series. That print went to Theodor Scheiwe and is illustrated in Jenkins, *Ukiyo-e Prints and Paintings: The Primitive Period, 1680–1745* (The Art Institute of Chicago, 1971), no. 30. The twelfth image, from the Buckingham Collection, is also illustrated in Jenkins's 1971 catalogue, no. 31.

22. Grabhorn owned two genuine Kaigetsudō prints, and his impression of the Questionable Kaigetsudō is reproduced in Edwin Grabhorn, *Figure Prints of Old Japan* (The California Book Club, 1959). It was also published by Jack Hillier, *Japanese Colour Prints* (London: Phaidon, 1966). The

Yamamoto example was also exhibited in Tokyo in 1964 at Shirokiya Nihonbashi, Tokyo, October 9–21, 1964: "International Exhibition of Ukiyo-e Masterpieces Depicting the Manners and Customs of Old Japan," sponsored by Nihon Keizai Shinbun and the Ukiyo-e Society of Japan, and published as no. 22 in the related 1969 catalogue. Additionally, it was included in the catalogue *Images du Temps qui Passe—Peintures et Estampes d'Ukiyo-e* (no. 27), presented at the Musée des Arts Decoratifs, Palais du Louvre, June 1–October 3, 1966. The catalogues for both exhibitions were prepared by three specialists in Japan, including Suzuki Jūzō and Harry Packard.

23. Julia Meech, "Edwin Grabhorn: Printer and Print Collector," *Impressions*, The Journal of the Japanese Art Society of America, 25 (2003): 64. See also, Julia Meech, "Edwin Grabhorn: Passionate Printer and Print Collector," in *The Printer's Eye: Ukiyo-e from the Grabhorn Collection*, edited by Laura W. Allen and Melissa M. Rinne (San Francisco: Asian Art Museum, 2013), 11–20.

24. Packard to Edwin Grabhorn, June 11, 1958, quoted in Julia Meech and Jane Oliver, eds., *Rare Correspondence: Letters from Harry Packard to Edwin Grabhorn, 1950–64*, in *Impressions*, The Journal of the Japanese Art Society of America, 36, Companion Issue (2015): 33.

25. Packard to Edwin Grabhorn, June 5, 1958, quoted in Meech and Oliver, eds., *Rare Correspondence*: 24.

26. One Gidwitz print we rejected was a Hiroshige print of a cuckoo flying in the rain, a variation of that scene in the Mann Collection (Mann catalogue no. 123). In a postscript to an April 3, 1973 letter, seven years before the transaction, Roger Keyes wrote to me: "The Gidwitz' have an impression of the Hiroshige panel print of the cuckoo flying in the rain, which seems to be printed from different blocks than yours. I suggested that they might get together one evening with you to compare impressions. The only other impression I have seen is in Honolulu, and from a small photograph it corresponds with theirs. Neither Ray [Lewis] nor I were convinced, however, that it was right, as I am sure yours is."

27. It was at the Le Véel sale that I renewed my friendship with Henry Steiner (b. 1934), the graphic designer who escaped with his family from Vienna in 1939 and settled in New York. Steiner designed many of the world's most famous logos, including those for IBM, HSBC, Hilton Hotels and others, and settled in Hong Kong in the early 1960s. Henry and I met (and competed) at several auctions over the years, as he built a collection of masterpieces, including prints from the 1974 Vever sale and the Chōkyōsai Eiri triptych *A Collection of Beautiful Streetwalkers from the Three Capitals* (*Sanka no tsu bijin awase*) from Christie's, New York, April 16, 1988, lot 363. Henry and his wife, Leela, visited us in Chicago in August 1980 and we, in turn, visited the Steiners in Hong Kong some years later. The Steiner Collection was sold in 2018 and 2019.

28. Soon after we returned to Highland Park, I was invited to David's junior high school to talk about our adventure. When I displayed snapshots of the visit to Myōshin-ji, including pictures of the Gilberts' two young daughters, one of David's classmates exclaimed: "Those are my cousins!" We had not realized the connection between the Gilberts (whose home was in a suburb about fifty miles from Highland Park) and David's classmate Julie Carson, who lived in Highland Park, until David's excited classmate reminded us.

29. For more about Amstutz, see Robert Sawers, "Swiss Bliss," *Impressions*, The Journal of the Japanese Art Society of America, 25 (2003): 75.

30. Dorothy loved to communicate by e-mail, always typing messages in **BOLD FACE**, using all capital letters. She also had a penchant for sending "unusual" holiday greetings. More than once, I received a photocopy of a piece of matzoh on Passover!!

31. The signed Kunimasa is reproduced as no. 213 in Michener's book and is in the Michener Collection in the Honolulu Museum of Art.

32. At the time of the Paris sale in 1992, I was volunteering in the Department of Asian Art at The Art Institute of Chicago, cataloguing the museum's eighty-plus Sharaku prints. While the Museum of Fine Arts, Boston, owns a few more Sharaku prints than the Art Institute, the Boston collection includes more duplicates, but fewer designs. I believe the Art Institute owns more designs by Sharaku than any other institution or private collection in the world.

33. As of the 2003 auction, neither I nor anyone at the museum knew when or where Huguette had acquired the print, nor the price she had paid. I learned that information several years later when her daughter, Anisabelle, sent me copies of annotated pages from the 1992 Paris auction catalogue. Had we known the actual price she paid, I wonder whether the director would have authorized a higher limit.

The 1992 auction included another impression of *Reflective Love* by Utamaro, less trimmed than the Vever impression that Huguette bought in 1974 and that was sold by her estate in 2003. The example

in the 1992 auction went for 2,400,000 F (about $443,000). I was not in Paris for that sale, but I made elaborate arrangements with a Parisian lawyer, formerly in my Chicago law firm, to bid for me. The bidding was aggressive and rose quickly beyond my limit. My representative did not have an opportunity to raise a hand.

34. See Howard Link, *The Theatrical Prints of the Torii Masters: A Selection of Seventeenth and Eighteenth-century Ukiyo-e* (Honolulu: Honolulu Academy of Arts, Tokyo: Riccar Art Museum, 1977), pl. 13, p. 49, for the Nelson-Atkins Museum impression. That version is also reproduced in Narazaki Muneshige, *Moronobu, Jihei, Kiyonobu, Kaigetsudō, Masanobu . . .* vol. 1 of *Ukiyoe taikei* (Compendium of ukiyo-e), pl. 30. The Museum of Fine Arts, Boston's print (RES.21.312) is identified on the museum's website as "Meiji-Taishō impression from Edo-period block."

35. Of the Nelson-Atkins impression, Howard Link, then the curator of Asian Art at the Honolulu Academy of Arts, wrote that "there can be little doubt as to the date [1701] of this singularly important design. But questions still remain about the actual date of printing, since the large sheet includes pigment the critics believe not to be used before the time of *nishiki-e* or full color prints (i.e., ca. 1765). As a tentative explanation, it has been suggested that this is a later reprinting by Emi-ya [the publisher] utilizing old blocks." Link, *The Theatrical Prints of the Torii Masters*, p. 26.

36. See Howard A. Link, with the assistance of Jūzō Suzuki and Roger S. Keyes, *Primitive Ukiyo-e from the James A. Michener Collection in the Honolulu Academy of Arts* (Honolulu: The University Press of Hawai'i, Honolulu, 1980), 264.

37. E-mail from Ken Caplan to the author on August 16, 2004.

38. Link, *The Theatrical Prints of the Torii Masters,* 48, caption to illustration 13.

39. Suzuki Jūzō first introduced this print to the scholarly world at the Chicago symposium on "Primitives" held in 1971. Suzuki remarked in his talk that the publisher Emiya issued four or five *tan-e* of elephant wrestling in the Bunka era, and of those, one is of the court noble Yamanaka Heikyūrō (played by Danjūrō?). The print was originally done in the Genroku era, but the block was probably also used for printing in the Bunka era. No materials exist to support a conclusion at this time. The Nelson-Atkins print has two collectors' seals and was once in the collection of Shokusanjin (Ōta Nanpo). *Ukiyo-e taikei*, vol. 1, 123.

40. Ōta Nanpo produced the first version of his famous *Various Thoughts on Ukiyo-e* (*Ukiyo-e ruikō*) in 1790. That collection of commentaries and biographies of ukiyo-e artists was circulated in handwritten copies and underwent numerous additions and alterations over the years.

41. There were several additional shows in the 1990s to which we loaned prints: Donald Jenkins's exhibition "The Floating World Revisited" in Portland in 1993; Sebastian Izzard's "Kunisada's World" at the Japan Society Gallery, New York, in 1993, organized by Japan Society, Inc. in collaboration with the Ukiyo-e Society of America (renamed Japanese Art Society of America); and Matthi Forrer's "Hiroshige" exhibition at the Royal Academy of Arts, London, in 1997, commemorating the 200th anniversary of Hiroshige's birth, among others. Then, in 2011, we loaned three Sharaku and one Toyokuni to the Tokyo National Museum exhibition "Sharaku" (May 1–June 12, 2011). We had planned to attend, but the Fukushima disaster intervened. In 2012, nine prints from the Mann Collection were included in "Awash in Color: French and Japanese Prints," at the Smart Museum of Art, University of Chicago, October 4, 2012 through January 20, 2013. The exhibition was organized by Chelsea Foxwell, an assistant professor of Art History at the University of Chicago, and Anne Leonard, a curator and the associate director of Academic Initiatives at the Smart Museum of Art. The focus of the exhibition was the development of color printing in France and Japan, with each culture flourishing independently of the other before they came into extensive contact.

42. An enlarged image of our Masanobu perspective print was placed near the entrance to the exhibition (see photo, page 149). The project was conceived by JASA to commemorate the thirty-fifth anniversary of its founding. After five years of organizing and producing the exhibition and catalogue, the show opened in 2008. For the guided tour of the exhibition on YouTube, google <https://www.youtube.com/watch?v=KCLNwbO_Nk4 >.

Phoebe Sacks posing in cap and gown for her Mann grandparents, who are sheltering in place, and her mother, taking the picture, to commemorate her 2020 graduation from the University of Wisconsin–Madison, closed during the COVID-19 pandemic. Photo: Julie Sacks

CATALOGUE OF THE MANN COLLECTION

All prints in the collection are Japanese, dated to the Edo period (1615–1868). Kabuki theaters mentioned in the entries were located in Edo (Tokyo) unless specified as being in Osaka. Under Provenance, "acquired" + date means the date the print entered the Mann Collection. Prints designed by artists active in Edo comprise catalogue entries 1–115; 118–53. Prints designed by artists active in Osaka comprise catalogue entries 116–17; 154–65.

The bibliographic and exhibition citations that are abbreviated under Provenance and Exhibited are given in full between pages 363 and 370.

The figure number listed at the end of given catalogue entries refers to a figure illustration between pages 15 and 148 in this volume.

The translations of poems and longer inscriptions, except where indicated otherwise, were provided by Alfred Haft, with suggestions on reading and interpretation from John Carpenter, Yoshinori Munemura and Akiko Yano. The translator requests that any errors be considered his own.

Attributed to Hishikawa Moronobu (1630/31?–1694)

Courtesan and Lover

c. 1680

Collector's seal illegible

Woodblock print from an erotic album (*shunga*), *sumizuri-e* with hand coloring; *ōban*, 30.4 x 35.8 cm

Provenance: Acquired from Sotheby's, London, November 15, 2001, lot 387

Published: Marks, no. 1

THE IMAGE BELONGS to an original set of twelve-plus sheets with identical scrolling-line border. Some, as here, have hand coloring contemporary to the print.

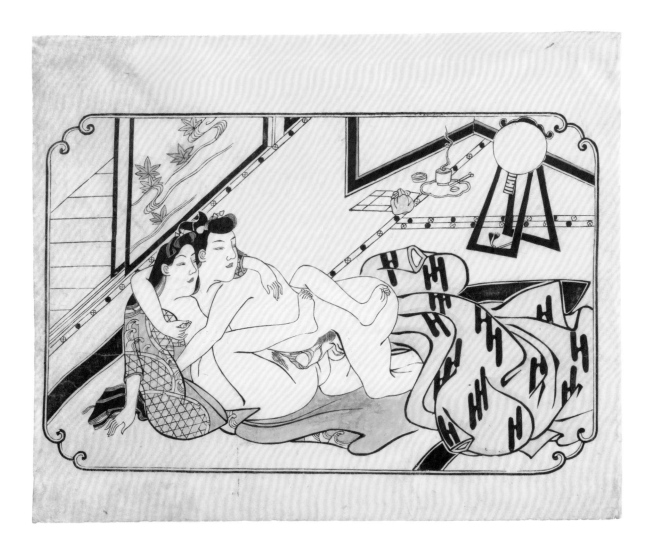

Attributed to Sugimura Jihei (act. c. 1681–98)

Samurai Embracing a Courtesan, Observed

1690s

Woodblock print from an erotic album (*shunga*), *sumizuri-e*; *ōban*,
27 x 37.2 cm

Provenance: Acquired from Kegan Paul, Trench, Trubner & Co.,
London, June 24, 1969

Published: Horioka, "An Essay on Sugimura Jihei," fig. 30; Jenkins,
The Primitive Period, cat. no. 25; Ōta Memorial Museum of Art, Tokyo,
The Mann Collection, cat. no. 2

Exhibited: The Art Institute of Chicago, "The Primitive Period," 1971;
Ōta Memorial Museum of Art, Tokyo, "The Mann Collection," 1994

Figures 25a, b, page 35

3   Attributed to Sugimura Jihei (act. c. 1681–98)

Courtesan and Samurai

1680s

Publisher: Hangiya Chōjirō of Toriaburachō [district in Edo]; the publisher's seal appears on the last sheet of the original complete album

Woodblock print from an erotic album (*shunga*), *sumizuri-e* with hand coloring; *ōban*, 26.6 x 36.2 cm

Provenance: Louis W. Black; John R. Gaines; acquired from Sotheby's, New York, Gaines, May 24, 1979

Published: Black, lot 4; Delay, p. 48; *Designed for Pleasure*, fig. 18, p. 39; Gaines, lot 432: Mann, *Impressions*, fig. 8; Ōta Memorial Museum of Art, Tokyo, *The Mann Collection*, cat. no. 1

Exhibited: Asia Society, New York, "Designed for Pleasure," 2008; Ōta Memorial Museum of Art, Tokyo, "The Mann Collection," 1994

THE SCENE PICTURES a woman attending to a young samurai, who is recovering from an illness.

The surrounding text reads:

> かしらはみな、白たへをいた〴〵くおやぢも、恋にはこびん［小鬢］の毛をなであげ、あなをのぞくおば〴〵も、色にはこしをつんのばし、朝夕た〻きがねを命のほん様も、此道にはじゆず［珠数］をなつきる、いわんやけつき［血気］をたねとして生をうけたるわか木の身、何とてをとなしからん、さかん成気をむりにをさへ、部屋ずみなんど〻いふすまひには、かならずきよら［虚労＝心神の衰弱する病］ををひきいだし、せうし［笑止］や、心なぐさめにとて、月花に心をうつさせ、古きふみ、やさしきさうし［草子］などにて、あしらはんとや、そんな事はむかし〻、今時は此みちにてみじかきいのちものばすは、たかきもひくきも、そつちもこつちも。

Kashira wa mina shirotae itadaku oyaji mo, koi ni wa kobin no ke o nadeage, ana o nozoku obaba mo, iro ni wa koshi o tsun-nobashi. Asayū tada kigane o inochi no hon'yō mo kono michi ni wa juzu o natsukiru. Iwanya kekki o tane to shite sei o uketaru wakaki no mi nani tote otonashikaran. Sakan naru ki o muri ni osae, heya-zumi nando to iu sumai ni wa kanarazu kyorō o ohiki-idashi sōshi ya. Kokoro nagusame ni tote tsuki-hana ni kokoro o utsusase, furuki-fumi yasashiki sōshi nado nite ashirawan to ya. Sonna koto wa mukashi mukashi. Ima-toki wa kono michi nite mijikaki inochi mo nobasu wa takaki mo hikuki mo, sotchi mo kotchi mo.

An old man capped in white hair will smooth his grizzled locks for love, and an old woman spying through peepholes will spring to her feet when passion strikes. Even those who claim, day and night, that the key to life is diffidence follow the way of love as they count on their rosaries. Need one ask, then, whether hot-blooded young people full of vim and vigor have any reason to remain demure? How ridiculous to live cooped in a room, certainly suffering from an emaciated body and a weak spirit, in a pointless effort to suppress a lusty nature! We hear

that long ago, people used to entertain themselves by turning their attentions to the moon and cherry blossoms, or managing with ancient books and simple tales, but that is all in the past. Nowadays, people high and low, near and far, are learning that the way to extend their brief lives is to pursue the way of love.

COLLECTOR'S COMMENTS

The inscriptions are introductory notes on the "Way of Love." Two other designs from the album, which likely comprised twelve prints, appear in Jenkins, *The Primitive Period*, cat. no. 30, from the Theodore Scheiwe Collection, and cat. no. 31, from The Art Institute of Chicago. Nine of the remaining designs are published in Izzard, *Early Images from the Floating World*, no. 22 and Addenda, no. 22. The Izzard catalogue accompanied the sale of prints from the Shibui Kiyoshi Collection. In 1926, Shibui made the discovery that Sugimura Jihei was a distinct artist whose work had been attributed previously to Hishikawa Moronobu.

Figure 59, pages 66–67

4 Torii Kiyonobu I (1664–1729)

The Actors Ichikawa Danjūrō II as Soga no Gorō, Sanogawa Mangiku I as a Courtesan and Fujimura Handayū II as a Courtesan in the kabuki play *The Beginning of the World: The Sogas Come of Age (Kaibyaku genpuku Soga),* performed at the Nakamura-za theater in the first lunar month, 1719

1719

Signed *Torii Kiyonobu hitsu*

Publisher: Komatsuya Denbei

Woodblock print with hand coloring and lacquerlike embellishment, *sumizuri-e urushi-e; chūban,* 19.9 x 28.3 cm

Provenance: Charles Salomon; H. P. and Edith P. Garland; acquired from Sotheby's, London, June 28, 1972

Published: Garland, lot 70; Ōta Memorial Museum of Art, Tokyo, *The Mann Collection,* cat. no. 3; Salomon, lot 1; Sotheby's, London, June 28, 1972, lot 43

Exhibited: Ōta Memorial Museum of Art, Tokyo, "The Mann Collection," 1994

A RELATED PRINT PUBLISHED by Sagamiya Yohei is in the Minneapolis Institute of Art (Mia) (Gale Collection, 74.1.22). It shows what appears to be the same kabuki scene of Danjūrō II as Soga no Gorō hiding behind a courtesan to avoid someone he has seen on the street, likely his brother. An inscription on the robe of one of the courtesans in the Mia print indicates they are in front of the Hishiya teahouse in the Yoshiwara pleasure district; both the Mann and Mia prints have the same chevron-patterned doorway curtain. For the Mia print, with the additional actor Katsuyama Matagorō, see the catalogue entry by Junko Mutō in Matthew Welch and Yuiko Kimura-Tilford, *Worldly Pleasures, Earthly Delights: Japanese Prints from the Minneapolis Institute of Art* (Minneapolis: Minneapolis Institute of Art, 2011).

The poem above the actors is a four-line Chinese poem (*kanshi*) with five characters per line. It probably was composed by a Japanese author:

綺羅靉日色
暁来遊陌頭
美人賞新歳
斎欲上青梅

The silk-gauze mist takes the color of the sun, / as the dawn brings pleasure-seekers by the hundreds. / The beautiful women praise the New Year / and the budding plum that has shunned desire.

5   Attributed to Torii Kiyonobu I (1664–1729)

*The Actors Nakamura Denkurō I Riding a Bull and
Matsumoto Kantarō I in a Female Role*

c. 1715

Woodblock print with hand coloring emphasizing orange pigment, *sumizuri-e tan-e*;
hosoban, 32.5 x 15.8 cm

Provenance: P. D. Krolik; acquired from Sotheby's, London, July 1, 1968, lot 2

Published: Krolik, lot 2; Ōta Memorial Museum of Art, Tokyo, *The Mann Collection*,
cat. no. 5

Exhibited: Ōta Memorial Museum of Art, Tokyo, "The Mann Collection," 1994

Torii Kiyomasu I (act. 1704–18?)

*The Actors Ichikawa Danzō I and Sakata Hangorō I
in a Kabuki Fight Scene over a Money Box*

c. 1715

Signed *Torii Kiyomasu hitsu*

Publisher: Nakajimaya, Sakaichō

Woodblock print with hand coloring and lacquerlike embellishment,
sumizuri-e urushi-e; *hosoban*, 34.8 x 15.9 cm

Provenance: Otto Laporte; acquired from Sotheby's, New York,
November 30, 1982

Published: Ōta Memorial Museum of Art, Tokyo, *The Mann Collection*,
cat. no. 4; Sotheby's, New York, November 30, 1982, lot 1

Exhibited: Ōta Memorial Museum of Art, Tokyo, "The Mann Collection," 1994

Torii Kiyomasu I (act. c. 1704–18?)

*Wrestling with an Elephant (Zōbiki): The Actors Ichikawa Danjūrō I as Yamanoue
Gennaisaemon and Yamanaka Heikurō I as Prince Suzuka (Suzuka no Ōji) in
the kabuki play The Courtesan Wang Zhaojun (Keisei Ōshōkun), performed
at the Nakamura-za theater in the first lunar month, 1701*

early 18th century

Signed *Torii Kiyomasu no zu*; seal *Kiyomasu*

Publisher: Emiya Kichiemon

Woodblock print with hand coloring emphasizing orange pigment, *sumizuri-e tan-e*;
hanging-scroll format (*kakemono-e*), 63.1 x 32.2 cm

Provenance: Adolphe Stoclet; acquired from Sotheby's, London, Stoclet,
June 8, 2004

Published: Foxwell et al., fig. 76; Stoclet 2004, lot 11

Exhibited: Smart Museum of Art, "Awash in Color," 2012–13

THE INSCRIPTION AT THE TOP of this print, signed by Tatekawa Enba (1743–1822),
was probably added in the early nineteenth century and gives imprecise details about
the actors and their roles. For the variants of this design and questions surrounding
the date of issuance, see figures 113–16 and pages 118–23 in this volume.

Figure 113, page 120

Okumura Masanobu (1686–1764)

A Courtesan Sitting on a Bedding Kimono (yogi) Entertaining
a Rapt Young Man with a Samisen

c. 1705–07

Woodblock print from an album, *sumizuri-e*; *ōban*, 27.1 x 37.7 cm

Provenance: Lilla Simmons Perry; acquired from Sotheby's, London, July 11, 1966

Published: Shibui, "Masanobu's Sumiye," 56; Ōta Memorial Museum of Art, Tokyo, *The Mann Collection*, cat. no. 6; Perry, "Introduction to a Catalogue: The Perry Collection of Japanese Prints," *Impressions*, The Journal of the Japanese Art Society of America, 14 (1988): fig. ill. p. 9; Sotheby's, London, July 11, 1966, lot 17

Exhibited: Ōta Memorial Museum of Art, Tokyo, "The Mann Collection," 1994

THE METROPOLITAN MUSEUM OF ART holds other impressions from the set, one with slight hand coloring (JP685; JP33). The Mann print is numbered in the lower right, indicating it is plate 6, presumably from a set of twelve. The Sotheby's, London, catalogue of the Perry Collection gives the series title as *Mirror of Yoshiwara Courtesans* (*Yoshiwara yūkun sugatami*) and states that the twelfth print is signed *Yamato eshi Okumura Masanobu* (Japanese artist Okumura Masanobu). In the *Impressions* essay cited above, the author identifies the man as the actor Matsumoto Kōshirō I.

Okumura Masanobu (1686–1764)

A Floating World Version of the Noh Play "The Potted Trees" (Ukiyo Hachinoki)

1710S

Signed *Okumura Masanobu zu*; seal *Masanobu*

Publisher: Komatsuya

Woodblock print with hand coloring, emphasizing safflower-red pigment, *beni-e*; *ōōban*, 31 x 54 cm

Provenance: Acquired from Christie's, New York, September 22, 1983, lot 15

Published: Delay, p. 76; *Designed for Pleasure*, fig. 40, p. 66; Ōta Memorial Museum of Art, Tokyo, *The Mann Collection*, cat. no. 7

Exhibited: Ōta Memorial Museum of Art, Tokyo, "The Mann Collection," 1994; Asia Society, New York, "Designed for Pleasure," 2008

THE SCENE IS AN "allusive picture" (*mitate-e*) adapted from the Noh play *The Potted Trees* (*Hachinoki*), in which an impoverished samurai sacrifices three treasured bonsai trees to light a fire in order to warm an unexpected guest who has arrived during a snowstorm. The samurai keeps a suit of armor, a rusted spear and a broken-down horse at the ready in case he is called to duty. At the end of the play, the guest is revealed as the regent of the country who restores the samurai to his former glory in appreciation for his loyalty. In Masanobu's version, a courtesan chats fondly with a client over sake warming on a brazier. The flowering plum tree and the narcissus in the bamboo vase indicate the New Year season. Her client holds a libretto of *The Potted Trees*, as though to suggest that he will restore her to glory by redeeming her contract and marrying her. The alcove contains three items that substitute for those of the samurai in the Noh play: a calligraphy by Fujiwara Teika (1162–1241), a torn pillow associated with the ninth-century poet Ono no Komachi and a broken samisen associated with the twelfth-century courtesan Ōiso no Tora, each with a rectangular label translated below:

浮世鉢木 [title]
Top right: みかきもり　えしのたく火の　よるはもえ　ひるは消つゝ
ものとこそ思へ
[御垣守　衛士の焚く火の　夜は燃え　昼は消えつゝ　物とこそ思え]
Bottom right: かけたりとも大いそとらかしゃみせん　[大磯虎が三味線]
Top center: そこねたり友定家のしきし　[損ねたりとも定家の色紙]
Bottom center: ゆれたりとも小町のまくら　[＿れたりとも小町の枕]
Cover of volume in man's hand: 鉢の木

Ukiyo Hachinoki [title] A Floating World Version of *The Potted Trees*

Top right: *Migakimori / eji no taku hi no / yoru wa moe / hiru wa kietsutsu / mono to koso omoe*

So simple yet true: / the imperial guardsman's / fire blazes by night, / but come day it barely glows, / reduced to dying embers.

Kaketari to mo Ōiso Tora ga samisen

Battered but still Ōiso Tora's samisen

Sokonetari to mo Teika no shikishi

Damaged but still a sheet of poetry (*shikishi*) by Teika

Yuretari to mo Komachi no makura

Unsteady but still Komachi's pillow

Hachinoki   The Potted Trees

Teika's poem, from his anthology *One Hundred Poems by One Hundred Poets*, likens the bonfire of imperial guardsmen to embers of burning love.

10 Okumura Masanobu (1686–1764)

The Actors Sanjo Kantarō II as Osome and Ichikawa Monnosuke I as Hisamatsu in the kabuki play *Double-suicide of the Lovers Osome and Hisamatsu in White Tie-dyed Sleeves (Osome Hisamatsu shinjū tamoto no shirashibori)*, performed at the Morita-za theater in 1720

c. 1720

Signed *Nihon gakō Okumura Masanobu shōhitsu* (from the authentic brush of Japanese artist Okumura Masanobu); seal *Okumura*

Publisher: Okumuraya Genroku; round seal *Kongen Okumura ban Tōrishiochō kongen Okumura ban kono hō no e nise-han sōrō aida hyōtan in itashi sōrō* (an original published by Okumura of Tōrishiochō; as my prints are being published spuriously, I have applied my gourd mark)

Woodblock print with hand coloring and metallic embellishment, *sumizuri-e urushi-e; hosoban*, 34 x 16.1 cm

Provenance: Robert Glauber; acquired from Robert Glauber, June 13, 1968

Published: Jenkins, *The Primitive Period*, cat. no. 144; Ōta Memorial Museum of Art, Tokyo, *The Mann Collection*, cat. no. 8

Exhibited: The Art Institute of Chicago, "The Primitive Period," 1971; Ōta Memorial Museum of Art, Tokyo, "The Mann Collection," 1994; The Art Institute of Chicago, "Connoisseurship of Japanese Prints," 2012

MANY KABUKI AND BUNRAKU puppet theater versions of the Osome-Hisamatsu story have been performed since their real-life models committed double-suicide around 1708. In some variations, noble characters in the drama intervene and they instead live happily ever after. Osome is the daughter of the proprietor of the prosperous Aburaya, a pawnshop in Osaka that also sold oil. Hisamatsu, who will turn out to be a samurai, is an apprentice at the shop. Both of these young lovers are betrothed to others but determine to be together, allowing for a full menu of circumstances involving selfishness, duty, mischief and sacrifice. The first kabuki play based on the lovers is *Love Suicides at the Devil's Gate (Shinjū Kimon kado)* of 1710. The basis for succeeding dramatic variations, the puppet play *Osome of the Aburaya of the White Tie-dyed Sleeves (Aburaya Osome tomoto no shirashibori)*, was written in 1711. For variants of the design of the print, see figures 39–42 and catalogue number 17 in this volume.

Figure 39, page 48

Attributed to Okumura Masanobu (1686–1764)

*The Actor Nakamura Kiyosaburō I as Yaoya Oshichi Holding the Libretto (tokiwazu)
for the Ballad-drama "The Greengrocer's Daughter, Oshichi, Beloved Cherry Blossom"
(Yaoya Oshichi koizakura)*

mid-to-late 1740s

Collector's seal of Hayashi Tadamasa

Woodblock print with hand coloring and lacquerlike embellishment, *sumizuri-e
urushi-e*; pillar-print format (*hashira-e*), 66.4 x 14.9 cm

Provenance: Hayashi Tadamasa; acquired from Merlin Dailey, East West Gallery,
Victor, New York, April 17, 1981, who acquired it from Sotheby's, New York,
January 17, 1981

Published: Hayashi, no. 304 (attributing the print to Shigenaga); Ōta Memorial
Museum of Art, Tokyo, *The Mann Collection*, cat. no. 12 (attributing the print to
Masanobu); Pins, no. 32; Sotheby's, New York, January 17, 1981, lot 4 (attributing
the print to Shigenaga); *Ukiyoe taisei*, vol. 3, no. 150

Exhibited: Ōta Memorial Museum of Art, Tokyo, "The Mann Collection," 1994

THE TRAGEDY OF THE greengrocer's daughter and the temple page is one of Japan's
enduring love stories that is often played on the kabuki and puppet stages. The story
is based on events in 1681 when the girl starts a fire to gain access to her lover and
is burned to death for her crime. The rough plot of the stage plays is that Oshichi,
daughter of a wealthy grocer, falls in love with Kichisaburō, a page at Kichijō-ji Temple, where her family sought sanctuary after their home was being rebuilt following a
great fire in Edo. Kichisaburō, of samurai class, loses his master's sword, with which
he has been entrusted, because it has been stolen by the man to whom Oshichi has
been promised in marriage to settle her father's debt. To prevent Kichisaburō from
committing ritual suicide, she determines to unlock the fire gates to his street in order
to reach him. The climax of the drama version of the story is her mounting the ladder
in the snow to sound a false fire alarm, for which she is sentenced to death.

The female-role actor (*onnagata*) Nakamura Kiyosaburō (1721–1777) also used the
name Kiyozō. There is an *ōban*-size print in red and green (*benizuri-e*) in the Museum
of Fine Arts, Boston dated 1750 that is catalogued as Nakamura Kiyozō I as Oshichi
with Onoe Kikugorō as Kichisaburō (21.7226). Another 1750 print by Masanobu
in *hosoban* size shows Nakamura Kiyosaburō I as Oshichi holding a puppet of the
character Kichisaburō (MFA 21.5782). Always an innovator, Okumura Masanobu conceived the "pillar print," as here, beginning in the early 1740s.

12   **Okumura Masanobu (1686–1764)**

Flower Vendor

mid-1740s

Signed *Hōgetsudō Tanchōsai Okumura Bunkaku Masanobu shōhitsu* (from the authentic brush of Hōgetsudō Tanchōsai Okumura Bunkaku Masanobu); seals *Tanchōsai* and *Hogetsudō Masanobu* (indistinct)

Woodblock print, emphasizing safflower-red pigment, *benizuri-e*; *ōōban*, 43.1 x 30.8 cm

Provenance: Takano H., Tokyo; acquired from Christie's, New York, June 27, 1985

Published: Christie's, New York, June 27, 1985, lot 18; Ōta Memorial Museum of Art, Tokyo, *The Mann Collection*, cat. no. 10; Parke-Bernet Galleries, New York, Takano, January 8, 1952, lot 97

Exhibited: Ōta Memorial Museum of Art, Tokyo, "The Mann Collection," 1994

THE 1952 TAKANO AUCTION CATALOGUE states that the image represents the actor Nakayama Tomisaburō I in the role of a female flower seller.

The poem reads:

桜色うつりにけりな草花売

Sakura iro / utsurinikeri na / sōka uri

The cherry blossom's / color has faded away: / the flower vendor.

13 Okumura Masanobu (1686–1764)

A Monkey Trainer of the Floating World on the Sumida River
(Sumidagawa ukiyo sarumawashi)

c. 1750

Signed *Hōgetsudō Okumura Bunkaku Masanobu shōhitsu* (from the authentic brush of Hōgetsudō Okumura Bunkaku Masanobu); seal *Tanchōsai*

Collector's seal of Henri Vever

Woodblock print emphasizing safflower-red pigment, *benizuri-e*; *ōban*, 32.1 x 44.6 cm

Provenance: Henri Vever; acquired from R. E. Lewis, Inc., San Francisco, purchased from Sotheby's, London at Vever 1, March 26, 1974

Published: Calza, no. 112; Delay, p. 74; *Designed for Pleasure*, fig. 53, p. 77 (detail, p. 56); Foxwell et al., fig. 82; Hillier, *Vever*, vol. 1, no. 41; Lane, no. 72; Ōta Memorial Museum of Art, Tokyo, *The Mann Collection*, cat. no. 11; Vever 1, lot 18; Vignier & Inada 1909, lot 139; von Seidlitz 1910, tipped-in illustration, pp. 58–59; von Seidlitz 1911, tipped-in illustration, pp. 34–35

Exhibited: Musée des Arts Decoratifs, Paris, 1909; Ōta Memorial Museum of Art, Tokyo, "The Mann Collection," 1994; Asia Society, New York, "Designed for Pleasure," 2008; Smart Art Museum, "Awash in Color," 2012–13

THE BOATING PARTY—a trained monkey in the prow, his handler, two female entertainers serenading them and a third poling the boat—are setting out for Mimeguri Shrine, shown in the background. The poems read:

船人にこがれて水に出し月
竿の歌裳にこがるゝうら紅葉

Funabito ni / kogarete mizu ni / ideshi tsuki

Sao no uta / suso ni kogaruru / ura-momiji

The rising moon / hangs on the water, longing / for the boatman.
The song of the oar / sends ripples through the first / crimson maple leaves.

Figure 53, pages 60–61

Okumura Masanobu (1686–1764)

Large Perspective Picture of a Second-floor Parlor in the New Yoshiwara, Looking toward the Embankment (Shin Yoshiwara nikai zashiki dote o mitōshi ō-uki-e)

c. 1745

Signed in the left margin *Tōbu Yamato gakō Hōgetsudō Tanchōsai Okumura Bunkaku Masanobu shōhitsu* (from the authentic brush of Hōgetsudō Tanchōsai Okumura Bunkaku Masanobu, artist of eastern Yamato [Japan]); seal *Tanchōsai*

Publisher: Okumuraya Genroku; inscribed in lower-right margin *Tōrishiochō akaki hyōtan-jirushi Okumura-ya Genroku hanmoto* (published by Genroku of the Okumuraya under the sign of the red gourd in Tōrishiochō)

Woodblock perspective print with hand coloring, emphasizing safflower-red pigment, *beni-e uki-e*; *ōōban*, 41.9 x 65.6 cm

Provenance: Pratt Institute, Brooklyn, New York, sold Kende Galleries, New York, November 30, 1946 (provenance given in the catalogue as "Yamanaka and Mallory collections"); Paolino Gerli; acquired from Sotheby's, New York, Gerli, April 28, 1971

Published: Delay, p. 75; *Designed for Pleasure*, fig. 51, pp. 74–75; Foxwell et al., fig. 81; Gerli, lot 1; Kende Galleries, November 30, 1946, Pratt Institute, lot 109; Mann, *Impressions*, fig. 3 and fig. 3 (detail); Marks, no. 16; Ōta Memorial Museum of Art, Tokyo, *The Mann Collection*, cat. no. 9

Exhibited: Ōta Memorial Museum of Art, Tokyo, "The Mann Collection," 1994; Asia Society, New York, "Designed for Pleasure," 2008; Smart Museum of Art, "Awash in Color," 2012–13

Figure 34, pages 44–45

15

Torii Kiyoshige (act. c. 1716–64)

The Actor Ichikawa Ebizō II (Danjūrō II) in the Shibaraku (Wait a Moment!) Scene as Shinozuka Iga no Kami Sadatsuna in the kabuki play *A Fair Wind in the Taiheiki Account (Junpū Taiheiki)*, performed at the Kawarazaki-za theater as the season premiere *(kaomise)* in the eleventh lunar month, 1736

1736

Signed *Torii Kiyoshige hitsu*; seal *Kiyoshige*

Publisher: Urokogataya Magobei

Woodblock print with hand coloring, *sumizuri-e*; *hashira-e*, 70.4 x 16.7 cm

Provenance: Yamamoto Hatsujirō, Ashiya, Kobe, Japan; acquired February 10, 1978

Published: Calza, no. 135; Delay, p. 153; Marks, no. 21; Nihon Keizai Shinbun and L'Union Central des Arts Decoratifs, *Images du Temps qui Passe*, cat. no. 54; Pins, slipcase illustration, plate 4 and no. 43; Shibui et al., *Masterpieces*, 1969, no. 62; Tokyo Olympics *Masterpieces*, 1964, cat. no. 44

Exhibited: Shirokiya Nihonbashi Department Store Galleries, Tokyo, "Masterpieces," 1964; Musée des Arts Decoratifs, Paris, "Images du Temps qui Passe," 1966

Figure 64, page 74

Okumura Toshinobu (act. c. 1717–50)

A Young Man-about-town Astride an Ox and Playing the Flute,
alluding to Hakoōmaru, the hero Soga no Gorō in his youth

1720s–30s

Signed *Yamato eshi Toshinobu* (Japanese artist Toshinobu)

Publisher: Izumiya Gonshirō

Woodblock print with hand coloring and metallic embellishment, *sumizuri-e*
urushi-e; *hosoban*, 33.6 x 16.1 cm

Provenance: Marumiya Collection, Japan (provenance given in Japan Ukiyo-e
Society catalogue cited below); acquired from Kondo Sentarō, Red Lantern
Shop, Kyoto, October 9, 1985

Published: Delay, p. 78; Japan Ukiyo-e Society, "An Exhibition of Masterpieces
of Ukiyo-e by the Japan Ukiyo-e Society / Ukiyoe meihin ten," *Ukiyoe geijutsu /*
Ukiyo-e Art 3 (1963): 11 and no. 49; Mann, *Impressions*, fig. 9; Ōta Memorial
Museum of Art, Tokyo, *The Mann Collection*, cat. no. 14; *Ukiyoe taikei*, vol. 1,
no. 180

Exhibited: Shirokiya Nihonbashi Department Store Galleries, Tokyo,
"Masterpieces," 1963; Ōta Memorial Museum of Art, Tokyo, "The Mann
Collection," 1994

Figure 87, page 96

Okumura Toshinobu (act. c. 1717–50)

The Actors Sanjō Kantarō II as Osome, Ichikawa Danjūrō II as Kamata Matahachi and Ichikawa Monnosuke I as Hisamatsu in the kabuki play *Double-suicide of the Lovers Osome and Hisamatsu in White Tie-dyed Sleeves (Osome Hisamatsu shinjū tamoto no shirashibori)*, performed at the Morita-za theater in 1720

1720

Signed *Yamato eshi* (Japanese artist) *Okumura Toshinobu hitsu*

Publisher's mark *Masuya*

Woodblock print with hand coloring and metallic embellishment, *sumizuri-e urushi-e; hosoban*, 32.7 x 16.1 cm

Provenance: Eddy Collection (provenance given in Gerli catalogue); Paolino Gerli; acquired from Adele and Willard Gidwitz, January 19, 1980

Published: Gerli, lot 6; Ōta Memorial Museum of Art, Tokyo, *The Mann Collection*, cat. no. 13

Exhibited: Ōta Memorial Museum of Art, Tokyo, "The Mann Collection," 1994

THERE IS ANOTHER PRINT by Toshinobu with the same publisher's mark, identified as Masuya, the literal reading of the two kanji, in the Honolulu Museum of Art (16080). For the play, see Mann catalogue no. 10.

18

Nishikawa Sukenobu (1671–1750)

Girl Playing with a Cat, from *River Grasses, a Picture Book (Ehon kawanagusa)*

1747

Publisher: Kikuya Kihei, Kyoto

Woodblock-printed book illustration with hand coloring; 23.3 x 12.8 cm

Provenance: Acquired from S. H. Mori Gallery, Chicago, March 14, 1964

Figure 19, page 31

19

Attributed to Nishikawa Sukenobu (1671–1750)

Couple Entwined in a Bedding Kimono (yogi)

c. 1711–16

Woodblock print with hand coloring, *sumizuri-e*; 26.1 x 42 cm

Provenance: Acquired from Richard Lane, November 15, 1971

Published: Delay, p. 47

FOR TWO PRINTS similar to this design, see pages 46–47 and figures 36–38 in this volume. It is probable that all three prints came from the same folding album.

Figure 36, page 47

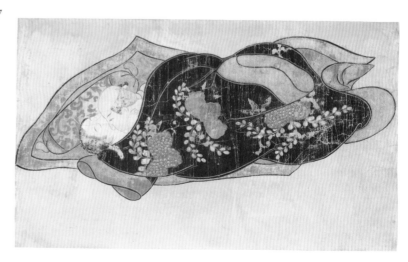

Katsukawa Terushige (act. 1716–36)

An Actor in the Role of a Puppeteer

1720s

Signed *Katsukawa Terushige*

Publisher: Izumiya Gonshirō

Woodblock print with hand coloring and traces of metallic embellishment, *sumizuri-e urushi-e*; *hosoban*, 31.2 x 15.8 cm

Provenance: Yamamoto Hatsujirō, Ashiya, Kobe, Japan, sold to Robert G. Sawers, London; acquired from Sotheby's, New York, June 26, 1981

Published: Nihon Keizai Shinbun and L'Union Central des Arts Decoratifs, *Images du Temps qui Passe,* cat. no. 60 (unillustrated; Yamamoto Hatsujirō, lender); Ōta Memorial Museum of Art, Tokyo, *The Mann Collection,* cat. no. 15; Shibui et al., *Masterpieces,* no. 67; Sotheby's, New York, June 26, 1981, lot 165; Tokyo Olympics *Masterpieces,* 1964, cat. no. 48

Exhibited: Musée des Arts Decoratifs, Paris, "Images du Temps qui Passe," 1966; Shirokiya Nihonbashi Department Store Galleries, Tokyo, "Masterpieces," 1964; Ōta Memorial Museum of Art, Tokyo, "The Mann Collection," 1994

IT IS NOT CERTAIN which actor appears in this print. The crest of wisteria, *fuji* in Japanese, points to Fujimura Handayū II, although the thick black border differs from the crest on other images of him. He was wildly popular at the time this print was designed. The Shibui *Masterpieces* catalogue cited above titles the print Yoshizawa Ayame II as the puppet master Yamanoi. The actor is listed as "possibly Fujimura Hanshirō" in the Sotheby's catalogue of 1981. The Ōta Museum catalogue of the Mann Collection does not name the actor or role.

21 Nishimura Shigenaga (c. 1697–1756)

The Actor Yamashita Kinsaku I as a Book Peddler

1720s

Signed *Nishimura Shigenaga ga*; seal *Shigenaga*

Publisher: Uemura Kichiemon; seal *Shiba Shinmei-mae Yokomachi hanmoto Emiya* (source of the print Emiya of Shiba Shinmei-mae)

Woodblock print with hand coloring and lacquer-like embellishment, *sumizuri-e urushi-e*; *hosoban*, 33.2 x 15.7 cm

Provenance: Robert Glauber; acquired from Robert Glauber, June 13, 1968

Published: Ōta Memorial Museum of Art, Tokyo, *The Mann Collection*, cat. no. 18

Exhibited: Ōta Memorial Museum of Art, Tokyo, "The Mann Collection," 1994

THE YELLOW SIGN at the top of the rack, *Shomotsu iro-iro*, advertises "a variety of books." In the peddler's hand is a volume of *Romance of the Three Kingdoms* (*Sangokushi* in Japanese), a Chinese historical novel that became popular during the Edo period. In the second tier, there are editions of *One Hundred Poems by One Hundred Poets* (*Hyakunin isshu*) and *Irotake* (Colorful bamboo). On the bottom tier are *Ōgibyōshi* (The rhythm of the fan), vol. 2 (*chū*) and *Niwatori* (The rooster). The last three are likely libretti of chanted narratives that accompanied a short dance.

Attributed to Nishimura Shigenaga (c. 1697–1756)

Bamboo and Tiger

c. 1725

Woodblock print with hand coloring, emphasizing safflower-red pigment, *benizuri-e*; *hosoban*, 32.5 x 15.4 cm

Provenance: John Mellor; acquired from Kegan Paul, Trench, Trubner & Co., London, October 23, 1967

Published: Delay, p. 62; Kegan Paul, *Japanese Prints*, 1967, cat. no. 3; Mann, *Impressions*, fig. 2; Mellor, lot 10; Ōta Memorial Museum of Art, Tokyo, *The Mann Collection*, cat. no. 18

Exhibited: Ōta Memorial Museum of Art, Tokyo, "The Mann Collection," 1994

FOR THE VARIANTS of this design, see pages 32–33 and figures 21–23 in this volume. The Mann version in safflower-red does not have black shadows nor metal filings on the bamboo. The bamboo leaves at the top of the impression in The Art Institute of Chicago are restorations. The three variants shown in the figure illustrations are considered editions of around 1725 of a contemporary print, now lost, issued with the signature of the artist Shigenaga or Okumura Masanobu.

Figure 21, page 32

Ishikawa Toyonobu (1711–1785)

The Actor Sanogawa Ichimatsu I as a Young Man-about-town Carrying a Lantern

c. 1740

Signed *Sojōdō Ishikawa Shūha Toyonobu zu*; seals *Ishikawa uji* (Ishikawa line) and *Toyonobu*

Publisher: Izumiya Ichibei

Collector's seal of Yamamoto Hatsujirō

Woodblock print with hand coloring, *sumizuri-e*; hanging-scroll format (*kakemono-e*), 58.1 x 22 cm

Provenance: Yamamoto Hatsujirō, Ashiya, Kobe, Japan; acquired February 10, 1978

Published: Calza, no. 136; Delay, p. 79; Keyes, *The Male Journey in Japanese Prints*, 1989, cat. no. 52; Ōta Memorial Museum of Art, Tokyo, *The Mann Collection*, cat. no. 17

Exhibited: Achenbach Foundation for the Graphic Arts, The Fine Arts Museums of San Francisco, "Rage, Power and Fulfillment: The Male Journey in Japanese Prints," 1989; Ōta Memorial Museum of Art, Tokyo, "The Mann Collection," 1994

Figure 66, page 75

Ishikawa Toyonobu (1711–1785)

Courtesan Parading with Her Girl Attendant

1750s

Signed *Sojōdō Ishikawa Shūha Toyonobu zu*; seals *Ishikawa uji* (Ishikawa line)
and *Toyonobu*

Publisher: Urokogataya Magobei

Color woodblock print in safflower-red and green, *benizuri-e*; *ōban*, 48.3 x 31.4 cm

Provenance: Murakami Takejirō (note on Stoclet mat stated "acheté à Murakami
15-2-13" [purchased from Murakami February 15, 1913]); Adolphe Stoclet; acquired
from Sotheby's, London, Stoclet, June 8, 2004

Published: Stoclet 2004, lot 44 (catalogue cover illustration)

THE POEM READS:

色かえぬまつはゆきにも馴染かな
Iro kaenu / matsu wa yuki ni mo / najimu kana
Steady, evergreen, / but the pine tree is also / intimate with snow.

興篠堂
石川秀苑豊信圖

25   **Torii Kiyohiro (act. 1737–76)**

Two Young Women on a Veranda Trimming Their Toenails and Washing Their Feet

c. 1760

Signed *Torii Kiyohiro hitsu*; seal *Kiyohiro*

Publisher: Maruya Kohei (Hosendō); printed to right of publisher's rectangular mark (*yama Maruko han*) *Tori Aburachō* [district in Edo] *Hosendō Maruya*

Collector's seal of Henri Vever

Color woodblock print in safflower-red and green, *benizuri-e*; *ōōban*, 42.5 x 30.2 cm

Provenance: Henri Vever; acquired from Sotheby's, London, Vever 4, October 30, 1997

Published: Hillier, *Vever*, vol. 1, no. 79; Japan, *Vever*, 1975, cat. no. 24; Japan, *Vever*, 1976, cat. no. 60; *Ukiyoe shūka*, vol. 12, no. 147; von Seidlitz 1911, tipped-in illustration, pp. 58–59; Vever 4, lot 10

Exhibited: Japan, "Vever," 1975

THE POEM IN the upper register of the print reads:

子を持たぬ内が女房の初桜

Ko o motanu / uchi ga nyōbo no / hatsu-zakura

That period before / she's had a child
is a wife's / early flowering.

Figure 107, page 112

The Actor Onoe Kikugorō I, called Baikō, as Issun Tokubei in the kabuki play
Prosperous Genji with Parted Hair (Furiwakegami suehiro Genji), performed
at the Ichimura-za theater in the first lunar month, 1760

1760

Signed *Torii Kiyohiro ga;* seal *Kiyohiro*

Publisher: Maruya Kuzaemon

Color woodblock print in safflower-red and green,
benizuri-e; hosoban, 39.6 x 17.2 cm

Provenance: Murakami Takejirō (note on Stoclet mat
stated "acheté à Murakami 8-12-09" [purchased from
Murakami December 8, 1909]); acquired from Sotheby's,
London, Stoclet, June 8, 2004

Published: Foxwell et al., fig. 83; Stoclet 2004, lot 52

Exhibited: Smart Museum of Art, "Awash in Color," 2012–13

TO THE LEFT of the actor's name and poetry name,
尾上菊五郎 梅幸 Onoe Kikugorō Baikō, is a poem:

> 貌なら顔なら千賀のむめ桜
>
> *Katachi nara / kao nara chiga no / mume zakura*
>
> A cherry-plum who, / for his form and figure, wins /
> many compliments.

189

27   **Torii Kiyohiro (act. 1737–76)**

An uncut triptych of a courtesan and her client adapted from the Noh play *Takasago*, the client (right) holding a mask of the old man Jō and the courtesan (left) holding a mask of the old woman Uba, with a potted pine symbolizing the pine-strewn beach of Takasago and auspicious objects in the center

1750s

Signed *Torii Kiyohiro hitsu* on each panel

Publisher: Enamiya

Color woodblock print in safflower-red and green, *benizuri-e*; uncut *hosoban* triptych, 30.9 x 44.7 cm

Provenance: Michele Stoclet, Barcelona (ex coll. Adolphe Stoclet); acquired from Sotheby's, London, June 7, 1966

Published: Marks, p. 16; Ōta Memorial Museum of Art, Tokyo, *The Mann Collection*, cat. no. 19; Stoclet 1966, lot 23

Exhibited: Ōta Memorial Museum of Art, Tokyo, "The Mann Collection," 1994

THE THREE POEMS from the right to left panels read:

> 寿や尉と紅梅とのうるわしき
> 千代八千代松竹しげき江戸鑑
> 福のよき日を得たり姥ざくら
> *Kotobuki ya / Jō to mume to no / uruwashiki*
> *Chiyo yachiyo / matsu take shigeki / Edo kagami*
> *Saiwai no / yoki hi o etari / Uba-zakura*
> A blessing indeed! / Old Jō and the plum blossom, / both in splendid form.
> The pine and bamboo / flourish for thousands of years: / models for Edo.
> An older cherry, / Uba has earned the lucky / days that lie ahead.

Jō and Uba are symbols of conjugal fidelity and venerable old age. Usually, they are portrayed raking and sweeping up the needles of ancient pine trees. In the Noh play *Takasago*, they represent the spirits of a pine at Takasago in Harima (present-day Hyōgo Prefecture) and a pine at Suminoe in Settsu (present-day Osaka Prefecture) that are separated in space, but joined in spirit. Kiyohiro's stylish modern client and courtesan hold masks and implements symbolizing the ancient couple, with Jō's rake substituted by a samisen. The triptych here is a later version of an earlier state, which was commissioned by a different publisher with alternate poems in the right and left panels and no poem in the center panel (Tokyo National Museum, *Tōkyō Kokuritsu Hakubutsukan zuhan mokuroku: Ukiyoe hanga hen / Illustrated Catalogues of Tokyo National Museum: Ukiyo-e Prints*, vol. 1 [Tokyo National Museum, 1974], no. 232).

Suzuki Harunobu (1725?–1770)

Cooling off by a River, a calendar print (*egoyomi*) for the second year,
Meiwa era, corresponding to 1765, the left panel of a diptych

1765

Date inscribed on the fan *Meiwa ni nen kinoto no tori no toshi* (Year of the Rooster,
Meiwa 2)

Color woodblock print; *chūban,* 26.2 x 19.4 cm

Provenance: Jules Chavasse (provenance given in Fuller sale catalogue); Gilbert
Fuller; acquired from Sotheby's, London, June 28, 1972

Published: Ōta Memorial Museum of Art, Tokyo, *The Mann Collection,* cat. no. 25;
Fuller, lot 44; Sotheby's, London, June 28, 1972, lot 47

Exhibited: Ōta Memorial Museum of Art, Tokyo, "The Mann Collection," 1994

SEVERAL INSTITUTIONS, including the Honolulu Museum of Art (21727a–b), have
the complete diptych, showing in the right panel another young woman retying her
obi beside an identical bamboo bench. The fan in the left panel of those versions has
been replaced by a crane roundel, indicating the calendar design was repurposed later
for commercial distribution.

Suzuki Harunobu (1725?–1770)

Couple Reading a Letter, alluding to the Chinese sage Sun Kang, and a calendar print (*egoyomi*) for the second year, Meiwa era, corresponding to 1765

1765

Seal *Shōhakusei in*

Color woodblock print; *chūban*, 27.1 x 20.4 cm

Provenance: Acquired from Robert G. Sawers, London, May 15, 1971

Published: Ōta Memorial Museum of Art, Tokyo, *The Mann Collection*, cat. no. 27

Exhibited: Ōta Memorial Museum of Art, Tokyo, "The Mann Collection," 1994

A YOUNG MAN by a room heater (*kotatsu*) is reading the end of a letter that bears the calendrical notations for Meiwa 2, Year of the Rooster, corresponding to 1765. His companion sits on top of the heater cover to read the beginning, idly holding her hairpin in her free hand as if to use it as a reading pointer. The scene alludes to the third- and fourth-century Chinese sage Sun Kang (Japanese, Sonkō), who had to study by moonlight reflected in the snow because he was too poor to buy oil for a lamp; Harunobu designed a similar calendar picture for 1765 of a beauty reading a scroll by a window next to snow-covered bamboo.

There is another impression in The Art Institute of Chicago (1932.205) with similar coloring to the Mann print and with the same seal, read as *Shōhakusei in.* It is the seal of a member of a poetry club of samurai and elite merchants who exchanged calendar prints and other allusive images (*mitate-e*) for amusement. David Waterhouse considered these two prints as the first states of the design, before subsequent prints with recarved letter, variant coloring and different or no seals. Other states of the print are in the Honolulu Museum of Art (06438, lacking calendar information and with different red seal) and in the Museum of Fine Arts, Boston (21.4596, catalogued as second state, with calendar information; and 06.462, catalogued as fourth state, lacking calendar information). A revised version of about 1768 has a closed window, different clothing and a standing screen inscribed with Harunobu's signature, among other differences (Hillier, *Utamaro*, no. 15).

30   **Suzuki Harunobu (1725?–1770)**

Evening Snow on the Floss Shaper (Nurioke no bosetsu),
from the series *The Eight Parlor Views (Zashiki hakkei)*

1766

Color woodblock print with embossing; *chūban*, 28.3 x 21.1 cm

Provenance: Hans Popper; acquired from Sotheby's, New York, Popper,
October 5, 1972

Published: Foxwell et al., fig. 86; Ōta Memorial Museum of Art, Tokyo, *The Mann
Collection*, cat. no. 23; Popper, lot 45

Exhibited: Ōta Memorial Museum of Art, Tokyo, "The Mann Collection," 1994;
Smart Museum of Art, "Awash in Color," 2012–13

LIKE MOST OF Harunobu's prints, this one is a visual conceit of a classic theme, here,
the "Evening Snow" image from the Chinese eleventh-century Eight Views of the
Xiao and Xiang Rivers. The Chinese landscapes were adapted in Japan as The Eight
Views of Ōmi, the Lake Biwa area east of Kyoto. This print represents "Evening Snow
on Mount Hira" in the Ōmi set. The white floss that the woman is stretching over the
black, rounded shaper symbolizes the mountain draped in snow and darkness. The
first state of the print has the signature *Kyosen* printed in the block and a red seal of
Okubo Jinshirō Tadanobu (1727–1777), poetry name Kyosen, the head of the Kikuren
poetry club, who commissioned the set. Harunobu designed numerous calendar
prints (see Mann catalogue no. 29) and allusive pictures for members of the poetry
circles. This is a later state of the print made for commercial release, with the Kyosen
signature and seal removed and slightly different design and coloration.

31   **Suzuki Harunobu (1725?–1770)**

Returning Sails of the Towel Rack (Tenuguikake no kihan),
from the series *The Eight Parlor Views (Zashiki hakkei)*

1766

Color woodblock print; *chuban*, 28.7 x 20.7 cm

Provenance: Acquired from Christie's, New York, March 22, 1984

Published: Christie's, New York, March 22, 1984, lot 426; Ōta Memorial Museum
of Art, Tokyo, *The Mann Collection*, cat. no. 22

Exhibited: Ōta Memorial Museum of Art, Tokyo, "The Mann Collection," 1994

THE IMAGE IS a play on "Returning Sails at Yabase" (*Yabase kihan*), one of the Eight
Views of Ōmi, that are referenced in Mann catalogue no. 30. The white hand towel
drying in the breeze on its wooden stand represents the sail of a boat returning to
harbor. This is a later state of the print without the signature and seal *Kyosen* of the
poetry club member who originally commissioned it from Harunobu in 1766.

30

31

32 Suzuki Harunobu (1725?–1770)

Young Woman Visiting a Shrine on a Stormy Night, alluding to the Noh play *Aridōshi*

late 1760s

Color woodblock print; *chūban*, 28.6 x 21.1 cm

Provenance: Walter Amstutz; acquired from Sotheby's, Tokyo, Amstutz, April 15, 1991

Published: Amstutz, lot 46; Calza, no. 21; *Designed for Pleasure,* fig. 55, p. 82; Foxwell et al., fig. 88; Ōta Memorial Museum of Art, Tokyo, *The Mann Collection,* cat. no. 24

Exhibited: Asia Society, New York, "Designed for Pleasure," 2008; Ōta Memorial Museum of Art, Tokyo, "The Mann Collection," 1994; Smart Museum of Art, "Awash in Color," 2012–13

THE SCENE OF A BEAUTY watching her lantern swing in the blustering rain outside a red *torii* gate is adapted from the Noh play *Aridōshi* by Zeami (1363–1443). In the play, the ninth-century poet Ki no Tsurayuki suddenly is caught in a storm with his horse collapsing beneath him. A shrine attendant appears carrying a lantern and informs Tsurayuki that he had failed to dismount before a shrine dedicated to the god Aridōshi, angering the deity, although a poem might appease him.

Tsurayuki then composes an impromptu poem:

Amagumo no / tachikasanereru /
yowa nareba / Ari to hoshi to mo /
omō beki ka wa

On a night like this, when rain clouds rise in layers in the sky,

How was I to know if there were stars?

Translation by Thomas Bienman Hara, *Zeami's Style: The Noh Plays of Zeami Motokiyo* (Stanford University Press, 1996), 106

The deity is appeased, and the attendant recounts the blessings of poetry and disappears. Tsurayuki realizes that the attendant was actually the deity Aridōshi and resumes his journey.

Other impressions of the print show the slanted rain implied in this version.

Figure 101, page 105

Suzuki Harunobu (1725?–1770)

Osen, a Younger Waitress and a Bush-Warbler Vendor at Kasamori Shrine

late 1760s

Signed *Suzuki Harunobu ga*

Color woodblock print; *chūban*, 27.6 x 21.1 cm

Provenance: Acquired from Christie's, New York, October 27, 1998

Published: Christie's, New York, October 27, 1998, lot 329

A CELEBRATED BEAUTY of the late 1760s–70s, Osen was a waitress at the Kagiya teahouse in the precincts of Edo's Kasamori Inari Shrine. Harunobu designed a number of prints of Osen at her stall near the shrine gate. The bird vendor and his cage point to the Buddhist practice of buying caged animals and releasing them to gain merit (*hōjō*) that was celebrated especially on the fifteenth day of the eighth lunar month.

The poem in the cloud reserve reads:

哀なと後たに見えぬむら鳥の
空にうき名の立まとうらん

*Aware nado / ato tani mienu /
muradori no / sora ni ukina no /
tachi-matou ran*

And what if rumors / circulate?
Rise above them, / like a flock
of birds / that takes to the sky,
leaving / sorrow and trouble
behind.

Suzuki Harunobu (1725?–1770)

Noda Jewel River in Mutsu Province (*Chidori no Tamagawa* [*Noda no Tamagawa*])
from an untitled series known as "Six Jewel Rivers" (*Mutamagawa*)

late 1760s

Signed *Harunobu ga*

Color woodblock print; *chūban*, 27.8 x 21 cm

Provenance: Acquired from Christie's, New York, October 27, 1998

Published: Christie's, New York, October 27, 1998, lot 328

THE YOUNG MAN fishing from a dock at night illustrates a poem by Tachibana Nagayasu (Monk Nōin, 968–c. 1051), one of the Thirty-six and the One Hundred Immortal Poets. His poem here is in the cloud reserve:

千鳥玉川　能因法師
夕されば塩風越してみちのくの野田の玉川千とり鳴なり

Chidori no Tamagawa Nōin Hōshi
Yū sareba / shio-kaze koshite / Michinoku no / Noda no Tamagawa /
chidori naku nari
Plover Jewel River, Priest Nōin
As evening draws in, / we hear the cry of plovers / through the ocean breeze /
crossing the Michinoku / Jewel River at Noda.

The Noda Jewel River is associated with the plover, *chidori*, here shown in the dark night sky.

Suzuki Harunobu (1725?–1770)

Young Man Writing a Poem under a Maple Tree,
alluding to the Tang-dynasty poet Bai Juyi

1760s

Signed *Harunobu ga*

Color woodblock print; *chūban*, 28.3 x 21.5 cm

Provenance: Hans Popper; acquired from Sotheby's, New York, Popper,
October 5, 1972

Published: Hillier 1970, cat. no. 110; Ōta Memorial Museum of Art, Tokyo,
The Mann Collection, cat. no. 21; Popper, lot 55

Exhibited: Philadelphia Museum of Art, "Harunobu," 1970; Ōta Memorial
Museum of Art, Tokyo, "The Mann Collection," 1994

LIKE MANY OTHER prints by Harunobu in the Mann Collection, this image is an allusive picture (*mitate-e*) representing a classical theme updated with Edo-period figures
in fashionable settings and dress. The young man here is writing a line from a poem
by the eighth-century Chinese poet Bai Juyi that refers to a remembrance of heating
wine over burning maple leaves and brushing away green moss to inscribe poems on
rocks. Burton Watson translated the poem in *Po Chü'i: Selected Poems* (New York:
Columbia University Press, 2000), no. 11:

Once when we were living this side of Daibo's peak,
we went several times to Xianyu Temple.
When Black River deeps were clear we could see right
    to the bottom,
where white clouds parted, the grotto's gaping mouth!
We heated wine among the trees, burning fall leaves,
brushed away green moss to inscribe poems on rocks.
I now regret those outings will never come again, and
envy your return by the chrysanthemum time.

Figure 30, page 40

Suzuki Harunobu (1725?–1770)

Woman Sweeping Discarded Love Letters to be Carried away by Her Ox

1760s

Color woodblock print; *chūban*, 27.8 x 21.5 cm

Provenance: Acquired from Herbert Egenolf, Ukiyo-e Gallery, Germany, January 11, 1983

Published: Ōta Memorial Museum of Art, Tokyo, *The Mann Collection*, cat. no. 26

Exhibited: Ōta Memorial Museum of Art, Tokyo, "The Mann Collection," 1994

THE SCENE IS NOT a simple picture of a young woman sweeping love letters to gather into woven baskets carried by her ox. It alludes to episode four "Tending the Ox" from *Ten Oxherding Songs* composed in China in the eleventh century. Popular with Zen Buddhists, the songs are themselves parables of enlightenment told as a herdsman's struggle to catch his runaway ox. The ox represents the True Self, recalcitrant at the outset and subdued by the fourth stage. There is another impression in the Honolulu Museum of Art (21739) titled "Parody of Herdboy Pictures" (*mitate bokudōzu*) from the collection of James Michener.

Suzuki Harunobu (1725?–1770)

Women Collecting Salt at Tagonoura with Mount Fuji in the Distance

late 1760s

Signed *Suzuki Harunobu ga*

Color woodblock print with embossing; *chūban*, 28 x 20.4 cm

Provenance: Walter Amstutz; acquired from Sotheby's, Tokyo, Amstutz, April 15, 1991

Published: Amstutz, lot 51; Calza, no. 181; Ōta Memorial Museum of Art, Tokyo, *The Mann Collection*, cat. no. 20

Exhibited: Ōta Memorial Museum of Art, Tokyo, "The Mann Collection," 1994

THE POEM IN THE CLOUD reserve is by Yamabe no Akahito, active in the early eighth century. It reads:

山辺赤人
田子のうらにうち出でてみれば白たえのふじの高根に雪はふりつゝ

Yamabe no Akahito
Tagonoura ni / uchi-idete mireba / shirotae no / Fuji no takane ni / yuki wa furi tsutsu

Yamabe no Akahito
Our journey takes us / farther along the coastline / of Tago Bay, where /
we see Fuji draped in white, / with snow falling at the peak.

38 **Ippitsusai Bunchō (act. 1765–92)**

The Actor Ichikawa Komazō II as Sano Genzaemon Tsuneyo in the kabuki play
The Unchanging Flowers and the Flourishing Potted Trees (*Kawaranu hana sakae
hachinoki*) by Sakurada Jisuke, performed at the Nakamura-za theater in the
eleventh lunar month, 1769

1769

Signed *Ippitsusai Bunchō ga*; seal *Mori uji*

Inscribed in ink upper left with date Meiwa 6, theater, play and actor

Publisher: Nishimuraya Yohachi (Eijudō)

Color woodblock print; *hosoban*, 31.8 x 14.6 cm

Provenance: Acquired from Kegan, Paul, Trench & Trubner, London,
June 24, 1969

Published: London Gallery, Ltd., Tokyo, *Important Japanese Prints from Kegan, Paul,
Trench & Trubner, London*, no. 13; Ōta Memorial Museum of Art, Tokyo, *The Mann
Collection*, cat. no. 28

Exhibited: London Gallery, Ltd., Tokyo, "Important Japanese Prints from Kegan,
Paul, Trench & Trubner, London," 1969; Ōta Memorial Museum of Art, Tokyo,
"The Mann Collection," 1994

39 **Ippitsusai Bunchō (act. 1765–92)**

To Ms. Katsuyama of the Kazusaya (*Kazusaya uchi Katsuyama-sama mairu*),
from an untitled series known as "Folded Love Letters (*fujibumi*)," the
shape of the cartouche upper right

c. 1770

Signed *Ippitsusai Bunchō ga*; seal *Mori uji*

Publisher: unmarked; others in the untitled series bear the mark of Nishimuraya
Yohachi (Eijudō)

Color woodblock print; *hosoban*, 32.6 x 15 cm

Provenance: Ernest Le Véel; acquired from Ader, Picard, Tajan, Paris, Le Véel 2,
October 24, 1980

Published: Japan Ukiyo-e Society, *Exposition Toulouse Lautrec et Utamaro*,
cat. no. 115; Le Véel 2, lot 15; Ōta Memorial Museum of Art, Tokyo, *The Mann
Collection*, cat. no. 31; *Ukiyoe shūka*, vol. 14, no. 316-12

Exhibited: Japan Ukiyo-e Society, "Exposition Toulouse Lautrec et Utamaro,"
Tokyo, 1980; Ōta Memorial Museum of Art, Tokyo, "The Mann Collection," 1994

EACH CARTOUCHE IN the series is shaped like a folded love letter to a courtesan of
a particular brothel, here read as *Kazusaya uchi Katsuyama-sama mairu* (加津さや内
可つ山様 参る; [love letter] to Ms. Katsuyama of the Kazusaya).

40   **Ippitsusai Bunchō (act. 1765–92)**

The Actor Ichikawa Yaozō II as Gunsuke, a footman (*yakko*) of the Yoshida family, in the kabuki play *The Mirror-Pond: Vestiges of the Soga* (*Kagamigaike omokage Soga*) by Sakurada Jisuke, performed at the Nakamura-za theater in the first lunar month, 1770

1770

Signed *Ippitsusai Bunchō ga*; seal *Mori uji*

Inscribed in ink upper right with date Meiwa 7, Spring, theater, play and actor

Publisher: Okumuraya

Color woodblock print; *hosoban,* 32.1 x 14.5 cm

Provenance: Hunter Collection, New York; Paolino Gerli; acquired from Sotheby's, New York, Gerli, April 28, 1971

Published: Gerli, lot 37; Ōta Memorial Museum of Art, Tokyo, *The Mann Collection,* cat. no. 29; *Ukiyoe shūka,* vol. 14, no. 77; *Ukiyoe taisei,* vol. 5, no. 222; Walpole Galleries, New York, Hunter Collection and others, April 11, 1919, lot 58

Exhibited: Ōta Memorial Museum of Art, Tokyo, "The Mann Collection," 1994

THE ROLE, DATE of the performance and theater are written in what is presumed to be a notation contemporary to the print.

41   **Ippitsusai Bunchō (act. 1765–92)**

The Actor Ichikawa Danjūrō IV as Kazusa Shichibei Kagekiyo Disguised as Enshū no hyakushō, kakezuri no Jūbei (the itinerant vendor Jūbei in Suruga province) in the kabuki play *The Mirror Pond: Vestiges of the Soga* (*Kagamigaike omokage Soga*) by Sakurada Jisuke, performed at the Nakamura-za theater in the first lunar month, 1770

1770

Signed *Ippitsusai Bunchō ga*; seal *Mori uji*

Publisher: Nishimuraya Yohachi (Eijudō)

Collector's seal of Henri Vever

Color woodblock print; *hosoban,* 32.2 x 15 cm

Provenance: Henri Vever (print purchased by R. E. Lewis, Inc. from Sotheby's, London, Vever 1, March 26, 1974); acquired from R. E. Lewis, Inc., San Francisco, March 26, 1974

Published: Hillier, *Vever,* vol. I, no. 230; Ōta Memorial Museum of Art, Tokyo, *The Mann Collection,* cat. no. 30; Vever 1, lot 98

Exhibited: Ōta Memorial Museum of Art, Tokyo, "The Mann Collection," 1994

42   **Isoda Koryūsai** (1735–1792)

Young Woman Dancing Okina

early 1770s

Signed *Koryūsai ga;* seal *Masakatsu*

Color woodblock print; pillar-print format (*hashira-e*), 66.2 x 11.5 cm

Provenance: Acquired from S. H. Mori Gallery, Chicago, November 26, 1962

Published: Ōta Memorial Museum of Art, Tokyo, *The Mann Collection,* cat. no. 32

Exhibited: Ōta Memorial Museum of Art, Tokyo, "The Mann Collection," 1994

THE DANCE IS AN hour-long performance by the white-haired old-man Okina character as a Shintō ritual for peace and prosperity in the Noh theater repertoire. At the time this print was made, the Okina dance commonly was staged at the start of a full day's Noh program.

43   **Katsukawa Shunshō** (1743?–1793)

The Actor Nakamura Nakazō I as Mikawaya Giheiji Kicking the Actor Nakamura Sukegorō II as Danshichi Kurobei in the kabuki play *Murder in the Back Street off Nagamachi (Nagamachi-ura),* Act 7 of the ballad-drama *Mirror of Osaka in the Summer Festival (Natsu matsuri Naniwa kagami),* performed as one act in *Mastery of the Fan in Kabuki (Ayatsuri kabuki ōgi)* at the Nakamura-za theater in the seventh lunar month, 1768

1768

Signed *Shunshō zu;* seal *Rin* in jar-shaped reserve

Collector's seal of Henri Vever

Color woodblock print; *chūban,* 27 x 20.5 cm

Provenance: Henri Vever (purchased by R. E. Lewis, Inc. from Sotheby's, London, Vever 1, March 26, 1974); acquired from R. E. Lewis, Inc., San Francisco, April 15, 1976

Published: Hillier, *Vever,* vol. 1, no. 255; Ōta Memorial Museum of Art, Tokyo, *The Mann Collection,* cat. no. 34; R. E. Lewis, Inc., *Fine Japanese Prints,* December 1974, no. 9; Vever 1, lot 109

Exhibited: The Art Institute of Chicago, "Connoisseurship of Japanese Prints," 2012; Ōta Memorial Museum of Art, Tokyo, "The Mann Collection," 1994

Katsukawa Shunshō (1743?–1793)

The Actor Ichikawa Yaozō II in an undetermined role

c. 1768

Seal *Rin* in jar-shaped reserve

Color woodblock print; *hosoban*, 32.5 x 15.1 cm

Provenance: Acquired from S. H. Mori Gallery, Chicago, March 14, 1964

Figure 18, page 31

Katsukawa Shunshō (1743?–1793)

Sumo Wrestlers of the Eastern Group: Nijigatake Somaemon, Sekiwaki Rank from Awa Province (Ashū) and Fudenoumi Kin'emon, Maegashira Rank from Kokura

c. 1782–83

Signed *Shunshō ga*

Publisher: Matsumura Yahei

Color woodblock print; *ōban*, 38.1 x 25.6 cm

Provenance: Carl Schraubstadter; acquired from Merlin Dailey, East West Gallery, Victor, New York, March 19, 1976

Published: Marks, no. 49; Ōta Memorial Museum of Art, Tokyo, *The Mann Collection*, cat. no. 37; Schraubstadter, March 8, 1948, lot 30 (a lot of five wrestler *ōban* by Shunshō)

Exhibited: Ōta Memorial Museum of Art, Tokyo, *The Mann Collection*, 1994

COLLECTOR'S COMMENTS

When examining this print at our home, Suzuki Jūzō commented to Roger Keyes that it must be an early impression because a carver's error, seen in the seal at the bottom center of the print, had not yet been corrected. The carver did not carve all the space around the characters, leaving a short mark that resembles a straight apostrophe to the left of the upper-right character. As the carving error eventually was addressed, most impressions do not have the small mark.

46   **Katsukawa Shunshō (1743?–1793)**

The Actor Nakamura Nakazō I as the Monk Raigō Ajari, a Buddhist Priest of the Onjō-ji Temple in the kabuki play *Forest of the Nue Monster: Target of the Eleventh Month* (*Nue no mori ichiyō no mato*), performed at the Nakamura-za theater in the eleventh lunar month, 1770

1770

Signed *Shunshō ga*; seal *Rin* in jar-shaped reserve

Color woodblock print; *hosoban*, 30.6 x 14.7 cm

Provenance: Ernest Le Véel; acquired from Ader, Picard, Tajan, Paris, Le Véel 2, October 24, 1980

Published: Le Véel 2, lot 18; Marks, no. 32; Ōta Memorial Museum of Art, Tokyo, *The Mann Collection*, cat. no. 33

Exhibited: Ōta Memorial Museum of Art, Tokyo, "The Mann Collection," 1994

47   **Katsukawa Shunshō (1743?–1793)**

The Actor Nakamura Sukegorō II as Matano no Gorō in the kabuki play *Conjoined Chrysanthemum Threads in Izu* (*Meotogiku Izu no kisewata*), performed as the season premiere (*kaomise*) at the Ichimura-za theater in the eleventh lunar month, 1770

1770

Signed *Shunshō ga*; seal *Rin* in jar-shaped reserve

Collector's seal of Albert Maroni

Color woodblock print on blue ground; *hosoban*, 32.6 x 15.1 cm

Provenance: Albert Maroni; acquired from Sotheby's, New York, May 13, 1983

Published: Maroni, lot 207; Sotheby's, New York, May 13, 1983, lot 325

48 Katsukawa Shunshō (1743?–1793)

The Actors Nakamura Nakazō I as Ōmi Kotota and Ōtani Hiroji III as Banba Chūta, retainers of the rival factions in the Soga brothers story, in the ballad-drama *The Plovers: Combing Hair at Midnight (Sono chidori yōwa no kamisuki)*, from part two of the kabuki play *A Soga Pattern Dyed to Order (Oatsuraezome Soga no hinagata)*, performed at the Nakamura-za theater in the third lunar month, 1774

1774

Signed *Shunshō ga* on each sheet

Color woodblock print; *hosoban* diptych, 29.5 x 13.9 cm (right sheet); 29.7 x 14.1 cm (left sheet)

Provenance: Frederic E. Church; Paolino Gerli; acquired from Adele and Willard Gidwitz, January 19, 1980

Published: Church, lot 152; Gerli, lot 40; Ōta Memorial Museum of Art, Tokyo, *The Mann Collection*, cat. no. 35

Exhibited: Ōta Memorial Museum of Art, Tokyo, "The Mann Collection," 1994

The Actor Onoe Matsusuke I as Retired Emperor Sutoku in the kabuki play
Returning Home in Splendor (*Katakaeru nishiki no wakayaka*), performed
at the Nakamura-za theater in the eleventh lunar month, 1780

1780

Signed *Shunshō ga*

Color woodblock print; *chūban*, 30.8 x 14.9 cm

Provenance: Maurice Cottle, MD, Chicago, gift to H. George Mann, 1960s

Published: Ōta Memorial Museum of Art, Tokyo, *The Mann Collection*,
cat. no. 36

Exhibited: Ōta Memorial Museum of Art, Tokyo, "The Mann Collection," 1994

50 Katsukawa Shunkō (1743–1812)

The Actor Ichimura Uzaemon IX in a Shibaraku (Wait a Moment!) Scene

1778

Signed *Katsukawa Shunkō ga*

Color woodblock print; *hosoban*, 30.6 x 15 cm

Provenance: Edith Ehrman; acquired from Parke-Bernet Galleries, New York, Ehrman, June 17, 1975

Published: Ehrman, lot 94; Marks, no. 44; Ōta Memorial Museum of Art, Tokyo, *The Mann Collection*, cat. no. 41

Exhibited: Ōta Memorial Museum of Art, Tokyo, "The Mann Collection," 1994

THE ACTOR ICHIMURA UZAEMON IX is easily identified from other prints by his broad face and lightning-bolt crest. The play in which he is performing is less certain. A version of the print showing the actor in a red robe, lacking the repeated Chinese character *shino* (bamboo shoot) in white here, has been catalogued by The Art Institute of Chicago as Araoka Hachirō in the play *Sakimasuya ume no kachidoki*, which opened the season at the Ichimura-za theater in the eleventh lunar month, 1778 (1939.872). However, there is a related print by Katsukawa Shunshō of Uzaemon in frontal Shibaraku pose wearing a black robe in the Museum of Fine Arts, Boston with the role given as Sasaki Tadaomi Araoka Genta in the same play (21.4350). The Ōta catalogue of the Mann Collection lists the name of the character as Shinozuka Iga no kami [Sadatsuna], who is a principal in the *Taiheiki* story.

Katsukawa Shunkō (1743–1812)

The Actor Matsumoto Kōshirō IV as the Sumo Wrestler Kaminari Tsurunosuke in the kabuki play *Plum Calendar Dawn of the Soga (Ume goyomi akebono Soga)*, performed at the Ichimura-za theater in the first lunar month, 1780

1780

Signed *Shunkō ga*

Collector's seal of Henri Vever

Color woodblock print, large-head picture (*ōkubi-e*), *ōban*, 37.2 x 25.1 cm

Provenance: Henri Vever; Sidney A. Tannenbaum; acquired from Christie's, New York, March 20, 1985

Published: Tannenbaum, lot 152; Hillier, *Vever*, vol. 1, no. 296; Ōta Memorial Museum of Art, Tokyo, *The Mann Collection*, cat. no. 43; Vever 2, lot 129; Yamaguchi et al., *Genshoku ukiyoe daihyakka jiten*, vol. 7, no. 214

Exhibited: Ōta Memorial Museum of Art Tokyo, "The Mann Collection," 1994

THE VEVER CATALOGUE identifies the play as *The Maple-leaf Fence of Takao Daimyōjin* (*Takao Daimyōjin momiji no magaki* [transliterated slightly differently therein]), performed at the Nakamura-za theater eight years later, in the spring of 1788. However, the *hosoban*-sized print of the same actor by Shunkō in the Museum of Fine Arts, Boston gives the play as the caption does here (21.6057). The MFA holds two impressions of a print by Katsukawa Shunshō of Kōshirō IV as the wrestler Tsurunosuke in striped robe with towel slung around his neck, also in the 1780 performance at the Ichimura-za theater.

Figure 119, page 127

Katsukawa Shunkō (1743–1812)

The Actor Segawa Kikunojō III in a Female Role, Dancing and Beating a Drum

c. 1781

Signed *Shunkō ga*

Color woodblock print; *hosoban*, 30.4 x 14.7 cm

Provenance: Acquired from R. E. Lewis, Inc., San Francisco, April 27, 1986

Published: R. E. Lewis, Inc., *Old Japanese Prints*, April 1986, no. 24; Ōta Memorial Museum of Art, Tokyo, *The Mann Collection*, cat. no. 42

Exhibited: Ōta Memorial Museum of Art, Tokyo, *The Mann Collection*, 1994

THERE IS A DIPTYCH by Katsukawa Shunshō in the Museum of Fine Arts, Boston (11.18921; 11.18934) that shows Kikunojō III as Onatsu in an outer robe with roundels of stylized chrysanthemums (*kiku*), a pun on his name, very similar to the print here, suggesting an identification of the same actor in the Mann print. Another image by Shunshō in The Art Institute of Chicago (1927.605) shows Kikunojō as Onatsu in an outer robe patterned with small, related roundels. Both institutions identify the play as *An Elopement: Chrysanthemum and Butterfly Lovers* (*Onatsu Seijūrō michiyuki hiyoku no kiku chō*), one of three alternate dance interludes in the main feature, *Flowers of Kabuki: The Eternal Soga* (*Kabuki no hana bandai Soga*), performed in the third lunar month, 1781, at the Ichimura-za theater.

The Actor Iwai Hanshirō IV as the Geisha Onaka Disguised as Akita Jonosuke Yoshikage in a Shibaraku (Wait a Moment!) Scene in the kabuki play *Memorial Service for Holy Nichiren: A Model of "The Potted Trees" (Mieikō nori no Hachinoki)*, performed at the Kawarazaki-za theater in the eleventh lunar month, 1791

1791

Signed *Shun'ei ga*

Publisher: Hariyama Shinshichi

Censor's seal *kiwame* (certified)

Color woodblock print; *hosoban*, 32.4 x 14.5 cm

Provenance: Acquired from Sotheby's, London, December 12, 1967

Published: Ōta Memorial Museum of Art, Tokyo, *The Mann Collection*, cat. no. 44; Sotheby's, London, December 12, 1967, lot 64

Exhibited: Ōta Memorial Museum of Art, Tokyo, "The Mann Collection," 1994

FOR THE NOH play to which the title of the play alludes, see Mann catalogue no. 9. The Art Institute of Chicago holds a large-head portrait (*ōkubi-e*) attributed to Shun'ei of Hanshirō IV in the same part represented here (1939.2206).

54   **Katsukawa Shun'ei (c. 1762–1819)**

The Wrestler Kagami-iwa Hamanosuke

1810

Signed *Shun'ei ga*

Publisher: Nishimuraya Yohachi (Eijudō)

Censor's seal *kiwame* (certified) and numeral *ni* (2)

Collector's seal of Henri Vever

Color woodblock print on gray ground; *ōban*, 38.4 x 26.2 cm

Provenance: Henri Vever; acquired from Sotheby Parke Bernet, New York, anonymous vendor in Gaines, May 24, 1979, lot 483

Published: Bickford, pl. 27B; Gaines, lot 483; Hillier, *Vever*, vol. 1, no. 322; Marks, p. 182 ; Ōta Memorial Museum of Art, Tokyo, *The Mann Collection*, cat. no. 49; Vever 2, lot 137

Exhibited: Ōta Memorial Museum of Art, Tokyo, "The Mann Collection," 1994

Katsukawa Shun'ei (c. 1762–1819)

An Actor of the Ichikawa Line

1795–96

Signed *Shun'ei ga*

Publisher: Tsuruya Kiemon

Censor's seal *kiwame* (certified)

Collector's seal of Hayashi Tadamasa

Color woodblock print; *aiban*, 33.2 x 22.9 cm

Provenance: Hayashi Tadamasa; Adolphe Stoclet (provenance given by Raymond E. Lewis); acquired from R. E. Lewis, Inc., San Francisco, June 23, 1980

Published: Ōta Memorial Museum of Art, Tokyo, *The Mann Collection*, cat. no. 45

Exhibited: Ōta Memorial Museum of Art, Tokyo, "The Mann Collection," 1994

THE ŌTA CATALOGUE gives the actor as Ichikawa Danjūrō VI playing Kinukawa Yasaburō, a role he debuted at the Miyako-za theater in the ninth lunar month of 1796 in the play *Rokusuke Hikosan gongen chikai no sukedachi*, known from its alternate title as *The Vow of Rokusuke*. Other sources suggest Ichikawa Yaozō III as Kamata Jirō disguised as Gotobei in *Yoshitsune Flowering again in Snow* (*Kaeribana yuki no Yoshitsune*) by Sakurada Jisuke, performed at the Miyako-za theater in the eleventh lunar month, 1795. While the crest on the actor's *kamishimo* vest does not have the *ya* character in the center as it appears in most images of Yaozō III, he does resemble the Yaozō in likenesses by Sharaku, Toyokuni I and Shun'ei.

Katsukawa Shun'ei (c. 1762–1819)

The Actor Ichikawa Yaozō III as Hayano Kanpei in the kabuki play *Treasury of the Loyal Retainers* (*Kanadehon Chūshingura*) by Takeda Izumo II, Miyoshi Shōraku and Namiki Senryū, performed at the Kiri-za theater in the fourth lunar month, 1795

Signed *Shun'ei ga*

Publisher: Iwatoya Kisaburō

Color woodblock print; *ōban*, 38.4 x 25.3 cm

Provenance: Acquired from Christie's, New York, April 16, 1988

Published; Christie's, New York, April 16, 1988, lot 334; Ōta Memorial Museum of Art, Tokyo, *The Mann Collection*, cat. no. 47

Exhibited: Ōta Memorial Museum of Art, Tokyo, "The Mann Collection," 1994

THE IDENTIFICATION OF the actor and role in this image is supported by another Shun'ei print by the same publisher in the Museum of Fine Arts, Boston, showing Yaozō III in the Kanpei role in black socks, leggings, black underrobe and red sash similar to those here (11.13917). The left sheet of a Shun'ei diptych in the MFA shows Yaozō, with the usual crest containing the character *ya,* in the same green-mountain-motif cloak and in black socks, clasping his hands (the role is listed as Soga no Gorō, but appears to be an unedited entry). The Ōta catalogue of the Mann print agrees with Yaozō in the Kanpei part. The impression in the Achenbach Foundation for the Graphic Arts, The Fine Arts Museums of San Francisco (1935-12-13), describes the figure as Morita Kan'ya VIII as Okaru's brother, Teraoka Heiemon, in the "Gion Teahouse" scene from Act VII of the same play performed also at the Miyako-za theater in the fourth month, 1795.

Katsukawa Shun'ei (c. 1762–1819)

The Actor Nakayama Tomisaburō I as Okaru in the kabuki play *Treasury of the Loyal Retainers* (*Kanadehon Chūshingura*) by Takeda Izumo II, Miyoshi Shōraku and Namiki Senryū, performed at the Kiri-za theater in the fourth lunar month, 1795

1795

Signed *Shun'ei ga*

Publisher: Iwatoya Kisaburō

Color woodblock print; *ōban*, 38.8 x 25.5 cm

Provenance: Charles Haviland; Walter Amstutz; acquired from Sotheby's, Tokyo, Amstutz, April 15, 1991

Published: Amstutz, lot 99; Haviland 1, lot 170, pl. VII; Ōta Memorial Museum of Art, Tokyo, *The Mann Collection*, cat. no. 48; *Ukiyo-e shūka*, vol. 14, no. 65

Exhibited: Ōta Memorial Museum of Art, Tokyo, "The Mann Collection," 1994

56

57

Katsukawa Shun'ei (c. 1762–1819)

The Actor Nakamura Nakazō II as Kawagoe Tarō Shigeyori in the kabuki play *Yoshitsune Flowering again in Snow* (*Kaeribana yuki no Yoshitsune*) by Sakurada Jisuke, performed as the season premiere (*kaomise*) at the Miyako-za theater in the eleventh lunar month, 1795

1795

Signed *Shun'ei ga*

Publisher: Tsuruya Kiemon

Censor's seal *kiwame* (certified)

Color woodblock print with gray ground; *aiban*, 33.9 x 22.6 cm

Provenance: Albert Maroni; acquired from Sotheby's, New York, April 14, 1983

Published: Marks, no. 72; Maroni, lot 171; Ōta Memorial Museum of Art, Tokyo, *The Mann Collection*, cat. no. 46; Sotheby's, New York, April 14, 1983, lot 330

Exhibited: Ōta Memorial Museum of Art, Tokyo, "The Mann Collection," 1994

THE ACTOR NAKAZŌ II (1759–1796) is recognizable by his cloak with signature over-lapping emblems known as "Nakazō stripes" (*Nakazō-jima*), which featured a stylized Chinese character for "person" (*hito*) repeated in sets of three. According to Andreas Marks, this print is the sole known impression of Nakazō from a Shun'ei set of three prints of popular actors performing in the play *Yoshitsune Flowering again in Snow* in the eleventh lunar month of 1795 (Marks, p. 236).

59   Katsukawa Shun'ei (c. 1762–1819) and Katsukawa Shunchō (act. c. 1780–1801)

The Actor Ichikawa Komazō II (Matsumoto Kōshirō IV)
and Two Women on an Evening Stroll

late 1780s

Signed *Shun'ei ga* (center) and *Shunchō ga* (right)

Color woodblock print; *aiban*, 32.5 x 23 cm

Provenance: Col. H. Appleton; acquired from Sotheby's, New York,
November 9, 1984

Published: Appleton, lot 1709, pl. XIV; Ōta Memorial Museum of Art, Tokyo,
The Mann Collection, cat. no. 50; Sotheby's, New York, November 9, 1984, lot 46

Exhibited: Ōta Memorial Museum of Art, Tokyo, "The Mann Collection," 1994

THERE ARE SEVERAL prints jointly designed by Shun'ei and Shunchō of famous actors in street attire accompanied by young women: a muted version of this design and another of Iwai Hanshirō IV in The Art Institute of Chicago (1938.545; 1925.2721) and a third in the British Museum of Ichikawa Danjūrō V showing his poem to a courtesan that has the emblem of the publisher Tsutaya Jūzaburō (1910,0614,0.12).

Katsukawa Shunchō (act. c. 1780–1801)

Ohisa of the Takashimaya

c. 1794

Signed *Shunchō ga*

Publisher: Tsuruya Kiemon

Color woodblock print with mica ground; *ōban*, 37.8 x 24.6 cm

Provenance: Frederic E. Church; Albert E. McVitty; Louis W. Black; acquired from Sotheby's, New York, Black, March 4, 1976

Published: Black, lot 107; Marks, no. 59; McVitty, lot 60; Ōta Memorial Museum of Art, Tokyo, *The Mann Collection*, cat. no. 51

Exhibited: Ōta Memorial Museum of Art, Tokyo, "The Mann Collection," 1994

OHISA, IMMORTALIZED by Kitagawa Utamaro in a similar print of her holding a fan, was a server at the Takashimaya, a teahouse in the Ryōgoku district of Edo owned by her father, who also operated a rice-cracker shop. The oak motif on her fan is the emblem of the shop. She is believed to have died at eighteen, shortly after Shunchō made this picture of her.

61   **Katsukawa Shunchō (act. c. 1780–1801)**

The Courtesan Morokoshi of the Echizenya Compared to a Peony, from the series *Courtesans Compared to Flowers,* implied by the flower in the right cartouche of each design

c. 1794

Publisher: Tsuruya Kiemon

Collector's seal of Albert Maroni

Color woodblock print, large-head picture (*ōkubi-e*); *ōban*, 37.6 x 25.1 cm

Provenance: Albert Maroni; acquired from Roland Koscherak, New York, June 27, 1964

Published: Maroni, lot 141; Ōta Memorial Museum of Art, Tokyo, *The Mann Collection,* cat. no. 52

Exhibited: Ōta Memorial Museum of Art, Tokyo, "The Mann Collection," 1994

62   **Torii Kiyonaga (1752–1815)**

The Actor Ichikawa Yaozō III at Leisure with Two Courtesans,
from an untitled series of eight actors shown offstage

c. 1782

Signed *Kiyonaga ga*

Collector's seal of Henri Vever

Color woodblock print; *aiban*, 31.9 x 22.2 cm

Provenance: Henri Vever; acquired from Christie's, New York, June 27, 1984

Published: Christie's, New York, June 27, 1984, lot 38; Hillier, *Vever*, vol. 1, no. 344;
Japan, *Vever*, 1975, no. 149; Ōta Memorial Museum of Art, Tokyo, *The Mann
Collection*, cat. no. 39; Vever 2, lot 146

Exhibited: Japan, "Vever," 1975; Ōta Memorial Museum of Art, Tokyo, "The Mann
Collection," 1994

Torii Kiyonaga (1752–1815)

The Actor Ichikawa Danjūrō V and His Family

c. 1782

Signed *Kiyonaga ga*

Color woodblock print; *ōban,* 39.5 x 26.5 cm

Provenance: Ernest Le Véel; acquired from Ader, Picard, Tajan, Paris, Le Véel 3, November 5, 1981

Published: Japan Ukiyo-e Society, *Exposition Toulouse Lautrec et Utamaro,* cat. no. 120; Le Véel 3, lot 9; Ōta Memorial Museum of Art, Tokyo, *The Mann Collection,* cat. no. 38

Exhibited: Japan Ukiyo-e Society, "Exposition Toulouse Lautrec et Utamaro," Tokyo, 1980; Ōta Memorial Museum of Art, Tokyo, "The Mann Collection," 1994

THE SENSATIONAL KABUKI star Ichikawa Danjūrō V (1741–1806), in the black gauze overcoat, is shown in private life walking with his family. His son, carried on the shoulder of Ichikawa Masugorō, appears to be about five years old, when he adopted the stage name Ichikawa Ebizō IV in *The Fifth Genji, the Tribute of the Long-sleeved Kimono* (*Godai Genji mitsugi*), performed as the season premiere (*kaomise*) at the Nakamura-za theater in the eleventh lunar month, 1782. After a relatively brief career, Ebizō IV, later Danjūrō VI, died at age twenty-two. The overcoat of Danjūrō V shows the crest of a carp swimming up-stream associated with the Danjūrō line; the square crest of nested rice measures associated with the Ichikawa family appears on the robes of Masugorō, with the additional character for "five," and of Ebizō. The women in the image have not been identified. Like most men of his stature, Danjūrō was an active member of a poetry club and founded the Mimasu Circle, named for his square crest of nested rice measures (*mimasu*) that identifies other Ichikawa actors in the Mann Collection (see Mann catalogue nos. 15, 53 and 80, for example). Here, he holds a fan inscribed with one of his poems. Danjūrō V was so serious about poetry that he retired from the stage to compose quietly, until being persuaded to return as a theatrical mentor.

Torii Kiyonaga (1752–1815)

A Party at the Komeikan Teahouse in the Shinagawa Pleasure District

c. 1790

Signed *Kiyonaga ga*

Publisher: Tsutaya Jūzaburō (Kōshodō)

Censor's seal *kiwame* (certified)

Color woodblock print; *ōban* triptych, 38.6 x 25.4 cm (right), 38.6 x 25.2 cm (center), 36.8 x 25.1 cm (left)

Provenance: Ernest Le Véel; acquired from Le Véel 2, October 24, 1980

Published: Japan Ukiyo-e Society, *Exposition Toulouse Lautrec et Utamaro*, cat. no. 121; Le Véel 2, lot 9; Ōta Memorial Museum of Art, Tokyo, *The Mann Collection*, cat. no. 40

Exhibited: Japan Ukiyo-e Society, "Exposition Toulouse Lautrec et Utamaro," Tokyo, 1980; Ōta Memorial Museum of Art, Tokyo, "The Mann Collection," 1994

THE CENTER SHEET of one of two impressions of the triptych at the Museum of Fine Arts, Boston (21.5593-95) lacks the black scroll box in the foreground and shows other smaller variations. The Komeikan teahouse, named in the plaque at the top of the center panel, was in Susaki in Shinagawa, one of the three main pleasure districts of Edo, along with Yoshiwara and Fukagawa. The entertainer is dancing a parodic *oni no nenbutsu* (demon intoning the name of Amida Buddha).

65   **Kitagawa Utamaro (1753?–1806)**

Diversions of the Four Seasons: The Color and Fragrance of Flowers (Shiki asobi hana no iroka), right panel of a diptych

c. 1783

Signed *Utamaro ga*

Collector's seal of Henri Vever

Color woodblock print; *ōban,* 36.8 x 24.2 cm

Provenance: Charles Haviland; Henri Vever; John R. Gaines; acquired from Sotheby's, New York, Gaines, May 24, 1979

Published: Haviland 1, lot 266, pl. XI; Hillier, *Vever,* vol. 2, no. 388; Ōta Memorial Museum of Art, Tokyo, *The Mann Collection,* cat. no. 53; Gaines, lot 548; Vever 1, lot 169

Exhibited: Ōta Memorial Museum of Art, Tokyo, "The Mann Collection," 1994

THE FIRST POEM (*kyōka*) on the fan is signed by Yomo no Akara, the pen name of Ōta Nanpo (1749–1823), a celebrated literatus, popular writer and head of the Yomo poetry circle. The second is by Akera Kankō (1740–1800), another samurai and leading light in the Edo *kyōka* world of the 1780s and 1790s. The right sheet in the Tokyo National Museum is registered as an Important Art Object.

The poems read:

四方赤良
春の夜のたゝ一時も千金にかへまし物を花か三文
Yomo no Akara
Haru no yo no / tada hito-toki mo / senkin ni / kaemashi mono o / hana ga san mon
Yomo no Akara
Though, as people say, / a thousand gold coins couldn't / buy even
one hour / of a spring night, three cents will / get you one cherry blossom.

朱楽漢江
天人も影向すてに花をえてまつたく雲の中の町かな
Akera Kankō
Tennin mo / yōgō sude ni / hana o ete / mattaku kumo no / Nakanochō kana
Akera Kankō
Manifestations / divine reach their floral peak / on Yoshiwara's / Main Street, quite enveloping / the quarter in clouds of pink.

Figure 63c, page 72

66 **Kitagawa Utamaro (1753?–1806)**

Woman Exhaling Smoke from a Pipe, from the series *Ten Types in the Physiognomic Study of Women (Fujo ninsō juppon)*

c. 1792–93

Signed *Sōkan Utamaro kōga* (thoughtfully drawn by Utamaro the physiognomist)

Publisher: Tsutaya Jūzaburō

Censor's seal *kiwame* (certified)

Color woodblock print with mica ground; *ōban*, 39.1 x 26 cm

Provenance: Acquired from Christie's, New York, November 2, 1996

Published: Christie's, New York, November 2, 1996, lot 522

Figure 103, page 108

67 **Kitagawa Utamaro (1753?–1806)**

The Courtesan Hanaōgi of the Gomeirō, from the series *Comparison of the Charms of Beauties (Bijin kiryō kurabe)*

1790s

Signed *Utamaro hitsu*

Publisher: Takasu Sōshichi

Censor's seal *kiwame* (certified)

Color woodblock print with mica ground; *ōban*, 37.8 x 25.1 cm

Provenance: Hans Popper; anonymous vendor, Sotheby's, New York, June 18, 1975; British Rail Pension Fund; acquired from British Rail Pension Fund at Sotheby's, London, December 8, 1987

Published: Mann, *Impressions,* fig. 11; *Masterpieces of Ukiyo-e in Foreign Collections,* no. 191; Ōta Memorial Museum of Art, Tokyo, *The Mann Collection,* cat. no. 54; Popper, lot 153; Shibui et al., *Masterpieces,* no. 233; Sotheby's, London, December 8, 1987, lot 9; Sotheby's, New York, June 18, 1975, lot 548; Tokyo Olympics *Masterpieces,* 1964, no. 174; *Ukiyoe taikei,* vol. 5, no. 181

Exhibited: Shirokiya Nihonbashi Department Store Galleries, Tokyo, "Masterpieces," 1964; Matsukaya Department Store Galleries, Tokyo, "Masterpieces of Ukiyo-e in Foreign Collections," 1972; Ōta Memorial Museum of Art, Tokyo, "The Mann Collection," 1994

Figure 99, page 102

Kitagawa Utamaro (1753?–1806)

Women in the Kitchen (Daidokoro)

c. 1795–96

Signed *Utamaro hitsu*

Publisher: Uemuraya Yohei

Collector's seal of Werner Schindler

Color woodblock print; *ōban* diptych, 36.1 x 48 cm

Provenance: Werner Schindler; acquired from Scholten Japanese Art, New York, March 11, 2004

Published: Kondō 1985, no. 56; Marks, no. 70

Exhibited: "Schindler Collection," Japan, 1985–86; The Art Institute of Chicago, "Connoisseurship of Japanese Prints," 2012

THERE ARE VARIANT states of the prints. In addition to the diptych, the Museum of Fine Arts, Boston has a single right sheet that lacks the wood bucket (21.7407-8; 11.14207). The single sheet is presumed to be the earlier state.

Pages 156–157

Kitagawa Utamaro (1753?–1806)

Peek-a-boo (Nozoki)

c. 1800

Signed *Utamaro hitsu*

Publisher: Omiya Gonkurō

Color woodblock print; *ōban*, 38.1 x 25.3 cm

Provenance: Louis Cartier; Huguette Berès; acquired from Sotheby's, London, October 24, 1977

Published: Berès, *Utamaro*, 1977, no. 110; Cartier, lot 164; Ōta Memorial Museum of Art, Tokyo, *The Mann Collection*, cat. no. 57; Sotheby's, London, October 24, 1977, lot 18

Exhibited: Berès, Paris, "Utamaro," 1977; Ōta Memorial Museum of Art, Tokyo, "The Mann Collection," 1994

Kitagawa Utamaro (1753?–1806)

*The Geisha Sankatsu of the Minoya and Her Lover Akaneya Hanshichi
(Akaneya Hanshichi, Minoya Sankatsu), from the series* True Feelings
Compared: The Founts of Love *(Jitsu kurabe iro no minakami)*

1790s

Signed *Utamaro hitsu*

Publisher: Nishimuraya Yohachi (Eijudō)

Censor's seal *kiwame* (certified)

Color woodblock print; *ōban*, 37.8 x 25.7 cm

Provenance: Arthur Davison Ficke; H. P. and Edith P. Garland; Paolino Gerli;
acquired from Adele and Willard Gidwitz, January 19, 1980

Published: Ficke 1920, lot 331; Garland, lot 134;
Gerli, lot 68; Ōta Memorial Museum of Art,
Tokyo, *The Mann Collection*, cat. no. 55

Exhibited: Ōta Memorial Museum of Art, Tokyo,
"The Mann Collection," 1994

HANSHICHI, THE SON of a sake shop owner in
Osaka and the husband of Osono, the prototypical
faithful wife, is still in love with his former girl-
friend, Sankatsu, a dancer at the Minoya house,
with whom he has a young daughter. After mur-
dering the man who had harassed Sankatsu, the
lovers ask for Osono's pardon on their way to com-
mit suicide together. The puppet, later kabuki, play
is based on an actual double-suicide of 1695.

The Courtesan Agemaki of the Miuraya Hiding Her Lover Yorozuya Sukeroku (Miuraya Agemaki, Yorozuya Sukeroku), from the series *True Feelings Compared: The Founts of Love (Jitsu kurabe iro no minakami)*

1790s

Signed *Utamaro hitsu*

Publisher: Nishimuraya Yohachi (Eijudō)

Censor's seal *kiwame* (certified)

Color woodblock print; *ōban*, 39 x 25.8 cm

Provenance: Acquired from Christie's, New York, March 20, 1986

Published: Christie's, New York, March 20, 1986, lot 22; Ōta Memorial Museum of Art, Tokyo, *The Mann Collection*, cat. no. 56

Exhibited: Ōta Memorial Museum of Art, Tokyo, "The Mann Collection," 1994

THE IMAGE IS from a series, like Mann catalogue 70, of half-length figures of famous lovers, here the high-ranking courtesan Agemaki of the Miuraya brothel and her married lover, the protagonist of various versions of the kabuki play *Sukeroku*.

Kitagawa Utamaro (1753?–1806)

Lovers in the Private Second-floor Room of a Teahouse,
from the album *The Poem of the Pillow (Utamakura)*

1788

Publisher: Tsutaya Jūzaburō

Color woodblock print from an erotic album (*shunga*); *ōban*, 26.5 x 37.8 cm

Provenance: Acquired from Robert G. Sawers, London, April 23, 1974

Published: Delay, p. 91; *Designed for Pleasure*, fig. 87, p. 125; Marks, pp. 26–27

Exhibited: Asia Society, New York, "Designed for Pleasure," 2008

ASANO SHŪGŌ AND TIMOTHY CLARK in their catalogue *The Passionate Art of Utamaro* remark on *The Poem of the Pillow* as a masterwork of ukiyo-e unique in the erotic genre. They explain that the title is a play on the "pillow word" (*makura-kotoba*) convention of classical Japanese poetry that can stand for a theme, sentiment, sound, place or other allusion. The preface of the album, attributed to Torai Sanna (1744–1810) using the pen name Profligate of Soggy Honjō (Honjō no Shitsubuka), is rife with such double-entendres:

> We hereby print pillow pictures in brocades of the East [prints] as a plaything of spring at court. With one glance the eye is startled, the heart throbs, the spirit leaps, pausing below the sash, pressing, pressing, entwining the legs like the reeds of Naniwa, from the jewel-comb box of Hakone onwards, it is akin to using the hips. Ah! Rather than some amateur at drawing, the brush of one who is skilled in the art of love, without pressing too hard, this is the way to move the hearts of men.
>
> Translation by Timothy Clark, *Utamaro*, cat. no. 489 and text volume, p. 279

The thirty-one-syllable light verse (*kyōka*) inscribed on the fan in this image is by Yadoya no Meshimori (Ishikawa Masamochi, 1754–1830):

蛤にはしをしっかとはさまれて鴫立ちかぬる秋の夕ぐれ

Hamaguri ni / hashi o shikka to / hasamarete / shigi tachi kanuru / aki no yūgure

With his beak firmly / clamped between the two hard shells /of a common clam, / one snipe will not be rising / into the autumn twilight.

The poem is a risqué parody of a classical poem (*waka*) by Saigyō (1118–1190):

心なき身にもあはれは知られけり鴫立つ沢の秋の夕暮れ

Kokoro naki / mi ni mo aware wa / shirarekeri / shigi tatsu sawa no / aki no yūgure

Even a person / as calloused as I must feel / the pathos of things, / seeing snipe rise from a marsh / into the autumn twilight.

For the relationship between Utamaro and his publisher Tsutaya Jūzaburō, see Julie Nelson Davis, "Tsutaya Jūzaburō: Master Publisher," in *Designed for Pleasure*, pp. 115–42.

Figure 55, page 63 and pages 240–241

Chōbunsai Eishi (1756–1829)

The Courtesan Konosato of the Takeya (Takeya Konosato), from the series
Six Blossoming Immortals of the Yoshiwara (Seirō bijin rokkasen)

c. 1794

Signed *Eishi zu*

Publisher: Nishimuraya Yohachi (Eijudō)

Censor's seal *kiwame* (certified)

Color woodblock print; *ōban,* 38.6 x 25.9 cm

Provenance: Louis Ledoux (sold after
Ledoux's death by Roland Koscherak,
New York); acquired from Robert G. Sawers,
London, June 15, 1971

Published: Ledoux, *Sharaku to Toyokuni,* no.
39; Mann, *Impressions,* fig. 4; Ōta Memorial
Museum of Art, Tokyo, *The Mann Collection,*
cat. no. 59

Exhibited: Ōta Memorial Museum of Art,
Tokyo, "The Mann Collection," 1994

KONOSATO HOLDS a small bag of incense;
other implements and a brazier for incense are
in front of her. The evanescence of her beauty
is symbolized by the bush clover (*hagi*), an
autumnal motif, in the round cartouche. The
title of the series plays on the theme of the Six
Immortal Poets, the Rokkasen.

74   **Chōbunsai Eishi (1756–1829)**

Ono no Komachi, from the series *Fanciful Representations of the Six Immortal Poets (Fūryū yatsushi Rokkasen)*

c. 1794

Signed *Eishi zu*

Publisher: Nishimuraya Yohachi (Eijudō)

Censor's seal *kiwame* (certified)

Collector's seal of Hayashi Tadamasa

Color woodblock print with yellow ground; *ōban,* 37.1 x 24.4 cm

Provenance: Hayashi Tadamasa; Gilbert Fuller; Paolino Gerli; acquired from Adele and Willard Gidwitz, January 19, 1980

Published: Fuller, lot 100; Gerli, lot 57; Marks, no. 60; Ōta Memorial Museum of Art, Tokyo, *The Mann Collection,* cat. no. 60

Exhibited: Ōta Memorial Museum of Art, Tokyo, "The Mann Collection," 1994

THE POEM in the square cartouche is by the ninth-century poet Ono no Komachi, the only female among the Six Immortal Poets (Rokkasen) and known for her skill, wit, great beauty and poignant decline in old age. Here, the fashionable Edo woman parodying Komachi is wearing a kimono tie-dyed with a pattern of speckled hemp leaves (*asa-no-ha kanoko*), an apt allusion to the sentiment of the verse. Komachi's poem reads:

色見へてうつらふもの八世の中の人のこゝろの花にそありける

*Iro miede / utsurou mono wa / yo no naka no /
hito no kokoro no / hana ni zo arikeru*

We cannot clearly see / the shifting colors / as they fade—the flowers /
in the hearts of those we love / in this fickle world of ours.

Translation by John T. Carpenter

244

Chōbunsai Eishi (1756–1829)

Picture of the Courtesan Hanamurasaki of the Tamaya Out Walking (Tamaya Hanamurasaki dōchū no zu), from the series *Comparison of Selected Beauties of the Yoshiwara (Seirō bisen awase)*

c. 1794

Signed *Eishi giga* (drawn for pleasure by Eishi)

Publisher: Iwatoya Kisaburō

Color woodblock print with mica ground; *ōban*, 38.7 x 24.9 cm

Provenance: Louis Ledoux (sold after Ledoux's death by Roland Koscherak, New York); William W. Collins; acquired from R. E. Lewis, Inc., San Francisco, December 10, 1974

Published: Jenkins 1973, no. 50; Ledoux, *Sharaku to Toyokuni,* no. 42

Exhibited: Japan Society, New York, "The Ledoux Heritage," 1973

Chōkyōsai Eiri (act. 1790s–early 1800s)

The Flowers of Edo: The Master of Yanagibashi (Edo no hana Yanagibashi natori)

c. 1795

Signed *Eiri ga*

Collector's seal of Theodor N. Scheiwe

Color woodblock print with mica ground, large-head picture (*ōkubi-e*); *ōban*, 36.8 x 25.2 cm

Provenance: Theodore N. Scheiwe; acquired from Christie's, New York, Scheiwe 1, March 21, 1989

Published: *Designed for Pleasure*, fig. 7, p. 194; Hempel 1959, no. 122; Hempel 1963, no. 66; Hempel 1964, pl. 6; Hempel 1972, pl. 188; Ōta Memorial Museum of Art, Tokyo, *The Mann Collection*, cat. no. 61; Scheiwe 1, lot 58 (catalogue cover illustration); Shibui et al., *Masterpieces*, no. 302; *Ukiyoe taikei*, vol. 6, pl. 54

Exhibited: Landesmuseum für Kunst und Kulturgeschichte, Münster, "Ausstellung japanischer Holzschnitte: Sammlung Theodor Scheiwe," 1959; Villa Hügel, Essen, "Ukiyo-e: die Kunst der heiteren vergänglichen Welt; Japan 17.–19. Jahrhundert, Sammlung Scheiwe," 1972; Ōta Memorial Museum of Art, Tokyo, "The Mann Collection," 1994; Asia Society, New York, "Designed for Pleasure," 2008

THE PORTRAIT is of the professional raconteur Tomimoto Buzendayū II (1754–1822), for whom the Tomimoto line of chanters was named. Here, he is beating out the rhythm of the song with his fan and fingers.

Figure 100, page 103

77

Ichirakutei Eisui (act. 1790–1823)

The Courtesan Hinazuru of the Chōjiya (Chōjiya uchi Hinazuru),
from the series *Beauties of the Five Seasonal Festivals (Bijin go sekku)*

c. 1800–1803

Signed *Ichirakutei Eisui ga*

Collector's seal of Hayashi Tadamasa

Color woodblock print; *ōban*, 38.7 x 24.5 cm

Provenance: Hayashi Tadamasa; Max Kade (provenance given in Lempertz catalogue); Fedor Sibeth; acquired from Lempertz Kunsthaus, Cologne, December 2, 1995

Published: Lempertz, December 2, 1995, lot 1323; *Ukiyoe taisei*, vol. 7, no. 603

Eishōsai Chōki (act. c. 1790s–early 1800s)

Mizue, a Geisha, and Moto, a Waitress at Yoshidaya
[in Shinmachi, Osaka] (Geiko Mizue Yoshidaya nakai Moto)

c. 1794

Signed *Chōki ga*

Publisher: Tsutaya Jūzaburō

Color woodblock print with mica ground; *ōban*, 37.3 x 24.9 cm

Provenance: Acquired from Christie's, New York, November 2, 1996

Published: Christie's, New York, November 2, 1996, lot 531; *Designed for Pleasure*,
fig. 5, p. 193 and frontispiece (detail); Marks, no. 58

Exhibited: Asia Society, New York, "Designed for Pleasure," 2008; The Art Institute
of Chicago, "Connoisseurship of Japanese Prints," 2012

Figure 104, page 109

79   **Eishōsai Chōki (act. c. 1790s–early 1800s)**

Three Geisha in Costume for the Niwaka Festival, from the series *Pageants at the Niwaka Festival in the Yoshiwara in Full Swing (Seirō Niwaka zensei asobi)*

c. 1794

Signed *Chōki ga*

Publisher: Tsuruya Kiemon

Censor's seal *kiwame* (certified)

Color woodblock print; *ōban,* 37.1 x 25.6 cm

Provenance: Art Museum, Bremen, sold Walpole Galleries, New York, 1922; Louis Ledoux (sold after Ledoux's death by Roland Koscherak, New York); acquired from Robert G. Sawers, London, May 15, 1971

Published: Delay, p. 134; Ledoux, *Sharaku to Toyokuni,* no. 24; Mann, *Impressions,* fig. 5; Ōta Memorial Museum of Art, Tokyo, *The Mann Collection,* cat. no. 58; Walpole Galleries, New York, November 10, 1922, lot 9

Exhibited: Ōta Memorial Museum of Art, Tokyo, "The Mann Collection," 1994

THE THREE WOMEN are dressed in men's costumes for three different skits in the Niwaka ("impromptu") Festival, a masquerade that took place in the Yoshiwara in the eighth month of the lunar calendar. Courtesans, their attendants, and sometimes geisha and brothel owners, performed the skits to the accompaniment of drums, flutes and samisen on floats, when they stopped at various establishments. The names and particulars of the skits are inscribed in the upper register of the print to the right of the title cartouche in the upper left. They read from right to left:

通り念仏
わか、かが、いと、さと、さの、ひやく、まさ、いほ、さき
花の瀧里の養老
かの、ふで、しげ、すが、あい、ゆき、八百、ひで
花貝らげ古卿の錦
くに　うた

Tōri Nenbutsu: Waka, Kaga, Ito, Sato, Sano, Hiyaku, Masa, Io, Saki
Street Nenbutsu: Waka, Kaga, Ito, Sato, Sano, Hyaku, Masa, Io, Saki [represented by the woman lower right]

Hana no taki sato no Yōrō: Kano, Fude, Shige, Suga, Ai, Yuki, Yao, Hide
The Yōrō Waterfall at the flowering village: Kano, Fude, Shige, Suga, Ai, Yuki, Yao, Hide [represented by the woman center]

Hana-kairage furusato kokyō no nishiki: Kuni, Uta
Returning home laden with honors, [with a sword sheathed] in shagreen: Kuni, Uta [represented by the woman lower left]

80 Tōshūsai Sharaku (act. 1794–95)

The Actor Ichikawa Ebizō as Takamura Sadanoshin, a father driven to suicide by the disgrace of his daughter, in the kabuki play *The Beloved Wife's Particolored Leading Rope (Koi nyōbō somewake tazuna)* by Miyoshi Shōraku and Yoshida Kanshi (the puppet master Yoshida Bunzaburō I), performed at the Kawarazaki-za theater in the fifth lunar month, 1794

1794

Signed *Tōshūsai Sharaku ga*

Publisher: Tsutaya Jūzaburō

Censor's seal *kiwame* (certified)

Color woodblock print with lacquerlike embellishment and dark mica ground, large-head picture (*ōkubi-e*); *ōban,* 38.4 x 25.4 cm

Provenance: Samuel Tuke; anonymous vendor, Sotheby's, London, June 28, 1972; acquired from R. E. Lewis, Inc., San Francisco, October 18, 1972

Published: Berès, *Sharaku,* cat. no. 19; *Designed for Pleasure,* fig. 96, p. 134; Forrer 2012, fig. 26; R. E. Lewis, Inc., *Twentieth Anniversary Catalogue,* 1972, no. 30; Ōta Memorial Museum of Art, Tokyo, *The Mann Collection,* cat. no. 64; Sotheby's, London, June 28, 1972, lot 111; Sotheby Parke-Bernet, *Art at Auction 1971–72,* p. 269; Tokyo National Museum, *Sharaku,* cat. no. 64, p. 113; Tuke, lot 228

Exhibited: Berès, Paris, "Sharaku," 1980; Ōta Memorial Museum of Art, Tokyo, "The Mann Collection," 1994; Asia Society, New York, "Designed for Pleasure," 2008; Tokyo National Museum, "Sharaku," 2011

THE PRINT SHOWS the aging superstar Ebizō (formerly Danjūrō V) as the Noh performer Sadanoshin, who commits suicide to atone for his daughter's illicit affair with a retainer of the Yurugi family. As a result, she is excused and promoted to wet nurse by the Yurugi. In the climax of the play, she must give up her chance of reuniting with the son from her liaison. The play was adapted for the kabuki stage in 1751 from a puppet play by Chikamatsu Monzaemon.

Figure 47, page 54

The Actor Matsumoto Kōshirō IV as the Fishmonger Gorobei in the ballad-drama *The Iris Hair-ornament of Remembrance (Hana-ayame omoi no kanzashi),* an interlude in the kabuki play *A Medley of Tales of Revenge (Katakiuchi noriai-banashi)* by Sakurada Jisuke, performed at the Kiri-za theater in the fifth lunar month, 1794

1794

Signed *Tōshūsai Sharaku ga*

Publisher: Tsutaya Jūzaburō

Censor's seal *kiwame* (certified)

Color woodblock print with dark mica ground, large-head picture (*ōkubi-e*); *ōban*, 37.3 x 24.8 cm

Provenance: Acquired from R. E. Lewis, Inc., San Francisco, December 15, 1979

Published: Berès, *Sharaku*, cat. no. 16; *Designed for Pleasure*, fig. 94, p. 221; Ōta Memorial Museum of Art, Tokyo, *The Mann Collection*, cat. no. 63; Tokyo National Museum, *Sharaku*, 2011, cat. no. 76, p. 125

Exhibited: Berès, Paris, "Sharaku," 1980; Ōta Memorial Museum of Art, Tokyo, "The Mann Collection," 1994; Asia Society, New York, "Designed for Pleasure," 2008; Tokyo National Museum, "Sharaku," 2011

Figure 50, page 57

Tōshūsai Sharaku (act. 1794–95)

The Actor Sakata Hangorō III as the Villain Fujikawa Mizuemon in the kabuki play *The Iris Soga of the Bunroku Era (Hana-ayame Bunroku Soga)* by Matsui Yūsuke, performed at the Miyako-za theater in the fifth lunar month, 1794

1794

Signed *Tōshūsai Sharaku ga*

Publisher: Tsutaya Jūzaburō

Censor's seal *kiwame* (certified)

Color woodblock print with mica ground, large-head picture (*ōkubi-e*); *ōban*, 38.9 x 25.3 cm

Provenance: Sidney Ward; acquired from Christie's, New York, December 3, 1982

Published: Christie's, New York, December 3, 1982, Ward, lot 1006; Ōta Memorial Museum of Art, Tokyo, *The Mann Collection*, cat. no. 62; Ward, *One Hundred Japanese Prints*, no. 61

Exhibited: Ōta Memorial Museum of Art, Tokyo, "The Mann Collection," 1994

SHARAKU SHOWS the corrupt Mizuemon pulling back his sleeves about to draw his sword. The drama is a reworking of a 1701 murder and reprisal (the latter sanctioned by the Tokugawa government) and the twelfth-century revenge tale of the Soga brothers. The kabuki play centers on the revenge over the period of some thirty years of Ishii Genzō, the subject of another Sharaku image, and his two brothers for the murder of their father by Mizuemon.

Figure 49, page 56

Tōshūsai Sharaku (act. 1794–95)

The Actor Sanogawa Ichimatsu III as Onayo, a Courtesan of the Gion District, Kyoto
in the kabuki play *The Iris Soga of the Bunroku Era (Hana-ayame Bunroku Soga)* by
Matsui Yūsuke, performed at the Miyako-za theater in the fifth lunar month, 1794

1794

Signed *Tōshūsai Sharaku ga*

Publisher: Tsutaya Jūzaburō

Censor's seal *kiwame* (certified)

Color woodblock print with mica ground, large-head picture (*ōkubi-e*);
ōban, 38.9 x 25.9 cm

Provenance: Sir Frank Athelstane Swettenham, presumed (provenance abbreviated
as "Swet." in Vignier & Inada, cited below); Henri Vever; acquired from Sotheby's,
London, post-sale Vever 4, October 30, 1997

Published: Berès, *Sharaku*, cat. no. 10; *Designed
for Pleasure*, fig. 95, p. 133; Hillier, *Vever*, vol. 2,
no. 587; Japan, *Vever*, 1975, cat. no. 186; Japan,
Vever, 1976, no. 470; Mann, *Impressions*, fig. 12;
Marks, no. 67; Vever 4, lot 124; Vignier & Inada,
1911, pl. LXXXIII; Tokyo National Museum,
Sharaku, cat. no. 42, p. 92; *Ukiyoe taisei*, vol. 8,
no. 11

Exhibited: Musée des Arts Decoratifs, Paris, 1911;
Japan, "Vever," 1975; Berès, Paris, "Sharaku," 1980;
Asia Society, New York, "Designed for Pleasure,"
2008; Tokyo National Museum, "Sharaku," 2011

Figure 108, page 113

Utagawa Toyokuni I (1769–1825)

*Tachibanaya (The Actor Ichikawa Yaozō III) as the Footman Shimobe Hatsuhei,
from the series* Images of Actors on Stage (Yakusha butai no sugata-e), *in the
kabuki play* The First Daybreak of the Year: Season-premiere Performance of the
Soga Drama (Hatsu akebono kaomise Soga) *by Kawatake Bunzō and others,
performed at the Miyako-za theater in the second lunar month, 1794*

1794

Signed *Toyokuni ga*

Publisher: Izumiya Ichibei (Kansendō)

Censor's seal *kiwame* (certified)

Color woodblock print with white mica ground; *ōban*, 36.9 x 24.8 cm

Provenance: Takano H., Tokyo; Gertrude Wickes Snellenburg, Philadelphia;
acquired from Sotheby Parke-Bernet, New York, October 2, 1973

Published: Ōta Memorial Museum of Art, Tokyo, *The Mann Collection*, cat. no. 66;
Sotheby Parke-Bernet, New York, Snellenburg, October 2, 1973, lot 144; Takano,
lot 145

Exhibited: Ōta Memorial Museum of Art, Tokyo, "The Mann Collection," 1994

TACHIBANAYA IN THE TITLE cartouche is the name of the house with which the actor
is affiliated (*yagō*).

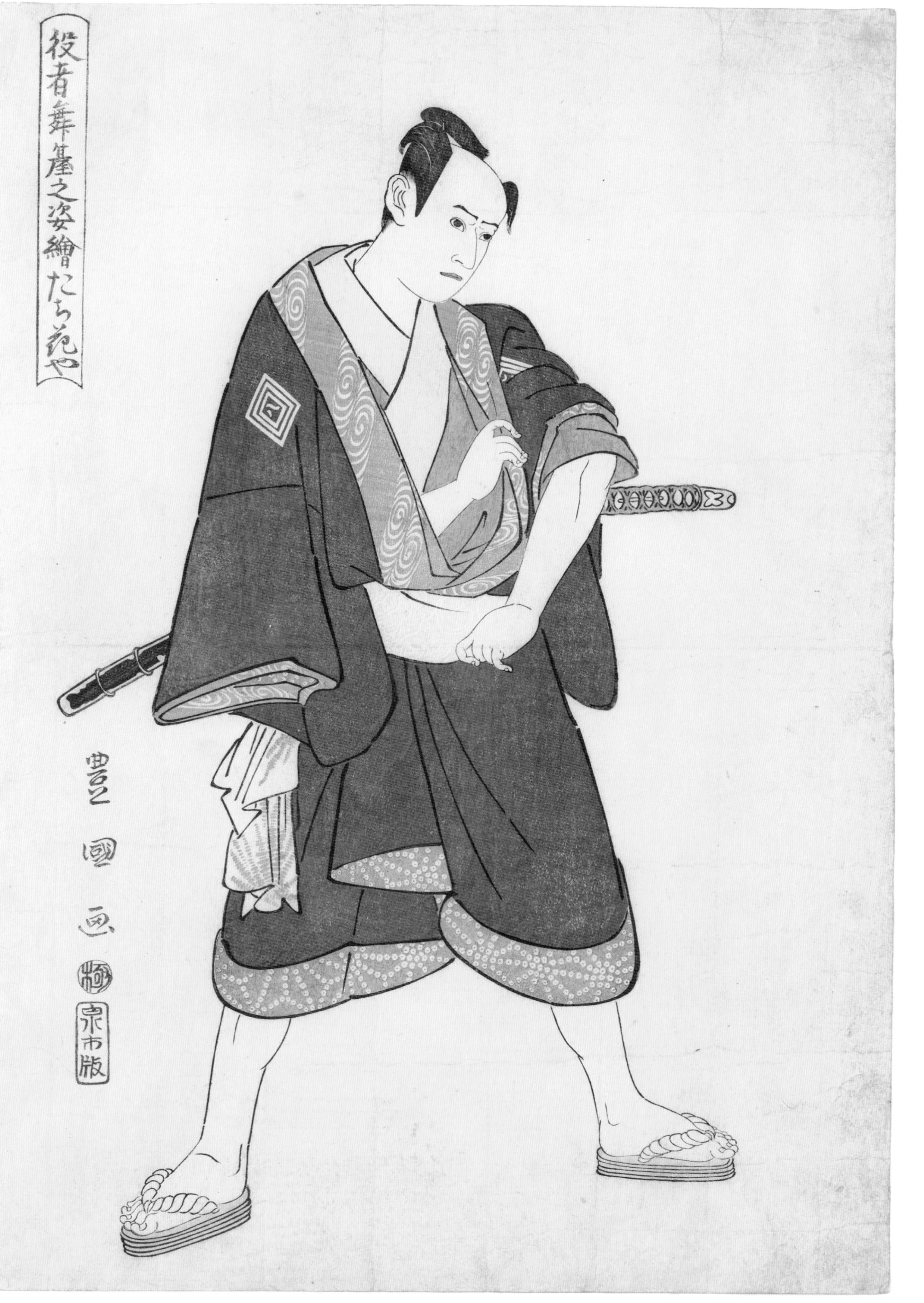
役者舞臺之姿繪 たち花や
豊國画
極
泉市版

Utagawa Toyokuni I (1769–1825)

Tachibanaya (The Actor Ichikawa Yaozō III) as the Villain Fuwa no Banzaemon, from the series *Images of Actors on Stage (Yakusha butai no sugata-e),* in the kabuki play *The Courtesan and the Three Umbrellas (Keisei sanbon karakasa),* performed at the Miyako-za theater in the seventh lunar month, 1794

1794

Signed *Toyokuni ga*

Publisher: Izumiya Ichibei (Kansendō)

Censor's seal *kiwame* (certified)

Collectors' seals of Hayashi Tadamasa and of Henri Vever

Color woodblock print with gray ground; *ōban,* 37.5 x 23.6 cm

Provenance: Hayashi Tadamasa; Henri Vever (print sold to R. E. Lewis, Inc. at Sotheby's, London, Vever 1, March 26, 1974); acquired from R. E. Lewis, Inc., San Francisco, March 1974

Published: Hillier, *Vever,* vol. 2, no. 625; Ōta Memorial Museum of Art, Tokyo, *The Mann Collection,* cat. no. 65; Tokyo National Museum, *Sharaku,* cat. no. 237; Vever 1, lot 272

Exhibited: Ōta Memorial Museum of Art, Tokyo, "The Mann Collection," 1994; Tokyo National Museum, "Sharaku," 2011

TACHIBANAYA IN THE TITLE cartouche is the name of the house with which the actor is affiliated (*yagō*). The number 4 (*yon*) appears below the publisher's mark, indicating the print's position in a set of five designed by Toyokuni of actors in this play.

Utagawa Toyokuni I (1769–1825)

The Actor Kataoka Nizaemon VII as Iyo no Tarō Disguised as Bantarō
in the kabuki play *Prosperous Rule of the Genji Clan Descended from
Emperor Seiwa (Seiwa nidai ōyose Genji)* by Katsu Hyōzō (Tsuruya
Nanboku IV), performed at the Miyako-za theater in the eleventh
lunar month, 1796

1796

Signed *Toyokuni ga*

Publisher: Izumiya Ichibei (Kansendō)

Color woodblock print; *ōban*, 37.2 x 23.4 cm

Provenance: Ernest Le Véel, acquired from Ader, Picard, Tajan, Paris,
Le Véel 2, October 24, 1980

Published: Japan Ukiyo-e Society, *Exposition Toulouse Lautrec et
Utamaro*, cat. no. 140; Le Véel 2, lot 59; Ōta Memorial Museum of Art,
Tokyo, *The Mann Collection*, cat. no. 67

Exhibited: Japan Ukiyo-e Society, "Exposition Toulouse Lautrec et
Utamaro," Tokyo, 1980; Ōta Memorial Museum of Art, Tokyo, "The
Mann Collection," 1994

Figure 117, page 125

Utagawa Toyokuni I (1769–1825)

The Actor Segawa Kikunojō III as the Fox, Okyaku, Disguised as a Wet Nurse
in the kabuki play *The Potted Trees That Trace Back to the Snow Maiden
(Yukionna keizu no hachinoki)* by Namiki Gohei, performed at the Kiri-za
theater in the eleventh lunar month, 1797

1797

Signed *Toyokuni ga*

Publisher: Murataya Jirobei

Censor's seal *kiwame* (certified)

Color woodblock print; *ōban*, 36.6 x 24.6 cm

Provenance: Merlin Dailey, East West Gallery, Victor, New York;
acquired from Doris Meltzer, New York, November 24, 1970

Published: Ōta Memorial Museum of Art, Tokyo, *The Mann
Collection*, cat. no. 69

Exhibited: Ōta Memorial Museum of Art, Tokyo, "The Mann
Collection," 1994

The Actors Segawa Kikunojō III as Naginoha and Sawamura Tetsunosuke I as Her Son, Inubōmaru in the kabuki play *A New Soga Kosode for the New Season (Kisohajime kosode Soga)* by Namiki Gohei, performed at the Kiri-za theater in the first lunar month, 1798

1798

Signed *Toyokuni ga*

Publisher: Izumiya Ichibei (Kansendō)

Collector's seal of Hayashi Tadamasa

Color woodblock print; *ōban*, 38.7 x 25.8 cm

Provenance: Hayashi Tadamasa; Ernest Le Véel, acquired from Ader, Picard, Tajan, Paris, Le Véel 2, October 24, 1980

Published: Japan Ukiyo-e Society, *Exposition Toulouse Lautrec et Utamaro*, cat. no. 142; Le Véel 2, lot 63

Exhibited: Japan Ukiyo-e Society, "Exposition Toulouse Lautrec et Utamaro," Tokyo, 1980

LIKE THE TITLES of most kabuki plays, the one represented by the print cannot be rendered conveniently in English. *Kisohajime* refers to the custom of donning new clothes for the new year. Variations of the Soga revenge drama regularly were mounted as season premieres (*kaomise*) at kabuki theaters. *Kosode Soga* refers to the episode in which the brothers in the story visit their mother; *kosode*, a form of kimono, connotes the mother and by extension, the scene.

89   Utagawa Toyokuni I (1769–1825)

The Actors Segawa Kikunojō III as Osome and Matsumoto Yonesaburō I as Her Lover Hisamatsu in the kabuki play *A Popular Song: Three Crests of Twinned Rings (Hayariuta hiyoku no mitsumon)* by Namiki Gohei, performed at the Kiri-za theater in the seventh lunar month, 1796

1796

Signed *Toyokuni ga*

Publisher: undetermined; publisher's mark *Yamaden*

Color woodblock print; *ōban*, 38.7 x 25.8 cm

Provenance: Ernest Le Véel, acquired from Ader, Picard, Tajan, Paris, Le Véel 2, October 24, 1980

Published: Le Véel 2, lot 62

Utagawa Toyokuni I (1769–1825)

The Actor Kataoka Nizaemon VII as Saibara Kageyu in Formal Kamishimo Vest in the kabuki play *The Chastity of the Yoshiwara-bred Courtesan (Kimigatete Yoshiwara sodachi)* by Namiki Gohei, performed at the Miyako-za theater in the seventh lunar month, 1795

1795

Signed *Toyokuni ga*

Publisher: Iseya Magobei

Censor's seal *kiwame* (certified), trimmed

Indistinct collector's seal on verso resembling Felix Frick monogram seal

Color woodblock print; *ōban*, 37.3 x 23.9 cm

Provenance: Osterritter Collection; Felix Frick; Fedor Sibeth; acquired from Lempertz Kunsthaus, Cologne, December 2, 1995 (giving provenance above)

Published: Lempertz, December 2, 1995, lot 1352

THIS HALF-LENGTH LIKENESS is one of five that Toyokuni produced in 1795. Nizaemon plays a villain planning to assume control of his master's household in a play that is itself a variation on *Disturbance in the Date Clan (Date sōdō)*.

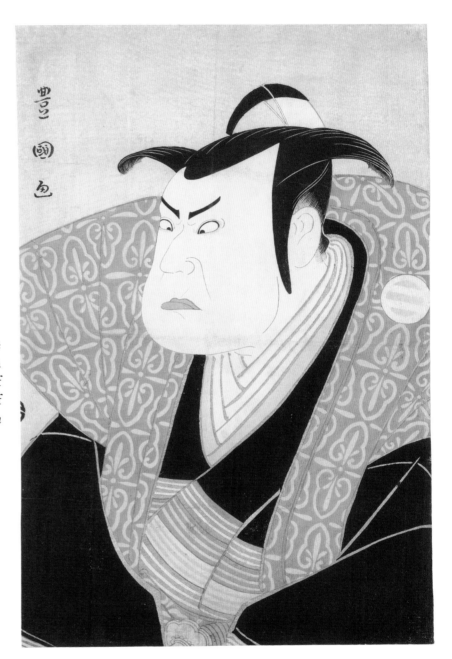

Utagawa Toyokuni I (1769–1825)

The Actors Arashi Ryūzō II as Konobei of Suma and Ichikawa Omezō I as Kujaku Saburō in the Guise of the Pilgrim Daisuke in the kabuki play *Yukihira and the Snow-covered Pine (Ginsekai matsu ni Yukihira)* by Namiki Gohei and Kanai Yūsuke, performed at the Kiri-za theater in the eleventh lunar month, 1796

1796

Signed *Toyokuni ga*

Publisher: undetermined; publisher's mark *Yamaden*

Color woodblock print; *ōban*, 38 x 25.6 cm

Provenance: Acquired from Adele and Willard Gidwitz, January 19, 1980

92   **Utagawa Toyokuni I (1769–1825)**

The Actors Segawa Kikunojō III as Oshizu of the Mizuchaya Teahouse and Ichikawa Yaozō III as the Songbird Seller Jirosuke (subtitled Mizuchaya Oshizu and Kotoriuri Jirosuke) in the dance interlude *Koizumō neya no torikumi* of the kabuki play *The Blossom Watchtower of the Tachibana Family (Hanayagura Tachibana keizu)* by Kanai Yūsuke, performed at the Ichimura-za theater in the eleventh lunar month, 1798

1798

Signed *Toyokuni ga*

Publisher: Nishimuraya Yohachi (Eijudō)

Censor's seal *kiwame* (certified)

Color woodblock print; *ōban*, 37.8 x 28.1 cm

Provenance: Acquired from Robert G. Sawers, London, December 21, 1967

Utagawa Toyokuni I (1769–1825)

The Actor Sawamura Sōjūrō III as Yukihira, one of three roles he took in the kabuki play *Yukihira and the Snow-covered Pine (Ginsekai matsu ni Yukihira)* by Namiki Gohei and Kanai Yūsuke, performed at the Kiri-za theater in the eleventh lunar month, 1796

1796

Signed *Toyokuni ga*

Publisher: Iseya Magobei

Censor's seal *kiwame* (certified)

Color woodblock print, the left sheet of a diptych; *aiban,* 32.9 x 22.3 cm

Provenance: Acquired from S. H. Mori Gallery, Chicago, March 20, 1965

Published: Ōta Memorial Museum of Art, Tokyo, *The Mann Collection,* cat. no. 68

Exhibited: Ōta Memorial Museum of Art, Tokyo, "The Mann Collection," 1994

Utagawa Toyohiro (1773–1828)

Fan Vendor

c. 1800

Signed *Toyohiro ga*

Color woodblock print; pillar-print format (*hashira-e*), 66.6 x 12 cm

Provenance: Acquired from Christie's, London, November 14, 2001

Published: Christie's, London, November 14, 2001, lot 155

Utagawa Kunimasa (c. 1773–1810)

The Actor Ichikawa Komazō III as the Warrior Endō Moritō in the kabuki play *Snow at Itsukushima (Itsukushima yuki)* by Sakurada Jisuke, the season premiere *(kaomise)* performed at the Kawarazaki-za theater in the eleventh lunar month, 1796

1796

Signed *Kunimasa ga*

Publisher: Yamaguchiya Chūsuke

Censor's seal *kiwame* (certified)

Color woodblock print, large-head picture *(ōkubi-e)*; *aiban*, 33.5 x 22.5 cm

Provenance: Isaac Dooman; acquired from Sotheby's, London, June 30, 1969

Published: Marks, p. 265; Ōta Memorial Museum of Art, Tokyo, *The Mann Collection*, cat. no. 87; Sotheby's, London, June 30, 1969, lot 169; *Ukiyo-e shūka*, vol. 9, no. 39; Walpole Galleries, Dooman, February 11, 1924, lot 171

Exhibited: Ōta Memorial Museum of Art, Tokyo, "The Mann Collection," 1994

96 Utagawa Kunimasa (c. 1773–1810)

The Actor Nakamura Noshio II as Tokume, the Wife of Gotobei in the kabuki play *Yoshitsune Flowering again in Snow (Kaeribana yuki no Yoshitsune)* by Sakurada Jisuke, performed at the Miyako-za theater in the eleventh lunar month, 1795

1795

Unsigned

Collectors' seals of Huguette Berès and of Henri Vever and two unidentified seals

Color woodblock print; *ōban*, 38 x 25.7 cm

Provenance: Henri Vever; Huguette Berès; acquired from Sotheby's, Paris, Berès 2, November 25, 2003

Published: Berès 2, lot 110; Hillier, *Vever*, vol. 2, no. 662; Vever 2, lot 274

ANOTHER STATE of this print with artist's signature, the seal of the publisher Uemuraya Yohei and censor's seal *kiwame* (certified) is in the Honolulu Museum of Art (21754). Notably, the Mann impression has no key-block line around the face.

Utagawa Kunisada (1786–1865)

The Actor Nakamura Utaemon III as the Monkey Trainer Yojirō (*Yojirō*), from the series *Great Performances* (*Ōatari kyōgen no uchi*), in a kabuki version of the puppet play *Recent Riverbed Rivalry* (*Chikagoro kawarano tatehiki*) (also known as *Horikawa* or *Oshun Denbei*) by Tamekawa Sōsuke, Tsutsukawa Hanji and Nakawa Shimesuke, performed at the Nakamura-za theater, 1807/08

c. 1808; possibly 1814/15

Signed *Gototei Kunisada ga*

Publisher: Kawaguchiya Uhei (Fukusendō)

Censor's seal *kiwame* (certified)

Color woodblock print with mica ground; *ōban*, 39.3 x 26.8 cm

Provenance: Takano H., Tokyo; anonymous vendor, Christie's, New York, June 27, 1985; anonymous vendor, Christie's, New York, October 17, 1990; acquired post-sale from Christie's, New York, March 25, 2003

Published: Christie's, New York, June 27, 1985, lot 95; Christie's, New York, October 17, 1990 lot 693; Christie's, New York, March 25, 2003, lot 269; *Designed for Pleasure*, fig. 3, p. 17; Takano, lot 85

Exhibited: Asia Society, New York, "Designed for Pleasure," 2008

NAKAMURA UTAEMON III gave this performance twice before the print was published: in 1808 and in 1814, both at the Nakamura-za theater. Sebastian Izzard suggests in *Kunisada's World* (p. 47) that the print more likely celebrates Utaemon's stellar debut on the Edo stage in 1808 rather than his later performance. The play was adapted from a popular puppet play based on a real-life love-suicide of 1703. Yojirō, the monkey trainer, is the brother of Oshun, a Kyoto courtesan, who is the female protagonist of the play.

Frontispiece

98

Utagawa Kunisada (1786–1865)

Dawn at the Wedded Rocks of Futamigaura (Futamigaura akebono no zu),
from an untitled series of landscapes

1830s

Signed *Kōchōrō Kunisada ga*; seals *Gototei* and *Kunisada*

Publisher: Yamaguchiya Tōbei (Kinkodō)

Censor's seal *kiwame* (certified)

Color woodblock print; *ōban*, 26.2 x 37.7 cm

Provenance: Acquired from Richard Kruml, London, June 1, 1982

Published: Izzard 1993, cat. no. 65/4, p. 138; Marks, no. 118, pp. 370–71; Ōta Memorial
Museum of Art, Tokyo, *The Mann Collection*, cat. no. 96

Exhibited: Japan Society Gallery, New York, "Kunisada's World," 1993; Ōta Memorial
Museum of Art, Tokyo, "The Mann Collection," 1994

99

Katsushika Hokusai (1760–1849)

Tama River in Musashi Province (Bushū Tamagawa), from the
series *Thirty-six Views of Mount Fuji (Fugaku sanjūrokkei)*

1830s

Signed *Hokusai Iitsu hitsu* (from the brush of Hokusai Iitsu)

Publisher: Nishimuraya Yohachi (Eijudō)

Color woodblock print; *ōban*, 25.7 x 37.1 cm

Provenance: Mrs. John Osgood Blanchard; Paolino Gerli; acquired from
Adele and Willard Gidwitz, January 19, 1980

Published: Blanchard, lot 200; Gerli, lot 92; Ōta Memorial Museum of Art,
Tokyo, *The Mann Collection*, cat. no. 71

Exhibited: Ōta Memorial Museum of Art, Tokyo, "The Mann Collection," 1994

100   **Katsushika Hokusai (1760–1849)**

Umezawa Manor in Sagami Province (Sōshū Umezawa-zai),
from the series *Thirty-six Views of Mount Fuji (Fugaku sanjūrokkei)*

1830s

Signed *saki no Hokusai Iitsu hitsu* (from the brush of Iitsu, the former Hokusai)

Publisher: Nishimuraya Yohachi (Eijudō)

Color woodblock print; *ōban*, 26.2 x 38.8 cm

Provenance: Acquired from Sotheby's, New York, March 25, 1998

Exhibited: Freer|Sackler, "Hokusai," 2012

Published: Sotheby's, New York, March 25, 1998, lot 138

101   **Katsushika Hokusai (1760–1849)**

Under the Well of the Great Wave off Kanagawa (Kanagawa oki nami ura)
["Great Wave"], from the series *Thirty-six Views of Mount Fuji (Fugaku sanjūrokkei)*

1830s

Signed *Hokusai aratame Iitsu hitsu* (from the brush of Iitsu, changed from Hokusai)

Publisher: Nishimuraya Yohachi (Eijudō)

Censor's seal *kiwame* (certified)

Color woodblock print; *ōban*, 26.1 x 38.4 cm

Provenance: Acquired post-sale from Christie's, New York, April 27, 1993

Published: Christie's, New York, April 27, 1993, lot 164; *Designed for Pleasure,*
fig. 127, p. 178; Ōta Memorial Museum of Art, Tokyo, *The Mann Collection*, cat. no. 73;
Yonemura, cat. no. 117

Exhibited: Ōta Memorial Museum of Art, Tokyo, "The Mann Collection," 1994;
Freer|Sackler, "Hokusai," 2006; Asia Society, New York, "Designed for Pleasure," 2008

Figure 137, pages 142–143

102　　**Katsushika Hokusai (1760–1849)**

Shower below the Summit (Sanka hakuu), from the series
Thirty-six Views of Mount Fuji (Fugaku sanjūrokkei)

1830s

Signed *saki no Hokusai Iitsu hitsu* (from the brush of Iitsu, the former Hokusai)

Publisher: Nishimuraya Yohachi (Eijudō)

Color woodblock print; *ōban,* 25.6 x 36.9 cm

Provenance: Acquired from Anders Rikardson, Sweden and Japan, March 1, 1983

Published: Ōta Memorial Museum of Art, Tokyo, *The Mann Collection,* cat. no. 72

Exhibited: Ōta Memorial Museum of Art, Tokyo, "The Mann Collection," 1994

Figure 5, page 20

103　　**Katsushika Hokusai (1760–1849)**

Kajikazawa in Kai Province (Kōshū Kajikazawa), from the series
Thirty-six Views of Mount Fuji (Fugaku sanjūrokkei)

1830s

Signed *saki no Hokusai Iitsu hitsu* (from the brush of Iitsu, the former Hokusai)

Publisher: Nishimuraya Yohachi (Eijudō)

Color woodblock print; *ōban,* 26.2 x 38.6 cm

Provenance: Acquired from Christie's, New York, March 22, 1984

Published: Christie's, New York, March 22, 1984, lot 463, Ōta Memorial Museum of Art, Tokyo, *The Mann Collection,* cat. no. 74

Exhibited: Ōta Memorial Museum of Art, Tokyo, "The Mann Collection," 1994

104

Katsushika Hokusai (1760–1849)

Mishima Pass in Kai Province (Kōshū Mishima goe), from the series *Thirty-six Views of Mount Fuji (Fugaku sanjūrokkei)*

1830s

Signed *saki no Hokusai Iitsu hitsu* (from the brush of Iitsu, the former Hokusai)

Publisher: Nishimuraya Yohachi (Eijudō)

Color woodblock print; *ōban*, 25.3 x 36.9 cm

Provenance: Acquired from Robert G. Sawers, London, March 9, 1973

Published: Ōta Memorial Museum of Art, Tokyo, *The Mann Collection*, cat. no. 75

Exhibited: Ōta Memorial Museum of Art, Tokyo, "The Mann Collection," 1994; Freer|Sackler, "Hokusai," 2012

105

Katsushika Hokusai (1760–1849)

Ushibori in Hitachi Province (Jōshū Ushibori), from the series *Thirty-six Views of Mount Fuji (Fugaku sanjūrokkei)*

1830s

Signed *saki no Hokusai Iitsu hitsu* (from the brush of Iitsu, the former Hokusai)

Publisher: Nishimuraya Yohachi (Eijudō)

Color woodblock print, all-blue picture (*aizuri-e*); *ōban*, 25.3 x 36.8 cm

Provenance: Acquired from S. H. Mori Gallery, Chicago, November 26, 1962

Published: Ōta Memorial Museum of Art, Tokyo, *The Mann Collection*, cat. no. 70; Forrer 1991, cat. no. 19; Forrer 2010, 2011, pl. 174; Yonemura, cat. no. 120

Exhibited: Royal Academy of Arts, London, "Hokusai," 1991; Ōta Memorial Museum of Art, Tokyo, "The Mann Collection," 1994; Freer|Sackler, "Hokusai," 2006; Freer|Sackler, "Hokusai," 2012

Figure 12, page 27

106   **Katsushika Hokusai (1760–1849)**

Cherry Blossoms at Yoshino (Yoshino), the flower image
from the series *Snow, Moon and Flowers (Setsugekka)*

1830s

Signed *saki no Hokusai Iitsu hitsu* (from the brush of Iitsu, the former Hokusai)

Publisher: Nishimuraya Yohachi (Eijudō)

Color woodblock print; *ōban*, 24.2 x 37 cm

Provenance: Acquired from Christie's, London, November 23, 1992

Published: Christie's, London, November 23, 1992, lot 54; Ōta Memorial Museum
of Art, Tokyo, *The Mann Collection*, cat. no. 81

Exhibited: Ōta Memorial Museum of Art, Tokyo, "The Mann Collection," 1994

Katsushika Hokusai (1760–1849)

Morning Glories (Asagao) and Tree Frog,
from an untitled series known as "Large Flowers"

early 1830s

Signed *saki no Hokusai Iitsu hitsu* (from the brush of Iitsu, the former Hokusai)

Publisher: Nishimuraya Yohachi (Eijudō)

Censor's seal *kiwame* (certified)

Collectors' seals of Hayashi Tadamasa and of Henri Vever

Color woodblock print; *ōban*, 25 x 37.5 cm

Provenance: Hayashi Tadamasa; Henri Vever; John R. Gaines; acquired from
Sotheby's, New York, Gaines, May 24, 1979

Published: Forrer 1991, cat. no. 55; Forrer 2010, 2011, pl. 211; Forrer and Bednarek
1996, p. 71; Gaines, lot 556 (catalogue cover illustration); Hillier, *Vever*, vol. 2, no. 698;
Marks, no. 125, p. 387; Ōta Memorial Museum of Art, Tokyo, *The Mann Collection*, cat.
no. 82; Vever 2, lot 287

Exhibited: Royal Academy of Arts, London, "Hokusai," 1991; Ōta Memorial Museum
of Art, Tokyo, "The Mann Collection," 1994

Figure 63b, pages 70–71

108

Katsushika Hokusai (1760–1849)

The Suspension Bridge on the Border of Hida and Etchū Provinces (Hietsu no sakai tsuribashi), from the series *Remarkable Views of the Bridges in All the Provinces (Shokoku meikyō kiran)*

1830s

Signed *saki no Hokusai Iitsu hitsu* (from the brush of Iitsu, the former Hokusai)

Publisher: Nishimuraya Yohachi (Eijudō)

Censor's seal *kiwame* (certified)

Color woodblock print; *ōban*, 25.8 x 38 cm

Provenance: McNair Scott; Hans Popper; acquired from Sotheby's, New York, Popper, October 5, 1972

Published: Forrer 1991, cat. no. 38; Forrer 2010, 2011, pl. 201; Forrer and Bednarek 1996, p. 67; Glendining & Co., London, McNair Scott, April 11, 1960, lot 101; *Masterpieces of Ukiyo-e in Foreign Collections,* cat. no. 297; Ōta Memorial Museum of Art, Tokyo, *The Mann Collection,* cat. no. 76; Popper, lot 215

Exhibited: "Masterpieces of Ukiyo-e in Foreign Collections," Japan, 1971; Royal Academy of Arts, London, "Hokusai," 1991; Ōta Memorial Museum of Art, Tokyo, "The Mann Collection," 1994

Katsushika Hokusai (1760–1849)

*Kirifuri Waterfall at Kurokami Mountain in Shimotsuke Province
(Shimotsuke Kurokamiyama Kirifuri no taki),* from the series
A Tour of Waterfalls in Various Provinces (Shokoku taki meguri)

1830s

Signed *saki no Hokusai Iitsu hitsu* (from the brush of Iitsu, the former Hokusai)

Publisher: Nishimuraya Yohachi (Eijudō)

Censor's seal *kiwame* (certified)

Color woodblock print; *ōban*, 38.1 x 25.8 cm

Provenance: Acquired from Sotheby's, New York, November 9, 1984

Published: Forrer 1991, cat. no. 39;
Forrer 2010, 2011, pl. 192; Forrer and
Bednarek 1996, p. 109; Sotheby's, New
York, November 9, 1984, lot 79; Ōta
Memorial Museum of Art, Tokyo, *The
Mann Collection,* cat. no. 79; Yonemura,
cat. no. 122

Exhibited: Royal Academy of Arts,
London, "Hokusai," 1991; Ōta
Memorial Museum of Art, Tokyo,
"The Mann Collection," 1994;
Freer|Sackler, "Hokusai," 2006

KIRIFURI (FALLING MIST) is one of eight
in Hokusai's series of spectacular waterfalls around Japan. There are four from
the set in the Mann Collection. Here, pil-
grims from Nikkō Shrine, north of Edo,
are admiring the fall. The publisher of the
series, Eijudō, has inserted some advertising into the image: his emblem appears
on the back of the coat of one figure and
on hats, and the syllable "Ei" appears on
other hats. Roger Keyes published a thor-
ough examination of the originals and
hard-to-detect Meiji-period (1868–1912)
facsimiles of the set in *Oriental Art* XVIII,
no. 2 (Summer 1972): 141–47.

Katsushika Hokusai (1760–1849)

The Waterfall Where Yoshitsune Washed His Horse at Yoshino in Yamato Province (Washū Yoshino, Yoshitsune uma arai no taki), from the series A Tour of Waterfalls in Various Provinces (Shokoku taki meguri)

1830s

Signed *saki no Hokusai Iitsu hitsu* (from the brush of Iitsu, the former Hokusai)

Publisher: Nishimuraya Yohachi (Eijudō)

Censor's seal *kiwame* (certified)

Color woodblock print; *ōban*, 38.7 x 26.4 cm

Provenance: Acquired from Sotheby's New York, November 9, 1984

Published: Sotheby's, New York, November 9, 1984, lot 81; Ōta Memorial Museum of Art, Tokyo, *The Mann Collection*, cat. no. 77

Exhibited: Ōta Memorial Museum of Art, Tokyo, "The Mann Collection," 1994

THE FAMOUS WARRIOR Minamoto no Yoshitsune (1159–1189) is said to have stopped at this waterfall to wash his horse during one of his campaigns. In his usual fashion, Hokusai uses common folk in a quotidian activity to allude to the legend.

111 **Katsushika Hokusai (1760–1849)**

*Kiyotaki Kannon Waterfall at Sakanoshita on the Tōkaidō Road
(Tōkaidō Sakanoshita, Kiyotaki Kannon), from the series
A Tour of Waterfalls in Various Provinces (Shokoku taki meguri)*

1830s

Signed *saki no Hokusai Iitsu hitsu* (from the brush of Iitsu, the former Hokusai)

Publisher: Nishimuraya Yohachi (Eijudō)

Censor's seal *kiwame* (certified)

Color woodblock print; *ōban*, 38.2 x 25.6 cm

Provenance: Mrs. M. A. Wilkinson; P. D. Krolik; acquired from Sotheby's,
London, July 1, 1968

Published: Sotheby's, London, Wilkinson, October 8, 1962, lot 331; Krolik, lot 49; Ōta Memorial Museum of Art, Tokyo, *The Mann Collection*, cat. no. 78

Exhibited: Ōta Memorial Museum of Art, Tokyo, "The Mann Collection," 1994

Katsushika Hokusai (1760–1849)

Aoigaoka Waterfall in the Eastern Capital (Tōtō Aoigaoka no taki), from
the series *A Tour of Waterfalls in Various Provinces (Shokoku taki meguri)*

1830s

Signed *saki no Hokusai Iitsu hitsu* (from the brush of Iitsu, the former Hokusai)

Publisher: Nishimuraya Yohachi (Eijudō)

Censor's seal *kiwame* (certified)

Color woodblock print; *ōban*, 36.2 x 25 cm

Provenance: Frank Lloyd Wright, by repute; acquired from Richard Stein,
date not recorded, 1960s

Published: Ōta Memorial Museum of Art,
Tokyo, *The Mann Collection*, cat. no. 80

Exhibited: Ōta Memorial Museum of Art,
Tokyo, "The Mann Collection," 1994

113   **Katsushika Hokusai (1760–1849)**

The Poem of Minamoto Muneyuki (Minamoto Muneyuki ason), from the series *One Hundred Poems by One Hundred Poets, Explained by the Nurse (Hyakunin isshu uba ga etoki)*

1830s

Signed *saki no Hokusai Manji* (Manji, the former Hokusai)

Publisher: Nishimuraya Yohachi (Eijudō)

Censor's seal *kiwame* (certified)

Collector's seal of Wakai Kenzaburō

Color woodblock print; *ōban*, 25.9 x 37.7 cm

Provenance: Wakai Kenzaburō; Ernest Le Véel; acquired from Ader, Picard, Tajan, Paris, Le Véel 2, October 24, 1980

Published: Forrer 1991, cat. no. 80; Forrer 2010, 2011, pl. 240; Forrer and Bednarek 1996, p. 86; Le Véel 2, lot 84; Museum of Decorative Arts, Copenhagen, cat. no. 119; Ōta Memorial Museum of Art, Tokyo, *The Mann Collection,* cat. no. 84; Yonemura, cat. no. 72

Exhibited: Museum of Decorative Arts, Copenhagen, "Hokusai," 1975; Royal Academy of Arts, London, "Hokusai," 1991–92; Ōta Memorial Museum of Art, Tokyo, "The Mann Collection," 1994; Freer|Sackler, "Hokusai," 2006

HOKUSAI SHOWS HUNTERS warming themselves by a fire on a snowy night to illustrate a poem by Minamoto Muneyuki (d. 939):

山里ハ冬そさみしさまさりけり人目も草も枯ぬと思へハ

Yamazato wa / fuyu zo samishisa / masari keri / hitome mo kusa mo / karenu to omoeba
A mountain village / turns all the bleaker in winter / as you notice / both the plants and the number of visitors / withering.

Figure 80, page 88–89

The Poem of Ariwara no Narihira (Ariwara no Narihira), from the series *One Hundred Poems by One Hundred Poets, Explained by the Nurse (Hyakunin isshu uba ga etoki)*

1830s

Signed *saki no Hokusai Manji* (Manji, the former Hokusai)

Publisher: Nishimuraya Yohachi (Eijudō)

Censor's seal *kiwame* (certified)

Color woodblock print; *ōban*, 25.2 x 36.5 cm

Provenance: Acquired from Gary Levine, New York, April 3, 1979 (acquired by Levine from Christie's, New York, November 28, 1978)

Published: Christie's, New York, November 28, 1978, lot 254; Ōta Memorial Museum of Art, Tokyo, *The Mann Collection,* cat. no. 83

Exhibited: Ōta Memorial Museum of Art, Tokyo, "The Mann Collection," 1994

Hokusai's image shows travelers crossing an arched bridge over the Tatsuta River in Yamato province (now Nara Prefecture), a reference to the ninth-century poet Ariwara no Narihira, one of the One Hundred Immortal Poets of Japan. His poem here reads:

ちはやぶる神代もきかず竜田川からくれなゐに水くくるとは

Chihayaburu / kami yo mo kikazu / Tatsutagawa / kara-kurenai ni / mizu kukuru to wa

Unheard of, even / in the days of the high and mighty / ancient gods: / the Tatsuta River's / waters dyed a China-red!

115 **Katsushika Hokusai (1760–1849)**

The Poem of Gonchūnagon Sadaie (Gonchūnagon Sadaie), from the series *One Hundred Poems by One Hundred Poets, Explained by the Nurse (Hyakunin isshu uba ga etoki)*

1830s

Signed *saki no Hokusai Manji* (Manji, the former Hokusai)

Publisher: Nishimuraya Yohachi (Eijudō)

Censor's seal *kiwame* (certified)

Color woodblock print; *ōban*, 26.3 x 38.1 cm

Provenance: Werner Schindler; acquired from Sebastian Izzard Asian Art LLC, New York, March 25, 2000

Published: Izzard 2000, cat. no. 32; Kondō 1985, no. 138

Exhibited: "Schindler Collection," Japan, 1985

GONCHŪNAGON (MIDDLE COUNCILLOR) Sadaie (Fujiwara Sadaie; Fujiwara Teika, 1162–1241), one of Japan's greatest poets, selected the One Hundred Poems on which Hokusai based his series of prints. Hokusai's image shows women gathering seawater and men stacking bundles of charcoal at a kiln to extract salt on a shoreline. The poem reads:

こぬ人をまつほの浦の夕なぎにやくやも塩のみもこがれつつ

Konu hito o / Matsuho no ura no / yūnagi ni / yaku ya moshio no / mi mo kogare tsutsu

Though she'll not arrive, / I wait, and desire consumes me, / like the flames that, / in Matsuo's evening calm, / reduce seaweed to salt-ash.

116 **Yashima Gakutei (1786?–1868)**

View of Boats Entering the Harbor at Mount Tenpō (Tenpōzan bansen nyūshin no zu), from the series *Famous Places of Naniwa [Osaka]: Fine Views of Mount Tenpō at a Glance (Naniwa meisho Tenpōzan shōkei ichiran)*

1830s

Signed *Gakutei*; seal *Gogaku*

Publisher: Shioya Kisuke (Kobundō), Osaka

Collectors' seals of Wakai Kenzaburō and of P. D. Krolik

Color woodblock print; *ōban*, 25.6 x 38.4 cm

Provenance: Wakai Kenzaburō; Col. H. Appleton; P. D. Krolik; acquired from Sotheby's, London, July 1, 1968

Published: Appleton, lot 449; Krolik, lot 61; Ōta Memorial Museum of Art, Tokyo, *The Mann Collection*, cat. no. 85

Exhibited: Ōta Memorial Museum of Art, Tokyo, "The Mann Collection," 1994

117 **Yashima Gakutei (1786?–1868)**

Sudden Shower at Mount Tenpō in Osaka (Ōsaka Tenpōzan yūdachi no kei), from the series *Famous Places of Naniwa [Osaka]: Fine Views of Mount Tenpō at a Glance (Naniwa meisho Tenpōzan shōkei ichiran)*

1830s

Signed *Gakutei*; seal *Gogaku*

Publisher: unmarked; Shioya Kisuke (Kobundō), Osaka

Censor's seal *kiwame* (certified)

Color woodblock print; *ōban*, 25.4 x 36.8 cm

Provenance: Acquired from The Art Institute of Chicago, November 30, 1967

Published: Marks, no. 130, pp. 398–99; Ōta Memorial Museum of Art, Tokyo, *The Mann Collection*, cat. no. 86

Exhibited: Ōta Memorial Museum of Art, Tokyo, "The Mann Collection," 1994

Figure 124, page 132

Utagawa Hiroshige (1797–1858)

Four sheets of thirty-one-syllable light verse (*kyōka*) and ten *surimono*, from the untitled series known as "Every Variety of Fish" (*Uo tsukushi*)

Album covers

early 1830s

Fish prints signed *Ichiryūsai Hiroshige ga*

Color woodblock prints originally mounted as an album; *surimono* with mica embellishments; *ōban*, 25.6 x 37 cm each

Original blue paper album covers, each 25.8 x 18.6 cm

Provenance: Adele and Willard Gidwitz, purchased disassembled from the original album from the Red Lantern Shop, Kyoto, 1970; *surimono* and paper covers acquired from the Gidwitzes, January 19, 1980; four sheets of poetry, gift to H. George Mann from Kondo Sentarō of the Red Lantern Shop, Kyoto, October 9, 1985

THE SHEETS OF LIGHT VERSE and fish prints were commissioned by an Edo poetry circle as a private edition, with deluxe printing and mica embellishments, to commemorate a *kyōka* competition. Each poem is preceded by the name(s) of the judge(s) in the poetry contest on the theme of seafood. Some poems were awarded extra points by a respective judge. Several poems from the printed poem sheets appear on the fish *surimono*, as Alfred Haft details on the following pages.

Kyōka clubs often held competitions. A theme would be set, and club members would submit their verses to a panel of judges (*hanja*) who awarded varying numbers of points to the poems they considered superior. Competitions were supported so enthusiastically, and held so often throughout the year, that one could make a living as a professional *kyōka* judge. Considerable effort—organizing, promoting, hosting, judging, documenting—went into the competitions, entirely separate from the effort required for the production of *kyōka surimono*. In some respects, *kyōka* during the late-Edo period was as much an industry as a pastime.

The poems on the Hiroshige "Large Fish" prints—presented here in the first, privately published edition—must have been thought the most successful among those submitted to a competition on the theme of "seafood," documented more fully in the four poetry sheets (catalogue nos. 118.1–4). The four poetry sheets suggest that when several club members happened to compose on the same topic, their poems would be grouped together; then, the various groups would be arranged in seasonal order (if the theme had a seasonal component) for initial publication as a record of the event. The *surimono* here follow the order of the subheadings given on the four sheets of *kyōka*.

葛花加三　葉穂加二　　雲鹿冨貴

波る淡い破れ露を
ちきるつて餻を
枝のの玉をとみつらき

葛花加三　葉穂加二
献ろれあをやつそうらやつも
三輪担耳喜

葛花加三　嚴足穂
ちのくつあをやき
うらふる

葛花加三　嚴足穂
これもはこちらいまて
かうらむ宅あくんの
細たもま合れ
あくれ
小くはは
千代垣素道

Detail of catalogue no. 118.11

Hiroshige's prints are unusual, in that they name the four judges behind the "seafood" competition—Kuzunone, Kuzubana, Kuzunoha and Noriho (perhaps the scholar of National Studies Nitei Noriho)—and also give each poem's score. This information appears more usually in the anthology published after a *kyōka* competition.

Numerous commercial editions of "Every Variety of Fish" were published slightly later by Eijudō (Nishimuraya Yohachi). A print by Hiroshige of swimming river trout (*ai*) with poem was added to the commercial sets, along with the deletion of the judges' names and points and adjustments to coloration and other elements of the designs. A supplement of nine prints with poems was released by Yamadaya Shōjirō around 1840–42.

118.1

SHEET 1. Spring. With the names of the two compilers, Komogaki (Suzugaki?) Makuzu and Toshigaki Maharu (*kyōka* by these poets appear at the end of the fourth sheet); twenty poems under the headings "sea bream" and "black sea bream / small sea bream" (*tai, kurodai / kodai*)

Figure 86, page 95

118.2

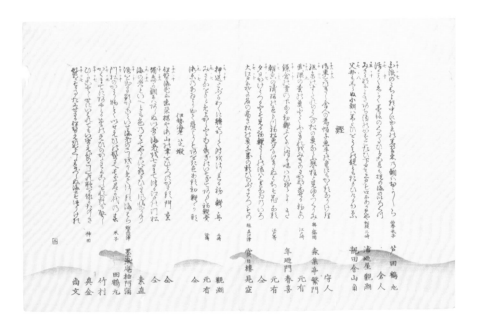

SHEET 2. Summer. Twenty-two poems: four under the previous heading and eighteen under the headings "bonito" and "spiny lobster / gray prawns" (*katsuo, Ise ebi / Shiba ebi*)

Four sheets of thirty-one-syllable light verse (*kyōka*) about various types of seasonal fish and shellfish; each type given as a heading followed by one or more poems; each poem followed by the poet's name and, occasionally, also the poet's location in smaller characters; each sheet numbered at bottom left

SHEET 3. Spring / summer / autumn / early winter. Twenty poems: three under the previous heading and seventeen under the headings "bartail flathead," "tiger prawn / horse mackerel," "abalone / halfbeak" and "gurnard" (*kochi, kuruma ebi / aji, awabi / sayori, kanagashira*)

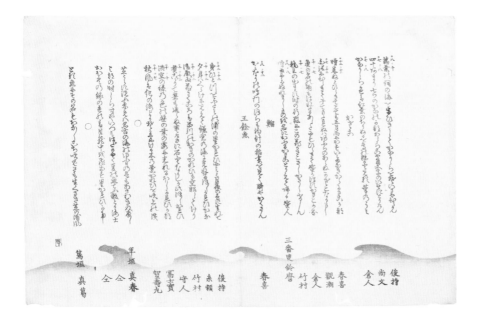

SHEET 4. Winter. Nineteen poems: three under the previous heading, twelve under the headings "rockfish," "gray mullet" and "right-eye flounder" (*kasago, bora, karei*), three by Toshigaki Maharu and one by Komogaki (Suzugaki?) Makuzu

Published: Ōta Memorial Museum of Art, Tokyo, *The Mann Collection*, cat. no. 117; Suzuki, *Utagawa Hiroshige*, no. 591

Exhibited: Ōta Memorial Museum of Art, Tokyo, "The Mann Collection," 1994

118.5   *Large Sea Bream and Red Pepper (Tai, Sanshō)*

Published: Ōta Memorial Museum of Art, Tokyo, *The Mann Collection*, cat. no. 118; Suzuki, *Utagawa Hiroshige*, no. 591

Exhibited: Ōta Memorial Museum of Art, Tokyo, "The Mann Collection," 1994

THE POEM READS:

葛廼根　巌足穂　*Kuzunone Iwa no Taruho*　Kuzunone; Iwa no Taruho
[Names of the judges that precede the poems in the album]

処女子か手玉もゆらにくり出す鯛の目はりもいとはひきけり

Otomego ga / tedama mo yura ni / kuri-idasu / tai no mehari mo / ito wa hiki keri

Just as thread secures / the rattling bean-bag toys tossed / by a little girl, / a line fixes the rolling, / big-eyed gaze of a sea bream.

静垣濤安
Shizugaki Namiyasu

This is a different poem from Namiyasu's contribution on the first of the four *kyōka* sheets in the Mann set—the sixth poem under the heading "sea bream" (*tai*). It uses an elaborate metaphor to link the big eyes of the sea bream with a girl's toy:

otomego is an unmarried girl

tedama is a girl's game, consisting of small, sewn sacks filled with beans or rice, intended to be tossed in the air

yura ni represents the sound of jewels rubbing against each other

kuri-dasu means to pay out rope, call out troops, disburse, go forth

mehari means "wide-eyed"

ito (string, line) *wa hiku* relates to fishing

tama no himo (or *tama no o*), a thread for stringing jewels together

An impression in the British Museum has a second poem; the print does not bear judges' marks (1902, 0212,0.392). There is also an impression of this print with second poem, lacking judges' marks, in the Waseda University Theatre Museum, image accessible at <ukiyo-e.org>.

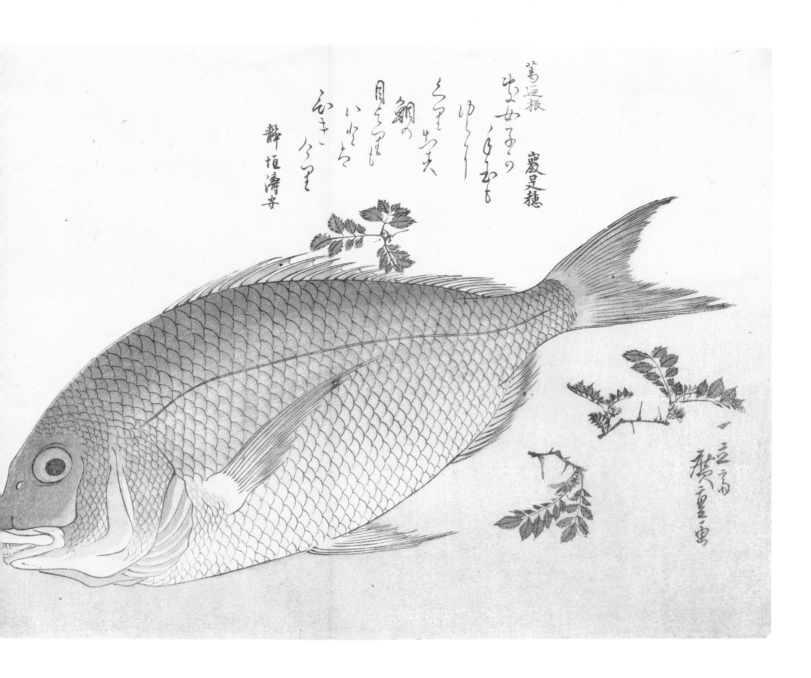

118.6   *Black Sea Bream, Small Sea Bream and Red Pepper (Kurodai, Kodai, Sanshō)*

Published: Ōta Memorial Museum of Art, Tokyo, *The Mann Collection*, cat. no. 119;
Suzuki, *Utagawa Hiroshige*, no. 591

Exhibited: Ōta Memorial Museum of Art, Tokyo, "The Mann Collection," 1994

THE TWO POEMS READ:

葛花　乗穂加三　*Kuzubana　Noriho ka san*

Kuzubana; Noriho: +3 [points]
[extra points for the poem awarded by judge Noriho]

もちの夜にすなとる蜑が小鯛つる影と大きく見ゆる黒鯛

Mochi no yo ni / sunadoru ama ga / kodai tsuru / kage to ōkiku / miyuru kurodai

The shadow of a fisherman / angling for small sea bream / on the night / of a full
autumn moon / looks like an enlarged blackhead sea bream.

富垣内安
Tomigaki Uchiyasu

葛花加二　乗穂加二　*Kuzubana ka ni　Noriho ka ni*

Kuzubana: +2 [points]; Noriho: +2 [points]

うつくしき小鯛に添し黒鯛は黒木にさしゝ桜とや見む

Utsukushiki / kodai ni soeshi / kurodai wa / kuroki ni sashishi / sakura to ya mimu

When they're accompanied / by lovely small sea breams, / don't the blackhead
sea breams / recall charcoal sticks dressed / with sprigs of cherry blossoms?

越後川袋花王菴芳志
Echigo Kawabukuro Kaōan Hōshi
Kaōan Hōshi from Kawabukuro
in Echigo Province

Mochi no yo, もちの夜 (望の夜), in the first line of the first poem refers to the full
moon on the fifteenth day of the eighth lunar month. The second poem appears on
the first of the four *kyōka* sheets in the Mann set—as the first poem under the heading
"black sea bream / small sea bream" (*kurodai / kodai*).

Both poems play on the "blackness" (*kuro*) of the blackhead seabream, the first by
introducing the imagery of a shadow, and the second by making reference to charcoal
sticks. The second poem alludes to depictions of the Ōharame (maidens of Ōhara)
peddling bundles of kindling fitted with sprigs of seasonal flowers. The poems are
about fish, but they evoke the literary themes of a fisherman and a young peasant
woman.

118.7

Blue Bonito and Saxifrage (Katsuo, Yukinoshita)

Published: Forrer 1997, cat. no. 84; Forrer 2017, pl. 208; Ōta Memorial Museum of Art, Tokyo, *The Mann Collection*, cat. no. 120; Suzuki, *Utagawa Hiroshige*, no. 591

Exhibited: Ōta Memorial Museum of Art, Tokyo, "The Mann Collection," 1994; Royal Academy of Arts, London, "Hiroshige," 1997

葛廼根　乘穗加三　*Kuzunone　Noriho ka san*

Kuzunone; Noriho: +3 [points]

朝かほの花たのいろのはつ鰹日の出ぬうちと夜通しに来る

Asagao no / hanada no iro no / hatsu-gatsuo / hi no denu uchi to / yo tōshi ni kuru

Morning-glory blue, / the season's first bonito / steadily travels / throughout the night to be certain / of arriving before dawn.

年廼門春喜

Toshinomon Haruki

葛花加三　乘穗加三　*Kuzubana ka san　Noriho ka san*

Kuzubana: +3 [points]; Noriho: +3 [points]

鎌くらの雪の下なる初鰹ふくめは消る味はひそよき

Kamakura no / yuki no shita naru / hatsu-gatsuo / fukumeba kieru / ajiwai zo yoki

Simply delicious! / That melt-in-your-mouth flavor / of the season's first / bonito from Under-the-Snow / at Kamakura.

年庵真千門

Nen'an Machikado

The second poem appears on the second of the four *kyōka* sheets in the set—as the fourth poem under the heading "bonito" (*katsuo*). Both poems mention "the season's first bonito" (*hatsugatsuo*), a delicacy that arrives in early summer (the fourth month in the Edo-period lunar calendar). The second poem mentions Kamakura because the area was known for its first bonito (over a century earlier, Bashō had composed a haiku on this subject). Yukinoshita, literally, "under the snow," is the location of Kamakura's famous Great Buddha (Daibutsu) and Tsurugaoka Hachiman Shrine. It is also the Japanese term for saxifrage, which begins to flower in early summer, coinciding with the arrival of the first bonito, hence its inclusion in the design.

118.8   *Spiny Lobster and Gray Prawns (Ise ebi, Shiba ebi)*

Published: Ōta Memorial Museum of Art, Tokyo, *The Mann Collection*, cat. no. 121; Suzuki, *Utagawa Hiroshige*, no. 591

Exhibited: Ōta Memorial Museum of Art, Tokyo, "The Mann Collection," 1994

THE TWO POEMS READ:

一点　巖足穂　*Itten　Iwa no Taruho*　1 point Iwa no Taruho

伊勢海老をとり逃せしはいせの海士の舟流したるおもひなるらむ

Ise ebi o / tori nigaseshi wa / Ise no ama no / fune nagashitaru / omoi naru ramu

Pushing his boat to sea, / does the seasoned fisherman / perhaps feel as though / he's trapping a spiny lobster / and then releasing the catch?

下野江戸崎緑樹園元有

Shimotsuke Edozaki Ryokujuen Motoari

Ryokujuen Motoari from Edozaki in Shimotsuke Province [d. 1861]

葛花加三　乗穂　*Kuzubana ka san　Noriho*

Kuzubana: +3 [points]; Noriho

汐ぬるみにえたつやうな夏の日にわきて出たる芝浦の蝦

Shio nurumi / nie-tatsu yōna / natsu no hi ni / wakite idetaru / Shiba ura no ebi

On a summer's day / hot enough to set the calm / salt-sea to boiling, / the prawns of Shiba Bay / come bursting forth from their shells.

年庵真千門

Nen'an Machikado

The first poem uses the term "*ise*" in two manners: first, referring to a location (*Ise ebi*, spiny lobster); second, to describe the fisherman in the phrase "*ise no*," literally meaning "of many currents," but here suggesting someone with long experience of the sea. The characters used for *ama* indicate that the subject is a fisherman.

Bartail Flathead and Miniature Eggplant (Kochi, Nasu)

Published: Ōta Memorial Museum of Art, Tokyo, *The Mann Collection*, cat. no. 122
Suzuki, *Utagawa Hiroshige*, no. 591

Exhibited: Ōta Memorial Museum of Art, Tokyo, "The Mann Collection," 1994

THE TWO POEMS READ:

葛花加二　乗穂加三　*Kuzubana ka ni　Noriho ka san*

Kuzubana: +2 [points]; Noriho: +3 [points]

春吹る風の名におふこちをこそ夏はみな人めつるなりけれ

Haru fukeru / kaze no na ni ou / kochi o koso / natsu wa minahito / messuru nari kere

The east winds of spring / arrive, true to form, with shoals / of flathead fish, /
but by summer, to be sure, / you'll find no trace of either.

良垣俊持
Yoshigaki Toshiji

葛花二　乗穂　*Kuzubana ni　Noriho*

Kuzubana: +2 [points]; Noriho

あらくうつ波の下より生れ出てこちはかしらのひしけたりけむ

Araku utsu / nami no shita yori / umare dete / kochi wa kashira no / hishigetari kemu

Flathead fish grow up / under wildly pounding waves, / so perhaps that is /
why their heads now appear / completely squashed and flattened.

真垣春友
Magaki Harutomo

These poems appear on the third of the four *kyōka* sheets in the Mann *surimono* set—as, respectively, the first and second poems under the heading "bartail flathead" (*kochi*). The imagery and seasonal words symbolize summer.

118.10   *Tiger Prawns, Horse Mackerels and Peppery Herb Garnish (Kuruma ebi, Aji, Yanagitade)*

Published: Forrer 1997, cat. no. 83; Forrer 2017, pl. 207; Ōta Memorial Museum of Art, Tokyo, *The Mann Collection*, cat. no. 123; Suzuki, *Utagawa Hiroshige*, no. 591

Exhibited: Ōta Memorial Museum of Art, Tokyo, "The Mann Collection," 1994; Royal Academy of Arts, London, "Hiroshige," 1997

THE POEM READS:

葛葉加一　乗穂加三　*Kuzunoha ka ichi*

Noriho ka san

Kuzunoha: +1 [point]; Noriho: +3 [points]

ちひさきをさいまきといふ車海
老柴うらにこそつみて送らめ

Chiisaki o / saimaki to iu / kuruma-ebi /
Shibaura ni koso / tsumite okurame

If there is one place / known for catching and shipping / mini tiger prawns / (what we call *saimaki*) / that is Shibaura.

年舎富春

Toshinosha Tomiharu

Saimaki (or *sayamaki*) is the smallest type of tiger prawn (*kuruma-ebi*). Shiba was the site of an important prawn industry. Shiba figures in a poem on another of the *surimono* set (Mann catalogue no. 118.8).

葛葉加一　粟穂加三

もろ山よりそをき
はいますきるよ
車はゑ
まちもら
みそほそ
はらそく
まそをゑ

尾舎冨春

118.11   *Abalone, Halfbeak and Peach Blossoms (Awabi, Sayori, Momo)*

Published: Izzard 1983, cat. no. 6; Ōta Memorial Museum of Art, Tokyo, *The Mann Collection*, cat. no. 124; Foxwell et al., cat. no. 104, p. 171; Suzuki, *Utagawa Hiroshige*, no. 591

Exhibited: Pratt Graphics Center, New York, "Hiroshige," 1983; Ōta Memorial Museum of Art, Tokyo, "The Mann Collection," 1994; Smart Museum of Art, "Awash in Color," 2012–13

THE THREE POEMS READ:

葛花加三　乗穂加三　*Kuzubana ka san　Noriho ka san*

Kuzubana: +3 [points]; Noriho: +3 points

波に洗ひ磯の巌にすりつけて鰒はおのか玉をみかける

Nami ni arai / iso no iwao ni / suritsukete / awabi wa onoga / tama o migakeru

Securely fastened / to the large boulders offshore, / and washed by the waves, / every abalone / is polishing its own pearl.

雲垣富士見
Kumogaki Fujimi

葛花三　乗穂加二　*Kuzubana san　Noriho ka ni*

Kuzubana: 3 points; Noriho: + 2 [points]

献立のあはせさよりも衣かへわたをぬきてそこしらへにける

Kondate no / awase sayori mo / koromogae / wata o nukite zo / koshirae ni keru

The pair of halfbeaks / on the menu have both had / the stuffing taken / out of them, like robes remade / for the first day of summer.

三輪垣甘喜
Miwagaki Amaki

葛花加二　巌足穂　*Kuzubana ka ni　Iwa no Taruho*

Kuzubana: +2 [points]; Iwa no Taruho

これもまたちひさてならむ岩あひの細きすきまのあはひとる海士

Kore mo mata / chiisate naramu / iwa-ai no / hosoki sukima no / awabi toru ama

He, too, probably / has to be on the small side, / the ocean diver / who retrieves abalone / from the crannies between rocks.

千代垣素直
Chiyogaki Sunao

The first poem appears on the third of the four *kyōka* sheets in the Mann set—as the first poem under the heading "abalone / halfbeak" (*awabi / sayori*). The word *awase* in the second line of the second poem indicates "a pair." *Wata nuki* refers to a lined kimono from which cotton padding has been removed; one changed into such a robe on the first day of the fourth lunar month (the start of summer). It has an alternate meaning of "to gut a fish," or, metaphorically, "to take the stuffing out." *Sayori* is the Japanese term for the halfbeak fish and is a spring seasonal word.

蔦花加三　葉穂加三　雲垣冨士見

波山淡い破れ嵐を
ちまらふて餘ら
　稚さの玉をとみつるを

蔦花加三　葉穂加二　三輪垣其喜
酔ふられあらさらさらさ
　あつくつめをとやき
　　　　てらうらふる

蔦花加二　巖足穂
ねもはゆこらいまて
かうらむ巖あくの
　細たまみ谷れ
　あらい
　小さらは里
千代垣素直

Red Gurnard, Right-eye Flounder and Bamboo Grass (Kanagashira, Konohagarei, Sasa)

Published: Ōta Memorial Museum of Art, Tokyo, *The Mann Collection*, cat. no. 125; Suzuki, *Utagawa Hiroshige*, no. 591

Exhibited: Ōta Memorial Museum of Art, Tokyo, "The Mann Collection," 1994

THE TWO POEMS READ:

葛廼根一点　*Kuzunone itten*　Kuzunone: 1 point

門にほす木の葉かれいも紅葉してうらの苫やの秋そ賑はふ

Kado ni hosu / konoha-garei mo / momiji shite / ura no tomaya no aki zo nigiwau

For the bayside thatched / huts, autumn is liveliest / when the *konoha* flounder / drying by the gates / change color like maple leaves.

下野江戸崎緑樹園元有
Shimotsuke Edozaki Ryokujuen Motoari
Ryokujuen Motoari from Edozaki
in Shimotsuke Province

葛花　乗穂加二　*Kuzubana*　*Noriho ka ni*
Kuzubana; Noriho: +2 [points]

ひのもとのふみのはしめのかなかしら先まな板にのせてひらかむ

Hinomoto no / fumi-no-hajime no / kanagashira / mazu manaita ni / nosete hirakamu

First things first, it seems: / calligraphy in Japan / commences with "*i*", / and filleting a gurnard / with the fish on the cutting board.

雀躍亭竹村
Jakuyakutei Chikuson (Takemura?)

In the first poem, *konoha-garei* is another term for ridged- or right-eye flounder (*meita-garei*) and a stack of dried, small flounder (5 cm long), also called *sasanoha-garei* and *ashinoha-garei*. *Tomaya* is a grass hut with reed thatching. The second poem appears on the third of the four *kyōka* sheets in the Mann set—as the first poem under the heading "gurnard" (*kanagashira*). The poet's name has previously been transcribed as Chikurin (竹林), however, the characters on the *surimono* and *kyōka* sheet read Chikuson (or Takemura, 竹村). The richly colored red gurnard is especially tasty in winter; hence, it is a winter seasonal word. *Hinomoto* is another word for Japan. The phrase *fumi no hajime* means "the first character one learns to write with a brush," usually indicating *i*, the first character in the premodern kana syllabary, sometimes called *kanagashira*.

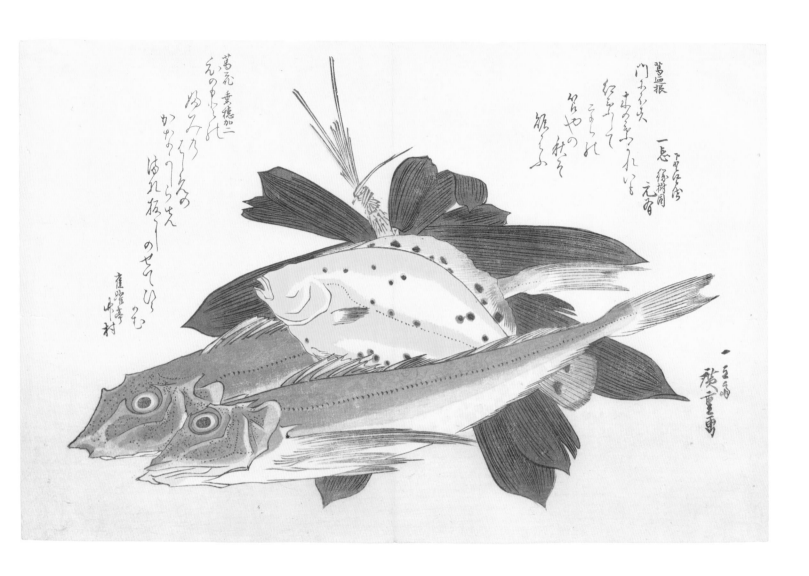

Gruntfish, Rockfish and Ginger (Isaki, Kasago, Shōga)

Published: Ōta Memorial Museum of Art, Tokyo, *The Mann Collection*, cat. no. 126; Suzuki, *Utagawa Hiroshige*, no. 591

Exhibited: Ōta Memorial Museum of Art, Tokyo, "The Mann Collection," 1994

THE TWO POEMS READ:

葛花二　乗穂加二　*Kuzubana ni　Noriho ka ni*
Kuzubana: 2 [points]; Noriho: +2 [points]

時来ぬと開きて見ても五月雨にほすいとまなきからかさこ哉
Tokiginu to / hirakite mite mo / samidare ni / hosu itoma naki / kara kasago kana
I unstitched them / to open them up, / but in this constant, early-summer rain / there is no chance for air-drying / the "Chinese umbrella fish."

年舎富春
Toshinosha Tomiharu

葛花加二　乗穂加二　*Kuzubana ka ni　Noriho ka ni*
Kuzubana: +2 [points]; Noriho: +2 [points]

生舟のたよりたのもし三崎はりいさきの魚を贈る友とち
Namabune no / tayori tanomoshi / Misaki-hari / isaki no uo o / okuru tomodochi
A generous friend / has sent via trustworthy / fish-transport vessel / a packet of three-line grunts, / the pride of Cape Misaki.

相州藤沢森節亭里人
Sōshū Fujisawa Morifushitei Satobito
Morifushitei Satobito of Fujisawa in Sagami Province

The first poem appears on the fourth of the four *kyōka* sheets in the Mann set—as the first poem under the heading "rockfish" (*kasago*); however, there the poet's name reads Haruki (春喜). The poet might have preferred not to use the same name on two different prints in the *surimono* set (see also Mann catalogue no. 118.14). Haruki and Tomiharu both suggest a "prosperous spring." The poet refers to the custom of unstitching robes to dry them in summer. In a pun he links *kasago* (rockfish) with *karakasa* (Chinese folding umbrella). In the second poem, *isaki* (gruntfish) is also a summer seasonal word. The young fish have three light-yellow stripes and are dark brown when mature. Cape Misaki, mentioned in the poem, is the tip of the peninsula at the head of Tokyo Bay in Kanagawa Prefecture.

118.14

Gray Mullet, Camellia and Spikenard Shoots (Bora, Tsubaki, Udo)

Published: Forrer 1997, cat. no. 82; Forrer 2017, pl. 209; Izzard 1983, cat. no. 5; Ōta Memorial Museum of Art, Tokyo, *The Mann Collection*, cat. no. 127; Suzuki, *Utagawa Hiroshige*, no. 591

Exhibited: Pratt Graphics Center, New York, "Hiroshige," 1983; Ōta Memorial Museum of Art, Tokyo, "The Mann Collection,"1994; Royal Academy of Arts, "Hiroshige," 1997

THE TWO POEMS READ:

一点　乗穂加三　*Itten　Noriho ka san*

1 point; Noriho: +3 [points]

田子のうらや不二の移れる波の上を下るもをかしすはしりの魚

Tagonoura ya / Fuji no utsureru / ha no ue o / kudaru mo okashi / subashiri no uo

Thoroughly charming / to see the "shallows-racers" / diving from the crests / of waves reflecting Fuji / at Tagonoura Bay.

檜垣百船

Higaki Momofune

"Shallows racers" (*subashiri*) is the literal name used in Edo for young *bora* (gray mullet) fish.

葛花加二　乗穂加二　*Kuzubana ka ni　Noriho ka ni*

Kuzubana: +2 [points]; Noriho: +2 [points]

神なりの鳴戸のほらも釣はりの稲妻を見て臍やちちめむ

Kaminari no / Naruto no bora mo / tsuri-hari no / inazuma o mite / heso ya chijimemu

If in the whirlpools / thundering at Naruto / a mullet espied / the lightning flash of a hook, / it would swim off, grumbling.

年廼門春喜

Toshinomon Haruki

The second poem appears on the fourth of the four *kyōka* sheets in the Mann set—as the only poem under the heading "gray mullet" (*bora*). The last four syllables of the poem there instead read *kakusan* (would hide away). The asparagus-like stalks behind the flowering branch in the print are Japanese *udo*, usually translated in English as spikenard for its spiked flowers. The cooked stalks of this wild herbaceous plant commonly accompany fish. *Udo* is a seasonal word for spring.

Figure 73, pages 84–85

Utagawa Hiroshige (1797–1858)

Sparrows and Camellias in Snow

1830s

Signed *Hiroshige hitsu*; red seal *Utagawa*

Publisher: Wakasaya Yoichi (Jakurindō); red seal below poem

Color woodblock print with embossing and areas without outlines; *ōtanzaku*, 37.1 x 16.7 cm

Provenance: Acquired from S. H. Mori Gallery, Chicago, April 5, 1966

Published: Delay, p. 253; Forrer 1997, cat. no. 108; Forrer 2017, p. 1 (detail); Izzard 1983, cat. no. 8b; Ōta Memorial Museum of Art, Tokyo, *The Mann Collection*, cat. no. 114

Exhibited: Pratt Graphics Center, New York, "Hiroshige," 1983; Ōta Memorial Museum of Art, Tokyo, "The Mann Collection," 1994; Royal Academy of Arts, London, "Hiroshige," 1997

THE CHINESE COUPLET in the upper register of the print reads:

烏鳶争食雀争窠
独立池辺風雪多

While the crows and kites spar for scraps, and the sparrows battle for nests, /
I stand alone beside the lake, in the howling wind and heavy snow.

Suzuki Jūzō remarks in *Utagawa Hiroshige* that the couplet is from a Chinese poem by Bai Juyi (772–846).

This design exists in several states, with shaded ground and snowflakes carved into the block, as here; solid gray ground without snowflakes; and gray ground with snowflakes. There are also prints with the publisher's seal of Sanoya Kihei, who is assumed to have taken over the production.

Utagawa Hiroshige (1797–1858)

Peacock and Peonies

1830s

Signed *Hiroshige hitsu*; seal *Ichiryūsai*

Publisher: Wakasaya Yoichi (Jakurindō)

Censor's seal *kiwame* (certified)

Color woodblock print with embossing; *ōtanzaku*, 38.3 x 17.4 cm

Provenance: Acquired from Kondo Sentarō, Red Lantern Shop, Kyoto, October 9, 1985

Published: Mann, *Impressions*, fig. 10; Marks, no. 126, p. 389; Ōta Memorial Museum of Art, Tokyo, *The Mann Collection*, cat. no. 113

Exhibited: Ōta Memorial Museum of Art, Tokyo, "The Mann Collection," 1994

THE LINE OF CHINESE poetry at the top of the image 牡丹花富貴者也 reads: "The peony is a man of wealth and standing." The characters 幽斎 "Yūsai" above the round censor's seal represent an alternate name of Hiroshige.

Figure 88, page 96

Utagawa Hiroshige (1797–1858)

Long-tailed Bird and Prunus Branch

1830s

Signed *Hiroshige hitsu*; poem sealed *Ōatari*
大当 and *Yūsai*

Publisher: Wakasaya Yoichi (Jakurindō)

Censor's seal *kiwame* (certified)

Color woodblock print; *ōtanzaku*,
38.1 x 17.6 cm

Provenance: Acquired from Carolyn Staley,
Seattle, October 22, 1997

Published: Foxwell et al., cat. no. 105 and
illustration back-cover flap; Staley, *Hiroshige
Masterworks*, cat. no. 71

Exhibited: Smart Museum of Art, "Awash
in Color," 2012–13

THE INSCRIPTION IS the second line of a
couplet by the Ming-dynasty poet Gao Qi
(Gao Jidi; 1336–1374) that reads:

> [萬花敢向雪中出] / 一樹独先天下春
>
> [Many flowers dare to bloom amidst
> the snow, / but] only one tree leads the
> world to spring.

The long-tailed bird has been identified as
Cissa erythrorhyncha, a member of the mag-
pie family.

Utagawa Hiroshige (1797–1858)

Performing Monkey and Cherry Blossoms

1830s

Signed *Hiroshige hitsu*

Publisher: Sanoya Kihei (Kikakudō)

Color woodblock print; *ōtanzaku*,
38.5 x 17.5 cm

Provenance: Acquired from Christie's, New
York, October 27, 1998

Published: Christie's, New York, October 27,
1998, lot 408

THE COUPLET at the top of the image consists
of two parallel phrases on the topic of "quietly
viewing the autumn mountains," taken from a
poem by Ki no Haseo (845–912) in the anthology *Chinese and Japanese Poems for Recitation*
(*Wakan rōeishū*), no. 458:

人煙一穂秋村僻
猿叫三聲曉峽深

Jin en issui no aki no mura sakareri
saru sakebite sansei akatsuki no kyō fukashi

Remote is the autumn village that yields
one trail of cooking smoke.

Deep is the dawn ravine that rings with
three cries from a gibbon.

Another state of this print has an extra falling
petal to the left of the monkey's platform.
Those with the seal of the publisher Jakurindō
(Wakasaya Yoichi) generally are taken to be
the earlier edition, yet, there exist impressions
with an extra petal and Kikakudō publisher's
seal (see Vever 1, lot 175).

Cuckoo in Rain

1830s

Signed *Hiroshige hitsu*

Publisher: Kawaguchiya Shōzō (Shōeidō)

Censor's seal *kiwame* (certified)

Color woodblock print; *chūtanzaku*, 37 x 12.2 cm

Provenance: Acquired from S. H. Mori, Gallery, Chicago, April 5, 1966

Published: Ōta Memorial Museum of Art, Tokyo, *The Mann Collection*, cat. no. 115

Exhibited: Ōta Memorial Museum of Art, Tokyo, "The Mann Collection," 1994

THE POEM READS:

二声は五百崎こへつほとゝぎす

Futagoe wa / Iosaki koetsu / hototogisu

The lesser cuckoo / sends an answering call / from distant Iosaki.

Lesser cuckoo is the English name for the bird *Cuculuys poliocephalus.*

124   **Utagawa Hiroshige (1797–1858)**

Mandarin Ducks and Bamboo in Snow

1830s

Signed *Hiroshige ga*

Publisher: Nishimuraya Yohachi (Eijudō)

Color woodblock print in fan reserve; *chūban*, 22.3 x 33 cm

Provenance: Acquired from Richard Kruml, London, October 1, 1980

Published: Izzard 1983, cat. no. 30; Ōta Memorial Museum of Art, Tokyo, *The Mann Collection*, cat. no. 133

Exhibited: Pratt Graphics Center, New York, "Hiroshige," 1983; Ōta Memorial Museum of Art, Tokyo, "The Mann Collection," 1994

THE POEM REFERS to the fidelity of mandarin ducks, which mate for life:

おし鳥の盃とちようす氷

Oshidori no / sakazuki to chiyo / usugōri

For mandarin ducks, / thin spring ice is a timeless / festive drinking cup.

Utagawa Hiroshige (1797–1858)

Full Moon over Takanawa (Takanawa no meigetsu), from the series
Famous Places in the Eastern Capital (Tōto meisho)

1830s

Signed *Ichiryūsai Hiroshige ga*

Publisher: Kawaguchiya Shōzō (Shōeidō)

Censor's seal *kiwame* (certified)

Color woodblock print; *ōban,* 24.8 x 37.8 cm

Provenance: Ernest Le Véel; acquired
from Ader, Picard, Tajan, Paris, Le Véel 2,
October 24, 1980

Published: Forrer, 1997, cat. no. 7;
Izzard 1983, cat. no. 4; Le Véel 2, lot 97;
Ōta Memorial Museum of Art, Tokyo,
The Mann Collection, cat. no. 101

Exhibited: Pratt Graphics Center, New York, "Hiroshige," 1983; Ōta Memorial
Museum of Art, Tokyo, "The Mann Collection," 1994; Royal Academy of Arts,
London, "Hiroshige," 1997

Utagawa Hiroshige (1797–1858)

Driving Rain, Shōno (Shōno hakuu), from the series
Fifty-three Stations of the Tōkaidō (Tōkaidō gojūsantsugi no uchi)

mid-1830s

Signed *Hiroshige ga*

Publisher: Takenouchi Magohachi
(Hōeidō)

Censor's seal *kiwame* (certified), trimmed
in left margin

Color woodblock print; *ōban,* 24.4 x 36.5 cm

Provenance: Acquired from Merlin Dailey,
East West Gallery, Victor, New York,
October 31, 1980

Published: Ōta Memorial Museum of Art,
Tokyo, *The Mann Collection,* cat. no. 103

Exhibited: Ōta Memorial Museum of Art, Tokyo, "The Mann Collection," 1994

127 Utagawa Hiroshige (1797–1858)

Clearing Weather after Snow, Kameyama (Kameyama yukibare), from the series *Fifty-three Stations of the Tōkaidō (Tōkaidō gojūsantsugi no uchi)*

mid-1830s

Signed *Hiroshige ga*

Publisher: Takenouchi Magohachi (Hōeidō)

Censor's seal *kiwame* (certified)

Color woodblock print; *ōban*, 25.5 x 37.5 cm

Provenance: John Stewart Happer; Adele and Willard Gidwitz, acquired January 19, 1980

Published: Happer, lot 133; Ōta Memorial Museum of Art, Tokyo, *The Mann Collection*, cat. no. 103

Exhibited: Ōta Memorial Museum of Art, Tokyo, "The Mann Collection," 1994

128 Utagawa Hiroshige (1797–1858)

Evening Snow, Kanbara (Kanbara yoru no yuki), from the series *Fifty-three Stations of the Tōkaidō (Tōkaidō gojūsantsugi no uchi)*

mid-1830s

Signed *Hiroshige ga*

Publisher: Takenouchi Magohachi (Hōeidō)

Censor's seal *kiwame* (certified)

Color woodblock print; *ōban*, 25.5 x 38.2 cm

Provenance: Acquired from David Caplan, Mita Arts Gallery Co., Ltd., Tokyo, January 1, 1980

Published: Ōta Memorial Museum of Art, Tokyo, *The Mann Collection*, cat. no. 102

Exhibited: Ōta Memorial Museum of Art, Tokyo, "The Mann Collection," 1994

Exit Willow at Shimabara (Shimabara deguchi no yanagi),
from the series *Famous Places in Kyoto (Kyōto meisho no uchi)*

1830s

Signed *Hiroshige ga*

Publisher: Kawaguchiya Shōzō (Shōeidō; Eisendō); red seal *Kawaguchi han*

Censor's seal *kiwame* (certified)

Color woodblock print; *ōban*, 25.2 x 37.8 cm

Provenance: Acquired from Sotheby's, London, April 2, 1980

Published: Izzard 1983, cat. no. 23; Ōta Memorial Museum of Art, Tokyo, *The Mann Collection*, cat. no. 112; Sotheby's, London, April 2, 1980, lot 92

Exhibited: Pratt Graphics Center, New York, "Hiroshige," 1983; Ōta Memorial Museum of Art, Tokyo, "The Mann Collection," 1994

130   **Utagawa Hiroshige** (1797–1858)

Cherry Trees in Full Bloom at Arashiyama (Arashiyama manka), from the series *Famous Places in Kyoto (Kyōto meisho no uchi)*

1830s

Signed *Hiroshige ga*

Publisher: Kawaguchiya Shōzō (Shōeidō; Eisendō); red seal *Kawaguchi han*

Censor's seal *kiwame* (certified)

Color woodblock print; *ōban,* 24 x 37.3 cm

Provenance: Acquired from S. H. Mori Gallery, April 1, 1965

Published: Forrer 1997, cat. no. 52; Ōta Memorial Museum of Art, Tokyo, *The Mann Collection,* cat. no. 110

Exhibited: Ōta Memorial Museum of Art, Tokyo, "The Mann Collection," 1994; Royal Academy of Arts, London, "Hiroshige," 1997

131   **Utagawa Hiroshige** (1797–1858)

Gion Shrine in Snow (Gionsha setchū), from the series *Famous Places in Kyoto (Kyōto meisho no uchi)*

1830s

Signed *Hiroshige ga*; seal *Ichiryūsai*

Publisher: Kawaguchiya Shōzō (Shōeidō; Eisendō)

Color woodblock print; *ōban,* 24.1 x 37.2 cm

Provenance: Walter Amstutz; acquired from Sotheby's, Tokyo, Amstutz, April 15, 1991

Published: Amstutz, lot 221; Ōta Memorial Museum of Art, Tokyo, *The Mann Colletion,* cat. no. 108

Exhibited: Ōta Memorial Museum of Art, Tokyo, "The Mann Collection," 1994

THIS STATE of the print lacks the blue censor's seal and blue publisher's mark in the margin.

Utagawa Hiroshige (1797–1858)

Yodo River (Yodogawa), from the series
Famous Places in Kyoto (Kyōto meisho no uchi)

1830s

Signed *Hiroshige ga*

Publisher: Kawaguchiya Shōzō (Shōeidō; Eisendō); red seal *Eisendō han*

Color woodblock print; *ōban*, 24.1 x 37.1 cm

Provenance: Walter Amstutz; acquired from Sotheby's, Tokyo, Amstutz, April 15, 1991

Published: Amstutz, lot 218; Ōta Memorial Museum of Art, Tokyo, *The Mann Collection,* cat. no. 109

Exhibited: Ōta Memorial Museum of Art, Tokyo, "The Mann Collection," 1994

THIS IS CONSIDERED a later state of the print lacking blue censor's seal and blue publisher's mark in the right margin.

Utagawa Hiroshige (1797–1858)

Twilight Shower at Tadasugawara (Tadasugawara no yūdachi), from the series *Famous Places in Kyoto (Kyōto meisho no uchi)*

1830s

Signed *Hiroshige ga*; seal *Ichiryūsai*

Publisher: Kawaguchiya Shōzō (Shōeidō; Eisendō)

Color woodblock print; *ōban*, 24.1 x 37.2 cm

Provenance: Walter Amstutz; acquired from Sotheby's, Tokyo, Amstutz, April 15, 1991

Published: Amstutz, lot 215; Forrer 1997, cat. no. 125; Ōta Memorial Museum of Art, Tokyo, *The Mann Collection,* cat. no. 111

Exhibited: Ōta Memorial Museum of Art, Tokyo, "The Mann Collection," 1994; Royal Academy of Arts, London, "Hiroshige," 1997

THIS IS CONSIDERED a later state of the print lacking blue censor's seal and blue publisher's mark in the right margin.

134

Utagawa Hiroshige (1797–1858)

Precincts of Kameido Tenman Shrine in Snow (Kameido Tenmangū keidai no yuki), from the series *Famous Places in the Eastern Capital (Tōto meisho)*

mid-1830s

Signed *Hiroshige ga*; seal *Ichiryūsai*

Publisher: Sanoya Kihei (Kikakudō)

Censor's seal *kiwame* (certified)

Color woodblock print; *ōban*, 26 x 38.2 cm

Provenance: Acquired from Adele and Willard Gidwitz, January 19, 1980

Published: Forrer 1997, cat. no. 10; Ōta Memorial Museum of Art, Tokyo, *The Mann Collection*, cat. no. 134

Exhibited: Ōta Memorial Museum of Art, Tokyo, "The Mann Collection," 1994; Royal Academy of Arts, London, "Hiroshige," 1997

135

Utagawa Hiroshige (1797–1858)

Evening Rain at Karasaki (Karasaki no yau), from the series
The Eight Views of Ōmi Province [Lake Biwa] (Ōmi hakkei no uchi)

mid-1830s

Signed *Hiroshige ga*

Publisher: Yamamotoya Heikichi (Eikyūdō); seal *Eikyūdō*

Censor's seal *kiwame* (certified)

Color woodblock print; *ōban*, 25.8 x 38.2 cm

Provenance: Acquired from Ayako Abe, Japan Gallery, New York, July 19, 1984

Published: Izzard 1983, cat. no. 28; Ōta Memorial Museum of Art, Tokyo, *The Mann Collection*, cat. no. 106

Exhibited: Pratt Graphics Center, "Hiroshige," 1983; Ōta Memorial Museum of Art, Tokyo, "The Mann Collection," 1994

MATTHI FORRER TRANSLATES the poem in the print's square cartouche as follows (*Hiroshige: Prints and Drawings*, 1997, cat. no. 71):

夜の雨に音をゆつりて夕風をよそになたつるから崎のまつ

Yo no ame ni / oto o yuzurite / yūkaze o / yoso ni na tatsuru / Karasaki no matsu

Yielding to the sound in the evening rain / and drawing near to the evening wind / he grows famous: / the pine tree of Karasaki.

136   **Utagawa Hiroshige (1797–1858)**

Lingering Snow on Mount Hira (Hira no bosetsu), from the series
The Eight Views of Ōmi Province [Lake Biwa] (Ōmi hakkei no uchi)

mid-1830s

Signed *Hiroshige ga*

Publisher: Yamamotoya Heikichi (Eikyūdō); seal *Eikyūdō*

Censor's seal *kiwame* (certified)

Color woodblock print; *ōban*, 25.6 x 38.2 cm

Provenance: Carl Schraubstadter; Paolino Gerli; acquired from Sotheby's,
New York, Gerli, April 28, 1971

Published: Delay, p. 243; Forrer 1997, cat. no. 72; Gerli, lot 184; Izzard 1983,
cat. no. 25; Ōta Memorial Museum of Art, Tokyo, *The Mann Collection,*
cat. no. 105; Schraubstadter, lot 284

Exhibited: Pratt Graphics Center, "Hiroshige," 1983; Ōta Memorial Museum
of Art, Tokyo, "The Mann Collection," 1994; Royal Academy of Arts, London,
"Hiroshige," 1997

MATTHI FORRER has transcribed the poem in the print's square cartouche as follows
(*Hiroshige: Prints and Drawings,* 1997, cat. no. 72):

雪はるる比良の高嶺の夕ぐれは花のさかりにすぐるころかな

Yuki haruru / Hira no takane no / yūgure wa / hana no sakari ni / suguru koro kana

When it clears after snowfall, / the tops of Mount Hira / at dusk surely surpass /
the beauty of cherry trees in bloom.

Evening Bell at Miidera Temple (Mii no banshō), from the series *The Eight Views of Ōmi Province [Lake Biwa] (Ōmi hakkei no uchi)*

mid-1830s

Signed *Hiroshige ga*

Publisher: Takenouchi Magohachi (Hoeidō); seal *Take*

Censor's seal *kiwame* (certified) in the gourd-shaped cartouche

Color woodblock print; *ōban*, 25.5 x 38.4 cm

Provenance: Acquired from Christie's, New York, September 22, 1983

Published: Christie's, New York, September 22, 1983, lot 167; Forrer 1997, cat. no. 68; Ōta Memorial Museum of Art, Tokyo, *The Mann Collection*, cat. no. 107

Exhibited: Ōta Memorial Museum of Art, Tokyo, "The Mann Collection," 1994; Royal Academy of Arts, London, "Hiroshige," 1997

ACCORDING TO MATTHI FORRER in his catalogue for the exhibition at the Royal Academy of Arts, this print has two versions: the earlier, printed in gray and soft colors, as here, and a later one in tints of gray and blue. He translates the poem in the print's square cartouche thus:

思ふその暁ちきるはしめそとまつきく三井の入あいのかね

Omou sono / akatsuki chigiru / hajime soto / mazu kiku Mii no / iriai no kane

I think that dawn has made a vow / to wait first outside / until it has heard / the evening bell of Mii Temple.

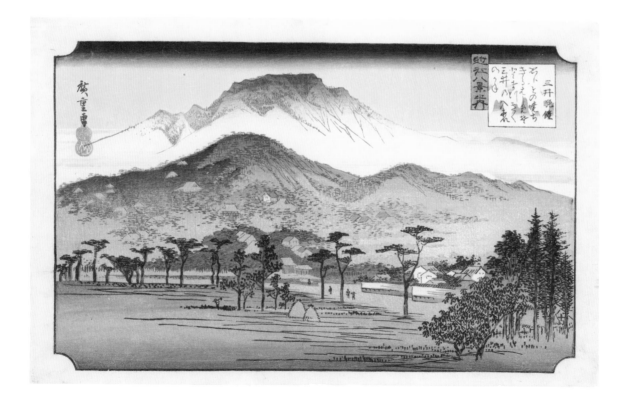

138 Utagawa Hiroshige (1797–1858)

Karuizawa, no. 19 from the series *The Sixty-nine Stations of the Kisokaidō*
(*Kisokaidō rokujūkyū tsugi no uchi*)

late 1830s

Signed *Hiroshige ga*; seal *Tōkaidō*

Publisher: Iseya Rihei (Kinjudō); *I se ri* inscribed on lantern hanging from horse
trappings; Takenouchi Magohachi (Hoeidō)

Color woodblock print; *ōban,* 23.6 x 35.9 cm

Provenance: Acquired from Adele and Willard Gidwitz, January 19, 1980

Published: Izzard 1983, cat. no. 35; Ōta Memorial Museum of Art, Tokyo, *The Mann
Collection,* cat. no. 129

Exhibited: Pratt Graphics Center, New York, "Hiroshige," 1983; Ōta Memorial
Museum of Art, Tokyo, "The Mann Collection," 1994

THE SERIES OF SEVENTY images (numbered in red cartouches next to the series title)
was initiated by the publisher Takenouchi Magohachi (Hoeidō) using designs commissioned from Keisai Eisen, beginning in 1835. Hiroshige was brought into the project in the later 1830s. Other impressions of *Karuizawa* have both the "Iseri" lantern
inscription and the red gourd-seal *Take-uchi* of Takenouchi Magohachi (see Museum
of Fine Arts, Boston, 21.5169). *Karuizawa* was one of the first images Hiroshige provided for the set, here using a seal pointing to his successful Tōkaidō Road series.

Nagakubo, no. 28 from the series *The Sixty-nine Stations of the Kisokaidō*
(*Kisokaidō rokujūkyū tsugi no uchi*)

late 1830s

Signed *Hiroshige ga*; seal *Ichiryūsai*

Publisher: Iseya Rihei; seal *Kinjudō*; and *Iseri* emblem on cloth on
back of horse on riverbank

late 1830s

Signed *Hiroshige ga*; seal *Ichiryūsai*

Censor's seal *kiwame* (certified), trace of circular edge left margin

Collector's seal of Henri Vever

Color woodblock print; *ōban*, 23.5 x 36.1 cm

Provenance: Henri Vever; acquired from Christie's, London,
November 23, 1992

Published: Christie's, London, November 23, 1992, lot 91; Hillier, *Vever*, vol. 3,
no. 929; Ōta Memorial Museum of Art, Tokyo, *The Mann Collection*, cat. no. 128;
Vever 1, lot 403

Exhibited: Ōta Memorial Museum of Art, Tokyo, "The Mann Collection," 1994

140   **Utagawa Hiroshige (1797–1858)**

Seba, no. 32 from the series *The Sixty-nine Stations of the Kisokaidō (Kisokaidō rokujūkyū tsugi no uchi)*

late 1830s

Signed *Hiroshige ga*; seal *Ichiryūsai*

Publisher: Iseya Rihei (Kinjudō)

Censor's seal *kiwame* (certified)

Color woodblock print; *ōban*, 23.6 x 36.7 cm

Provenance: Acquired from Adele and Willard Gidwitz, January 19, 1980

Published: Izzard 1983, cat. no. 38b; Ōta Memorial Museum of Art, Tokyo, *The Mann Collection*, cat. no. 130

Exhibited: Pratt Graphics Center, New York, "Hiroshige," 1983; Ōta Memorial Museum of Art, Tokyo, "The Mann Collection," 1994

141   **Utagawa Hiroshige (1797–1858)**

Suhara, no. 40 from the series *The Sixty-nine Stations of the Kisokaidō (Kisokaidō rokujūkyū tsugi no uchi)*

late 1830s

Signed *Hiroshige ga*; seal *Ichiryūsai*

Publisher: Iseya Rihei; seal *Kinjudō*

Color woodblock print; *ōban*, 24.3 x 36.7 cm

Provenance: Acquired from Robert G. Sawers, London, June 5, 1979

Published: Ōta Memorial Museum of Art, Tokyo, *The Mann Collection*, cat. no. 131

Exhibited: Ōta Memorial Museum of Art, Tokyo, "The Mann Collection," 1994

Utagawa Hiroshige (1797–1858)

Ōi, no. 47 from the series *The Sixty-nine Stations of the Kisokaidō*
(*Kisokaidō rokujūkyū tsugi no uchi*)

late 1830s

Signed *Hiroshige ga*; seal *Ichiryūsai*

Publisher: Iseya Rihei; seal *Kinjudō*

Censor's seal *kiwame* (certified)

Color woodblock print; *ōban*, 24.8 x 37.6 cm

Provenance: Acquired from Robert G. Sawers, London, July 2, 1982

Published: Forrer 1997, cat. no. 117; Ōta Memorial Museum of Art, Tokyo,
The Mann Collection, cat. no. 132

Exhibited: Ōta Memorial Museum of Art, Tokyo, "The Mann Collection," 1994;
Royal Academy of Arts, London, "Hiroshige," 1997

Utagawa Hiroshige (1797–1858)

Fuji River in Snow (Fujikawa setchū)

mid-1840s

Signed *Hiroshige hitsu*; seal *Ichiryūsai*

Publisher: Sanoya Kihei (Kikakudō)

Color woodblock print; *ōban* vertical diptych (hanging scroll format, *kakemono-e*), 74.2 x 25 cm

Provenance: Acquired from Richard Kruml, London, March 26, 1981

Published: Izzard 1983, cat. no. 54; Ōta Memorial Museum of Art, Tokyo, *The Mann Collection*, cat. no. 135

Exhibited: Pratt Graphics Center, New York, "Hiroshige,"1983; Ōta Memorial Museum of Art, Tokyo, "The Mann Collection," 1994

144 **Utagawa Hiroshige** (1797–1858)

Poem by Bai Juyi, from the series *Chinese and Japanese Poems for Recitation* (*Wakan rōeishū*)

c. 1840

Signed *Hiroshige hitsu*; seal *Ichiryūsai*

Publisher: Jōshūya Kinzō

Censor's seal *kiwame* (certified)

Color woodblock print; *ōban*, 37.5 x 25.7 cm

Provenance: Louis Ledoux (sold after Ledoux's death by Roland Koscherak, New York); acquired from Robert G. Sawers, London, May 7, 1971

Published: Delay, p. 244; *Designed for Pleasure*, fig. 11, p. 28; Forrer 1997, cat. no. 124; Izzard 1983, cat. no. 48; Jenkins 1973, cat. no. 62; Ledoux, *Landscapes*, pl. 10; Ledoux, *Hokusai and Hiroshige*, no. 52; Mann, *Impressions*, fig. 6; Ōta Memorial Museum of Art, Tokyo, *The Mann Collection*, cat. no. 136

Exhibited: Grolier Club, New York, "Landscapes," 1924; Japan Society, New York, "The Ledoux Heritage," 1973; Pratt Graphics Center, New York, "Hiroshige," 1983; Ōta Memorial Museum of Art, Tokyo, "The Mann Collection," 1994; Royal Academy of Arts, London, "Hiroshige," 1997; Asia Society, New York, "Designed for Pleasure," 2008

THE INSCRIPTION is a couplet by Bai Juyi (772–846), included as entry no. 376 in the classical poetry anthology *Wakan rōeishū*, and referenced in the Noh play *The Potted Trees* (*Hachinoki*). (For *The Potted Trees*, also see Mann catalogue number 9.)

雪似鵞毛飛散乱
人被鶴氅立徘徊

Snow like goose-down flies and scatters;
People coated in crane feathers arise and wander.

Donald Jenkins, in *The Ledoux Heritage*, notes that Hiroshige's imagery derives from the Chinese painting tradition of imaginary landscapes.

Page 154 (detail)

145   **Utagawa Hiroshige (1797–1858)**

Fireworks, Ryōgoku Bridge (Ryōgoku hanabi), from the series
One Hundred Views of Famous Places in Edo (Meisho Edo hyakkei)

1858; date seal for the eighth lunar month, Year of the Horse

Signed *Hiroshige ga*

Publisher: Uoya Eikichi

Censor's seal *aratame* (inspected)

Color woodblock print; *ōban,* 35 x 23.2 cm

Provenance: G. Wynkoop (provenance given by R. E. Lewis); acquired from
R. E. Lewis, Inc., San Francisco, October 4, 1974

Published: Forrer 2017, pl. 124; Ōta Memorial Museum of Art, Tokyo, *The Mann
Collection,* cat. no. 138

Exhibited: Ōta Memorial Museum of Art, Tokyo, "The Mann Collection," 1994

Figure 56, page 64

146   **Utagawa Hiroshige (1797–1858)**

Fireworks, Ryōgoku Bridge (Ryōgoku hanabi), from the series
One Hundred Views of Famous Places in Edo (Meisho Edo hyakkei)

1858; date seal for the eighth lunar month, Year of the Horse

Signed *Hiroshige ga*

Publisher: Uoya Eikichi

Censor's seal *aratame* (inspected)

Color woodblock print; *ōban,* 36 x 24.4 cm

Provenance: G. Wynkoop (provenance given by R. E. Lewis); acquired from R. E.
Lewis, Inc., San Francisco, October 4, 1974

Published: Forrer 1997, cat. no. 96; Ōta Memorial Museum of Art, Tokyo, *The Mann
Collection,* cat. no. 139

Exhibited: Ōta Memorial Museum of Art, Tokyo, "The Mann Collection," 1994;
Royal Academy of Arts, London, "Hiroshige," 1997

Figure 57, page 64

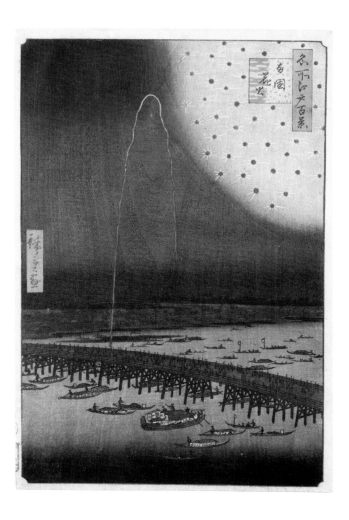

Utagawa Hiroshige (1797–1858)

Drum Bridge and "Setting Sun Hill," Meguro (Meguro Taikobashi Yūhinooka),
from the series *One Hundred Views of Famous Places in Edo (Meisho Edo hyakkei)*

1857; date seal for the fourth lunar month, Year of the Snake

Signed *Hiroshige ga*

Publisher: Uoya Eikichi

Censor's seal *aratame* (inspected) combined with date seal

Color woodblock print; *ōban*, 35 x 23.7 cm

Provenance: Acquired from Nagatani, Inc., Chicago, June 7, 1961

Published: Forrer 2017, p. 12 (detail)

Figure 6, page 21

Utagawa Hiroshige (1797–1858)

Sudden Shower over Ōhashi Bridge, Atake (Ōhashi Atake no yūdachi),
from the series *One Hundred Views of Famous Places in Edo (Meisho Edo hyakkei)*

1857; date seal for the ninth lunar month, Year of the Snake

Signed *Hiroshige ga*

Publisher: Uoya Eikichi

Censor's seal *aratame* (inspected)

Color woodblock print; *ōban*, 36.9 x 24.7 cm

Provenance: Adele and Willard Gidwitz; acquired from Adele and Willard Gidwitz,
January 19, 1980

Published: Forrer 1997, cat no. 95; Forrer 2017, pl. 132; Ōta Memorial Museum of Art,
Tokyo, *The Mann Collection*, cat. no. 137; *Designed for Pleasure*, fig. 26, p. 201

Exhibited: Ōta Memorial Museum
of Art, Tokyo, "The Mann Collec-
tion," 1994; Royal Academy of Arts,
London, "Hiroshige," 1997; Asia
Society, New York, "Designed for
Pleasure," 2008

Figure 72, page 82

149 **Utagawa Kuniyoshi (1797–1861)**

Mount Fuji on a Fine Day off the Coast of Tsukuda (Tsukuda oki kaisei no Fuji),
from the series *Thirty-six Views of Mount Fuji from the Eastern Capital*
(Tōto Fujimi sanjūrokkei)

c. 1843

Signed *Ichiyūsai Kuniyoshi ga*

Publisher: Murataya Jirobei (Eiyudō); seal *Mura*

Color woodblock print; *ōban*, 24.1 x 37 cm

Provenance: Robert Glauber, sold Sotheby's, London, November 5, 1968; acquired
from Robert G. Sawers, London, June 5, 1979

Published: Mann, *Impressions*, fig. 7; Ōta Memorial Museum of Art, Tokyo,
The Mann Collection, cat. no. 99; Sotheby's, London, November 5, 1968, lot 27

Exhibited: Ōta Memorial Museum of Art, Tokyo, "The Mann Collection," 1994

THE HAIKU INSCRIBED above the flying cormorant (between the series and print
titles) reads:

舟道に動いて涼し不二の影

Funa michi ni / ugoite suzushi / Fuji no kage

Refreshingly cool, / this ride along the channel, / in sight of Fuji.

新日庵琴雅
Shinnichi-an Kotomasa

Page 14 (detail)

150   **Utagawa Kuniyoshi (1797–1861)**

The Brave Woman Okane of Ōmi Province (Ōmi no kuni no yūfu Okane)

c. 1834

Signed *Ichiyūsai Kuniyoshi ga*

Publisher: Yamaguchiya Tobei (Kinkodō)

Censor's seal *kiwame* (certified)

Color woodblock print; *ōban*, 26 x 38 cm

Provenance: Acquired from Sotheby's, New York, June 26, 1981

Published: Ōta Memorial Museum of Art, Tokyo, *The Mann Collection*, cat. no. 97; Sotheby's, New York, June 26, 1981, lot 393

Exhibited: Ōta Memorial Museum of Art, Tokyo, "The Mann Collection," 1994

151   **Utagawa Kuniyoshi (1797–1861)**

View of the Tamura Ferry on the Ōyama Road, Sagami Province (Sōshū Ōyama michi Tamura no watashi no kei)

c. 1842

Signed *Ichiyūsai Kuniyoshi ga*

Publisher: Wakasaya Yoichi (Jakurindō)

Collector's seal of Wakai Kenzaburō

Color woodblock print; *ōban*, 24.9 x 36.5 cm

Provenance: Wakai Kenzaburō; Basil W. Robinson; acquired from Merlin Dailey, East West Gallery, Victor, New York, December 24, 1985

Published: Ōta Memorial Museum of Art, Tokyo, *The Mann Collection*, cat. no. 100

Exhibited: Ōta Memorial Museum of Art, Tokyo, "The Mann Collection," 1994

152

Utagawa Kuniyoshi (1797–1861)

Surugadai, from the series *Famous Places in the Eastern Capital (Tōto meisho)*

1830–35

Signed *Ichiyūsai Kuniyoshi ga*

Publisher: Kagaya Kichiemon

Censor's seal *kiwame* (certified)

Color woodblock print; *ōban,* 24.5 x 36.3 cm

Provenance: Acquired from Christie's, New York, April 26, 1995

Published: Christie's, New York, April 26, 1995, lot 241

153

Utagawa Kuniyoshi (1797–1861)

In the Snow at Tsukuhara, Sado Island (Sashū Tsukahara setchū), from the series *Abridged Illustrated Biography of the Monk Nichiren (Kōsō goichidai ryakuzu)*

c. 1835–36

Signed *Ichiyūsai Kuniyoshi hitsu;* artist's seal of *toshidama* emblem of Utagawa lineage within box

Publisher: Iseya Rihei

Censor's seal *kiwame* (certified)

Color woodblock print; *ōban,* 24.8 x 37.2 cm

Provenance: Acquired from Richard Kruml, London, April 5, 1982

Published: Marks, no. 124; Ōta Memorial Museum of Art, Tokyo, *The Mann Collection,* cat. no. 98

Exhibited: Ōta Memorial Museum of Art, Tokyo, "The Mann Collection," 1994

COLLECTOR'S COMMENTS

The image shows the monk Nichiren, founder of the Nichiren sect of Japanese Buddhism, struggling up a mountain in heavy snow, during his exile on Sado Island. Yoshida Teruji proposed that Kuniyoshi, an adherent of the sect, designed his ten prints on Nichiren to commemorate the five-hundred-fiftieth anniversary of Nichiren's death. This impression generally is considered the second state, lacking a horizon line, but there are differences of opinion on which of the known designs is the earliest. In the Mann example, an embossed, uninked horizon line is visible in raked light. It seems logical that the impressions with the inked horizon line are the earlier and that someone involved in the process removed it from subsequent prints. The composition is thought to be based on an illustration in the book *Bunpō's Landscape Album (Bunpō sansui gafu),* by Kawamura Bunpō (1779–1821), published posthumously in 1824.

154 **Ryūkōsai Jokei (act. 1776–1809)**

The Actor Onoe Shinshichi I as Ōboshi Yuranosuke, the leader of the Forty-seven
Loyal Retainers, in the kabuki play *Young Sprout from The Treasury of the Loyal
Retainers (Chūshin futabagura),* performed as the season premiere (*kaomise*)
at the Naka no Shibai theater, Osaka, in the eleventh lunar month, 1792

1792

Publisher: Shioya Rinbei; marks *yama* (mountain), *Shio Rin*

Collector's seal of Pierre Barboutau on verso

Color woodblock print; *hosoban,* 31.4 x 14.4 cm

Provenance: Pierre Barboutau; Adolphe Stoclet; acquired from Sotheby's, London,
Stoclet, June 8, 2004

Published: Barboutau, lot 980; Gerstle and Yano, no. 8; Stoclet 2004, lot 342

155 **Ryūkōsai Jokei (act. 1776–1809)**

The Actor Kanō Hinasuke I

c. 1793

Publisher: Ōsakaya Sashichi; marks *yama* (mountain) and *chidori* (plover bird)

Color woodblock print; *hosoban,* 31.2 x 14.2 cm

Provenance: Richard Kruml, London; acquired from Roger Keyes,
November 3, 2000

THE CATALOGUE RAISONNÉ compiled by Gerstle and Yano of the works of Ryūkōsai
states that the role and performance are still uncertain, and dates the print as above.
Elsewhere, the print has been catalogued as Kanō Hinasuke I (Arashi Koroku III) as
the wrestler Tatsugadake in the kabuki play *Kiyomizu Yogaichō District in the Imperial
Capital (Miyako Kiyomizu Yogaichō),* performed at the Naka no Shibai theater, Osaka,
in the second lunar month, 1792 (see Museum of Fine Arts, Boston, 21.6298).

二葉藏
大星由良之助
尾上新七

156

Ryūkōsai Jokei (act. 1776–1809)

The Actor Ichikawa Danzō IV as Ōboshi Yuranosuke in the kabuki play *Forty-seven Poems on Folding Fans Fired off in Quick Succession* (*Ōgi no yakazu shijūshichihon*), performed at the Naka no Shibai theater, Osaka, in the third lunar month, 1797

1797

Color woodblock print; *hosoban*, 30.9 x 14.1 cm

Provenance: Acquired from Christie's, New York, October 22, 1993

Published: Christie's, New York, October 22, 1993, lot 27; Gerstle and Yano, no. 38; Ōta Memorial Museum of Art, Tokyo, *The Mann Collection*, cat. no. 90

Exhibited: Ōta Memorial Museum of Art, Tokyo, "The Mann Collection," 1994

157

Ryūkōsai Jokei (act. 1776–1809)

The Actor Kanō Hinasuke I as Akizuka Tatewaki in the kabuki play *A Courtesan's Mutsu Jewel River* (*Keisei Mutsu no Tamagawa*) by Namiki Jūsuke, performed at the Kado no Shibai theater, Osaka, in the second lunar month, 1793

1793

Signed *Ryūkōsai ga*

Publisher: Shioya Rinbei; marks *yama* (mountain), *Shio Rin*

Color woodblock print; *hosoban*, 31.4 x 14 cm

Provenance: Acquired from Richard Kruml, London, August 11, 1980

Published: Gerstle and Yano, no. 19b; Ōta Memorial Museum of Art, Tokyo, *The Mann Collection*, cat. no. 91; Schwab, *Osaka Prints*, no. 1

Exhibited: Ōta Memorial Museum of Art, Tokyo, "The Mann Collection," 1994

158   **Ryūkōsai Jokei (act. 1776–1809)**

The Actor Onoe Shinshichi I (Fujaku) as Isshiki Yūki no Kami in the kabuki play *Courtesans, Weeping Willows and Cherry Trees (Keisei yanagi zakura)* by Tatsuoka Mansaku and Chikamatsu Tokuzō, premiered at the Naka no Shibai theater, Osaka, in the first lunar month, 1793

1793

Publisher: Shioya Chōbei; mark *Shio Chō han*

Color woodblock print; *hosoban*, 32.5 x 14.5 cm

Provenance: Acquired from Richard Kruml, London, January 26, 1979

Published: Richard Kruml, *Japanese Prints*, catalogue 21, London, 1978, no. 10; Schwab, *Osaka Prints*, no. 4; Ōta Memorial Museum of Art, Tokyo, *The Mann Collection*, cat. no. 89

Exhibited: Ōta Memorial Museum of Art, Tokyo, "The Mann Collection," 1994

THE IMAGE IS one of five prints that Ryūkōsai designed from the play represented. Shinshichi played Isshiki, father of the courtesan Hinaji, and two other parts.

159   **Ryūkōsai Jokei (act. 1776–1809)**

The Actor Ichikawa Danzō IV in an undetermined role

c. 1793

Signed *Ryūkōsai*

Publisher: Shioya Rinbei; marks *yama* (mountain), *Shio Rin*

Collector's seal of Theodor N. Scheiwe

Color woodblock print; *hosoban*, 31.9 x 14.3 cm

Provenance: Theodor N. Scheiwe; acquired from Christie's, New York, Scheiwe 1, March 26, 1998, lot 262

Published: Christie's, New York, March 26, 1998, lot 262; Gerstle and Yano, no. 33a; Hempel 1959, no. 176, p. 106; Hempel 1972, no. 400, p. 237; Scheiwe 1, lot 160

Exhibited: Landesmuseum für Kunst und Kulturgeschichte, Münster, "Ausstellung japanischer Holzschnitte: Sammlung Theodor Scheiwe," 1959; Villa Hügel, Essen, "Ukiyo-e: die Kunst der heiteren vergänglichen Welt: Japan 17.–19. Jahrhundert, Sammlung Scheiwe," 1972

160   **Ryūkōsai Eishō (act. mid-1790s?–early 1830s?)**

The Actor Arashi Hinasuke II in an undetermined role

c. 1796–1801

Signed *Ryūkōsai Eishō*

Woodblock print with stenciled coloring, *kappazuri-e; chūban*, 29.6 x 18 cm

Provenance: Acquired from Kegan Paul, Trench, Trubner & Co., London, October 31, 1967

Published: Gerstle and Yano, no. 46; Kegan Paul, *Japanese Prints*, 1967, cat. no. 81; Ōta Memorial Museum of Art, Tokyo, *The Mann Collection*, cat. no. 88

Exhibited: Ōta Memorial Museum of Art, Tokyo, "The Mann Collection," 1994

GERSTLE AND YANO explain in their catalogue raisonné of the work of Ryūkōsai Jokei that the role and play depicted here are as yet undetermined. There is also confusion over the artist's signature on the print: whether this is a design by Jokei using the variant name Eishō or, as they postulate, a different artist active even some twenty years beyond Jokei's last dated work of 1809.

Figure 24, page 34

161   **Shunkōsai Hokushū (act. 1802–32)**

The Actors Arashi Kichisaburō II (Rikan) as Prince Koretaka (right) *and Nakamura Utaemon III (Shikan) as Katō Masakiyo* (left) *in the respective kabuki plays* The Time Is Now for an Ariwara Line Revival (Toki ni saikō Ariwara keizu) *and* Eight Battle Formations to Defend Honjō Castle (Hachijin shugo no Honjō), *performed in the ninth lunar month, 1820*

1820

Signed *Shunkōsai Hokushū ga*

Color woodblock print; *ōban*, 38.6 x 25.6 cm

Provenance: Acquired from The Eighth Written Bid Auction, Tokyo, Ukiyo-e Dealers Association of Japan, no. 89, October 1989

ARASHI KICHISABURŌ II (Rikan) and Nakamura Utaemon III (Shikan) had not acted together in more than twenty years when Hokushū was commissioned by the publisher to design this fantasy double portrait. Because of their large followings, they are shown together, although each actor was performing in a different play in a different theater in Osaka at the time: Kichisaburō in *Toki ni saikō Ariwara keizu* at the Horie theater and Utaemon in *Hachijin shugo no Honjō* at the Kado no Shibai theater. The artist has captured their real-life rivalry in their rather challenging expressions. According to Roger Keyes (*The Theatrical World of Osaka Prints*, 13), the actors were persuaded to appear together in the autumn of 1821, but Kichisaburō died before the play could be mounted.

There is another version of the print with brass embellishments from a limited, special edition.

Shunkōsai Hokushū (act. 1802–32)

The Actors Nakamura Utaemon III as Kanawa Gorō Imakuni and Arashi Koroku IV as Omiwa in the kabuki play *Mounts Imo and Se: Exemplary Women's Virtues (Imoseyama onna teikin)* by Chikamatsu Hanji, Matsuda Baku and others, performed at the Kado no Shibai theater, Osaka in the third lunar month, 1821

1821

Signed *Shunkōsai Hokushū ga*; seal *Yoshinoyama*

Collector's seal of Theodor N. Scheiwe

Color woodblock print with gold ground and with embellishments of silver and copper powders; *ōban*, 39.3 x 26.3 cm

Provenance: Theodor N. Scheiwe; acquired from Christie's, New York, Scheiwe 1, March 21, 1989, lot 162

Published: *Designed for Pleasure*, fig. 128, p. 180; Hempel 1972, no. 405, p. 240; Marks, no. 99, p. 349; Ōta Memorial Museum of Art, Tokyo, *The Mann Collection*, cat. no. 94; Scheiwe 1, lot 162

Exhibited: Villa Hügel, Essen, "Ukiyo-e: die Kunst der heiteren vergänglichen Welt; Japan 17.–19.; Jahrhundert, Sammlung Scheiwe," 1972; Ōta Memorial Museum of Art, Tokyo, "The Mann Collection," 1994; Asia Society, New York, "Designed for Pleasure," 2008

WITH ITS METALLIC embellishments, this print is from a limited, special edition. The version in the Museum of Fine Arts, Boston is a later state, without metallic powder (Museum of Fine Arts, Boston, 11.35374). The scene shows Gorō, a retainer of the powerful Fujiwara family, about to stab Omiwa, who has been spurned by Iruka of the rival Soga clan. Gorō has mistaken her for someone else. Her dying words promise that they will aid in the overthrow of their mutual enemy, Iruka.

163 Shunkōsai Hokushū (act. 1802–32)

The Actor Asao Gakujūrō, Changing His Name from Yūjirō, as Mashiba Hisatsugu
in the kabuki play *The Golden Gate and the Paulownia Crest* (*Kinmon gosan no kiri*)
by Namiki Gohei, performed at the Kado no Shibai theater, Osaka, in the second
lunar month, 1822

1822

Signed *Shunkōsai Hokushū*; seal *Hokushū*

Color woodblock print; *ōban*, 38 x 26.5 cm

Provenance: Acquired from Christie's, New York, October 8, 1988

Published: Christie's, New York, October 8, 1988, lot 325; Ōta Memorial Museum of
Art, Tokyo, *The Mann Collection*, cat. no. 95

Exhibited: Ōta Memorial Museum of Art, Tokyo, "The Mann Collection," 1994

THE INSCRIPTION RECORDS the actor's name change from Asao Yūjirō to Asao
Gakujūrō. The two poems above his head are signed *Enjaku*, Gakujūrō's pen name, and
Shōkoku-an. The seal in the middle left of the print is that of the engraver, Funaki
Kasuke, and reads: "Kasuke, pupil of Hokushū" (*Hokushū monjin hori Kasuke*).

The inscription and poems read:

真柴久次　勇次郎改　浅尾額十郎
名花凡三十餘種

このゆふべ浅黄ざくらと驕らばや　延若
誰もすくあさを桜に花多し　小黒庵

Mashiba Hisatsugu Yūjirō aratame Asao Gakujūrō
Meika oyoso sanjū yo shū
Mashiba Hisatsugu Yūjirō changing to Asao Gakujūrō
Thirty-or-so Varieties of Famous Flowers

[First poem]
Kono yūbe / asagi-zakura to / ogoraba ya
Yesterday evening, / he could have boasted the title: / *asagi* cherry.

Enjaku

[Second poem]
Dare mo sugu / asa o sakura ni / hana ōshi
Everyone hopes that the mornings / will soon see the cherries / covered
in blossoms.
(Everyone hopes that Asao / will soon be crowned / in cherry blossoms.)

Shōkoku-an

Asagi is a pale-blue color associated during the Edo period with robes worn by rural samurai; *asagi-zakura* is a variety of flowering cherry, with white blossoms tinged with pale blue. The second poem turns on a pun: *asa o* あさを［朝を］ ("the morning") and Asao 浅尾 (the actor's name). A famous scene in the play *Kinmon gosan no kiri* takes place at the height of cherry-blossom season, hence the two poems associate Asao Gakujūrō with cherry blossoms.

164   Shunkōsai Hokushū (act. 1802–32)

The Actors Ichikawa Ebijūrō II as Ki no Haseo (right), *Nakamura Utaemon III as Kujaku Saburō* (center) *and Fujikawa Tomokichi* (left) *as Kōbai hime,* in the kabuki play *Famous Trees of Tenmangū Shrine* (*Tenmangū aiju no meiboku),* performed at the Kado no Shibai theater, Osaka, in the first lunar month, 1828

1828

Signed *Shunkōsai Hokushū* on each sheet; seal *Yoshinoyama*

Censor's seal *kiwame* (certified)

Color woodblock print triptych; *ōban,* 38 x 79.5 cm

Provenance: Acquired from Israel Goldman, London, June 18, 1998

Published: Goldman, *Japanese Prints and Paintings,* 1998, no. 12

165 Shunbaisai (Shunkōsai) Hokuei (act. 1824?–37)

The Osaka Actor Arashi Rikan II as Danshichi Kurobei in the night murder scene of the kabuki play *Mirror of Naniwa [Osaka]: The Summer Festival (Natsu matsuri Naniwa kagami),* performed at the Chikugo no Shibai theater, Osaka, in the fifth lunar month, 1832

1832

Signed *Shunkōsai Hokuei*; seal *Shunkō*

Engraver: Kasuke (Funaki Kasuke)

Poem signed *Rikan*

Censor's seal *kiwame* (certified)

Color woodblock print; *ōban*, 37.5 x 24.1 cm

Provenance: Acquired from Israel Goldman, London, October 29, 2000

Published: *Designed for Pleasure,* fig. 133, p. 185; Goldman, *Japanese Prints, Recent Acquisitions,* Catalogue 6, 2000, no. 13; Marks, no. 120

Exhibited: Asia Society, New York, "Designed for Pleasure," 2008

THE CATALOGUE FOR the exhibition "Designed for Pleasure" describes this scene as Kurobei making bloody tracks in the snow after killing his father-in-law, who constantly taunted him. The poem, signed *Rikan,* the actor's name, likens the character Kurobei to young bamboo shoots that can survive the fiercest storm. The poem reads:

> はか竹や雨のおもさをくにもせず　璃寛
>
> *Wakatake ya / ame no omosa o / ku ni mo sezu*
>
> Even in heavy rain, / the young bamboo / does not suffer.
>
> Rikan
>
> Translation by John T. Carpenter, in
> *Designed for Pleasure: The World of Edo
> Japan in Prints and Paintings, 1680–1860,* 205

BIBLIOGRAPHY AND EXHIBITION CITATIONS

Publications and exhibitions cited in the catalogue entries of the Mann Collection and the collector's memoir appear below. Catalogue numbers below the citations refer to the catalogue entries of the Mann Collection in this volume.

The Art Institute of Chicago. "Connoisseurship of Japanese Prints." Exhibition, March 10–May 27, 2012. [No catalogue].
Mann catalogue nos. 10, 43, 68, 78

The Art Institute of Chicago, "The Primitive Period," 1971
The Art Institute of Chicago. "Ukiyo-e Prints and Paintings: The Primitive Period, 1680–1745." An exhibition in memory of Margaret O. Gentles, November 6–December 26, 1971. Catalogue by Donald Jenkins.
Mann catalogue nos. 2, 10

The Art Institute of Chicago. *The Great Eastern Temple: Treasures of Japanese Buddhist Art from Tōdai-ji.* Catalogue of an exhibition, June 28–September 7, 1986, organized by Yutaka Mino, with contributions from John M. Rosenfield, William H. Coaldrake, Samuel C. Morse, and Christine M. E. Guth. Chicago: The Art Institute of Chicago, in association with Indiana University Press, 1986.

Amstutz
Sotheby's, Tokyo, April 15, 1991. *Japanese and Chinese Prints: The Collection of Walter Amstutz.*
Mann catalogue nos. 32, 37, 57, 131–33

Appleton
Sotheby's, London, June 20–23, 1910. Sotheby, Wilkinson and Hodge. *Catalogue of an Exceedingly Fine and Valuable Collection of Japanese Colour Prints Representative of Nearly All of the Best Artists, the Property of Col. H. Appleton (late Royal Engineers), Naval and Military Club, London.*
Mann catalogue nos. 59, 116

Asano Shūgō and Timothy Clark. *The Passionate Art of Kitagawa Utamaro / Utamaro.* London: British Museum Press for the Trustees of the British Museum; Tokyo: Asahi Shinbun, 1994.
Mann catalogue no. 72 (note)

Asia Society, New York, "Designed for Pleasure," 2008
Asia Society, New York and Japanese Art Society of America. "Designed for Pleasure: The World of Edo Japan in Prints and Paintings, 1680–1860." Exhibition, February 27–May 4, 2008.
Mann catalogue nos. 3, 9, 13, 14, 32, 72, 75, 78, 80, 81, 83, 97, 101, 144, 148, 162, 165

Barboutau
Hôtel Drouot, Paris, March 31–April 3, 1908. *Art Japonais, Collection Pierre Barboutau, Objects d'Art, Estampes, Peintures, Tissus Anciens, Vente Publique.*
Mann catalogue no. 154

Berès 1
Sotheby's, Paris, November 27, 2002. *Collection Huguette Berès: Estampes, Dessins et Livres Illustrés Japonais (première vente).*

Berès 2
Sotheby's, Paris, November 25, 2003. *Collection Huguette Berès: Estampes, Dessins et Livres Illustrés Japonais (seconde vente).*
Mann catalogue no. 96

Berès, *Utamaro*, 1977
Galerie Huguette Berès, Paris. With an introduction by Jack Hillier. *Utamaro: Estampes, Livres Illustrés.* Catalogue of an exhibition, March 16–April 6, 1977, Wildenstein [Galleries], London. Paris: Galerie Berès, n. d. [printed December 1976].
Mann catalogue no. 69

Berès, *Sharaku*, 1980
Galerie Huguette Berès, Paris. *Sharaku: Portraits d'Acteurs 1794–1795.* Catalogue of an exhibition, October 17–November 15, 1980. Catalogue by Roger Keyes, Eiko Kondō et al.
Mann catalogue nos. 80, 81, 83

Bickford, Lawrence. *Sumo and the Woodblock Print Masters.* Tokyo; London: Kodansha International, 1994.
Mann catalogue no. 54

Black
Sotheby Parke Bernet, New York, March 4, 1976. *The Louis W. Black Collection of Japanese Prints and Property of Other Owners.*
Mann catalogue nos. 3, 60

Blanchard
American Art Galleries, New York, April 5–6, 1916. *Illustrated Catalogue of the Notable Collection of Japanese Color Prints, The Property of Mrs. John Osgood Blanchard.*
Mann catalogue no. 99

British Museum. "Shunga: Sex and Pleasure in Japanese Art." Exhibition, October 3, 2013–January 5, 2014. Catalogue edited by Timothy Clark, Andrew Gerstle, Aki Ishigami and Akiko Yano.

Calza, Gian Carlo. *Stampe Populari Giapponese.* Milan: Electa Editrice, 1979.
Mann catalogue nos. 13, 15, 23, 32, 37

Cartier
Ader, Etienne, auctioneer, and André and Guy Portier, specialists. *Succession de M. Louis Cartier: Objets d'Art et Estampes d'Extrême-Orient, Laques du Japon . . . Très Belle Suite d'Estampes Japonaises d'Utamaro . . . Estampes Chinoises . . . .* Catalogue of an auction at Hôtel Drouot, Paris, March 16, 1962.
Mann catalogue no. 69

Centre Culturel du Marais and Centre de Recherches par les Expositions et le Spectacle (C.R.E.S.). *Le Fou de Peinture: Hokusai et Son Temps, Dessins, Estampes, Peintures . . . .* Catalogue of an exhibition, Centre Culturel du Marais, Paris, October 6, 1980–January 4, 1981.

Christie's, London, November 23, 1992. *Japanese Prints from a Private Collection.*
Mann catalogue nos. 106, 139

———, November 14, 2001. *Japanese Art and Design.*
Mann catalogue no. 94

Christie's, New York, November 28, 1978. *Japanese and South Asian Works of Art.*
Mann catalogue no. 114

———, December 2–4, 1982. *Important Chinese and Japanese Works of Art.*
Mann catalogue no. 82

———, September 22, 1983. *Fine Japanese Prints, Paintings, Screens and Works of Art.*
Mann catalogue nos. 9, 137

———, March 22, 1984. *Important Japanese Works of Art.*
Mann catalogue nos. 31, 103

———, June 27, 1985. *Fine Japanese Prints.*
Mann catalogue nos. 12, 97

Christie's, March 20, 1986. *Fine Japanese Paintings, Screens, Swords and Sword Fittings.*
Mann catalogue no. 71

———, April 22, 1987. *Fine and Important Japanese Prints from Various Collections.*

———, April 16, 1988. *Fine and Important Japanese Prints and Works of Art.*
Mann catalogue no. 56

———, October 8, 1988. *Fine Japanese Prints and Works of Art.*
Mann catalogue no. 163

———, October 17, 1990. *Japanese and Korean Works of Art.*
Mann catalogue no. 97

———, April 27, 1993. *Japanese Prints, Illustrated Books and Manuscripts.*
Mann catalogue no. 101

———, October 22, 1993. *Japanese Prints.*
Mann catalogue no. 156

———, April 27, 1994. *Japanese Works of Art.*

———, April 26, 1995. *Japanese Prints, Paintings and Works of Art.*
Mann catalogue no. 152

———, November 2, 1996. *Japanese Prints.*
Mann catalogue nos. 66, 78

———, March 26, 1998. *Japanese Works of Art.*
Mann catalogue no. 159

———, October 27, 1998. *Japanese Screens, Paintings and Prints; Japanese Prints from the Estate of a Private East Coast Collector.*
Mann catalogue nos. 33, 34, 122

———, March 25, 2003. *An Important Collection of Japanese Prints.*
Mann catalogue no. 97

———, September 18, 2013. *Japanese and Korean Art.*

Church
Parke-Bernet Galleries, New York, February 25–26, 1946. *Japanese Prints: Important Primitives and Works by Harunobu, Koryusai, Hokusai, Hokkei, Kuniyoshi, and Others; Actor Prints by Shunyei, Shunsho and Shunko; Hiroshige Landscapes, Bird and Flower Prints . . . Collection of Frederic E. Church.*
Mann catalogue no. 48

Clark, Timothy, Andrew Gerstle, Aki Ishigami and Akiko Yano, eds. *Shunga: Sex and Pleasure in Japanese Art.* Catalogue of an exhibition, British Museum, October 3–January 5, 2014. Leiden: Hotei Publishing, 2013.

Cottle, Thomas J. *When the Music Stopped: Discovering My Mother.* Albany: State University of New York Press, 2004.

Delay
Delay, Nelly. *L'Estampe Japonaise.* Paris: Editions Hazan, 1993.
Mann catalogue nos. 3, 9, 13–16, 19, 22, 23, 72, 79, 119, 136, 144

Designed for Pleasure
Meech, Julia and Jane Oliver, eds. *Designed for Pleasure: The World of Edo Japan in Prints and Paintings, 1680–1860.* Catalogue of an exhibition, Asia Society, New York, February 27–May 4, 2008. New York: Asia Society and Japanese Art Society of America in association with University of Washington Press, Seattle and London, 2008.
Mann catalogue nos. 3, 9, 13, 14, 32, 72, 76, 78, 80, 81, 83, 97, 101, 144, 148, 162, 165

Ehrman
Sotheby's, New York, June 18, 1975. *The Edith Ehrman Collection of Japanese Prints.*
Mann catalogue no. 50

Eskenazi, Ltd. *Chinese Ceramics from the Cottle Collection.* Catalogue of an exhibition, Eskenazi, Ltd., Foxglove House, Piccadilly, London, November 28–December 15, 1973. London: Eskenazi, Ltd., 1973.

Ficke, Arthur Davison. *Chats on Japanese Prints.* London and New York: Frederick A. Stokes, Co., 1915.

Ficke 1920
Anderson Galleries, New York, February 10–11, 1920. *Illustrated Catalogue of an Exceptionally Important Collection of Rare and Valuable Japanese Color Prints together with a Few Paintings of the Ukiyoe School: The Property of Arthur Davison Ficke.*
Mann catalogue no. 70

Forrer 1991
Forrer, Matthi. *Hokusai: Prints and Drawings.* Catalogue of an exhibition, Royal Academy of Arts, London, November 15, 1991–February 9, 1992. London: Royal Academy of Arts and Prestel, 1991.
Mann catalogue nos. 107–09, 113

Forrer 1997
———. *Hiroshige: Prints and Drawings.* With essays by Suzuki Jūzō and Henry D. Smith II. Catalogue of an exhibition, Royal Academy of Arts, London, July 3–September 28, 1997. London: Royal Academy of Arts; Munich: Prestel, 1997.
Mann catalogue nos. 118.7, 118.10, 118.14, 119, 125, 130, 133, 134, 136, 137, 142, 144, 146, 148

Forrer 2010, 2011
———. *Hokusai.* Munich; New York: Prestel, 2010. French edition, Paris: Editions Hazan, 2011.
Mann catalogue nos. 105, 107–09, 113

Forrer 2012
———. "Tōshūsai Sharaku, the Man, His Works and Tsutaya Jūsaburō." *Andon,* Journal of the Society for Japanese Arts, 92 (June 2012): 5–29, fig. 26.
Mann catalogue no. 80

Forrer 2017
———. *Hiroshige.* Munich; London; New York: Prestel, 2017. French edition, Paris: Editions Citadelles & Mazenod, 2017.
Mann catalogue nos. 118.7, 118.10, 118.14, 119, 145, 147 (detail), 148

Forrer and Bednarek 1996
Forrer, Matthi and Catherine Bednarek. *Hokusai.* Paris: Bibliothèque de l'Image, 1996.
Mann catalogue nos. 107–09, 113

Foxwell, Chelsea, Anne Leonard, David Acton et al. *Awash in Color: French and Japanese Prints.* Catalogue of an exhibition, Smart Museum of Art, University of Chicago, October 4, 2012–January 20, 2013. Chicago: Smart Museum of Art, University of Chicago, 2012.
Mann catalogue nos. 7, 13, 14, 26, 30, 32, 118.11, 121

Freer|Sackler, "Hokusai," 2006
Freer Gallery of Art and Arthur M. Sackler Gallery, Smithsonian Institution, Washington, DC. "Hokusai." Exhibition, March 4–May 14, 2006. Catalogue by Ann Yonemura.
Mann catalogue nos. 101, 105, 109, 113

Freer|Sackler, "Hokusai," 2012
———. "Hokusai: Thirty-six Views of Mount Fuji." Exhibition, March 24–June 17, 2012. [No catalogue].
Mann catalogue nos. 100, 104–05

Fuller
Parke-Bernet Galleries, New York, November 20, 1945. *Japanese Prints: Primitives from 1680–1764, Full Color Prints from Harunobu to Utamaro and Toyokuni, 1765–1805, Landscapes from 1820 to 1859, the Noted Collection of Gilbert Fuller, Boston.*
Mann catalogue nos. 28, 74

Gaines
Sotheby Parke Bernet, New York, May 23–25, 1979. *Important Japanese and Other Asian Works of Art, Including the Collection of John R. Gaines, Lexington, Kentucky.*
Mann catalogue nos. 3 (Gaines), 54 (anonymous vendor), 65 (Gaines), 107 (Gaines)

Garland
Parke-Bernet Galleries, New York, April 12, 1945. *Japanese Prints by Hiroshige, Harunobu, Shunman, Sharaku, Kiyonaga, Hokusai and Others: Collected by the late Mr. & Mrs. H. P. Garland, Saco, Maine . . . together with an Important Print Shonenko by Hokusai, the Property of a Well-known New York Private Collector.*
Mann catalogue nos. 4, 70

Gerli
Parke-Bernet Galleries, New York, April 28, 1971. *Important Japanese Color Prints, The Property of Signor Paolino Gerli.*
Mann catalogue nos. 14, 17, 40, 48, 70, 74, 99, 136

Gerstle and Yano
Gerstle, Andrew and Akiko Yano, eds. *Ryūkōsai zuroku: Kamigata yakusha nigao-e no reimei / Ryūkōsai Catalogue: The Dawn of Osaka Actor Likeness Prints.* Nishinomiya: Mukogawa Joshi Daigaku Kansai Bunka Kenkyū Sentā (Kansai Cultural Center, Mukogawa Women's University), 2009.
Mann catalogue nos. 154–57, 159, 160

Gilbert, Jeffrey. *The Heritage of Art Photography in Japan.* Vol. 2 of *Nihon shashin zenshū / The Complete History of Japanese Photography.* Tokyo: Shogakukan, 1985–88.

Glendining & Co., London, April 11–12, 1960. *Catalogue of Fine Japanese Coloured Prints and Japanese Sword Furniture, also Relative Books Sold by Direction of RG McNair Scott, Esq.*
Mann catalogue no. 108

Goldman, Israel. *Japanese Prints, Recent Acquisitions.* Catalogue 4. London: Israel Goldman, 1998.
Mann catalogue no. 164

———. *Japanese Prints, Recent Acquisitions.* Catalogue 6. London: Israel Goldman, 2000.
Mann catalogue no. 165

Grabhorn, Edwin. *Figure Prints of Old Japan: A Pictorial Pageant of Actors & Courtesans of the Eighteenth Century Reproduced from the Prints in the Collection of Marjorie and Edwin Grabhorn.* Book Club of California series no. 103. San Francisco: Printed by the Grabhorn Press for the Book Club of California, 1959.

Grolier Club, New York, "Landscapes"
"Japanese Landscape, Bird, and Flower Prints and *Surimono* from Hokusai to Kyōsai." Exhibition, The Grolier Club, New York, 1924. Catalogue by Louis V. Ledoux.
Mann catalogue no. 144

Happer
Sotheby's, London, June 14–18, 1909. Sotheby, Wilkinson & Hodge. *Catalogue of the Valuable Collection of Japanese Colour Prints: The Property of John Stewart Happer . . . Second and Final Portion.*
Mann catalogue no. 127

Haviland 1
Hôtel Drouot, Paris. *Collection Ch. Haviland, Estampes Japonaises, Peintures des Ecoles Classiques et de quelques Maitres de l'Ukiyo-e, Première Vente.* November 1922.
Mann catalogue nos. 57, 65

Hayashi
Galerie Durand-Ruel, Paris, February 1, 1902. *Collection Hayashi: Objets d'Art du Japon et de la Chine: Peintures, Livres . . . .*
Mann catalogue no. 11

Hayashi Yoshikazu and Richard Lane, eds. *Kōshoku hana-zakari . . .* (Eroticism in full bloom). Vol. 22 of *Teihon ukiyo-e shunga meihin shūsei* (The complete masterworks of ukiyo-e erotica). Tokyo: Kawade Shobō, 1998. Accessible online at <http://www.slownet.ne.jp/sns/area/pc/reading/ukyoe/200803111153-9380870.html>.
Mann catalogue no. 3 (note)

Hempel 1959
Hempel, Rose. *Ausstellung japanischer Holzschnitte: Sammlung Theodor Scheiwe.* Catalogue of an exhibition at the Landesmuseum für Kunst und Kulturgeschichte, Münster, 1959. Münster: Aschendorff, 1959.
Mann catalogue nos. 76, 159

Hempel 1963
———. *Holzschnittkunst Japans: Landschaft, Mimen, Kurtisanen . . .* Stuttgart: Belser, 1963.
Mann catalogue no. 76

Hempel 1964
———. *Okubi-e: Portraits im japanischen Farbholzschnitt.* Stuttgart: Belser, 1964.
Mann catalogue no. 76

Hempel 1972
———. *Ukiyo-e: die Kunst der heiteren vergänglichen Welt; Japan 17.–19. Jahrhundert, Sammlung Scheiwe.* Catalogue of an exhibition at Villa Hügel, Essen, March 17–June 30, 1972. Recklinghausen: Bongers, 1972.
Mann catalogue nos. 76, 159, 162

———. *Meisterwerke des Japanische Farbholzschnitte: Die Sammlung Otto Riese.* Munich; New York: Prestel, 1993.

Hillier, Jack. *Japanese Colour Prints.* London: Phaidon, 1966.

Hillier 1970
———. *Suzuki Harunobu: An Exhibition of His Colour-Prints and Illustrated Books on the Occasion of the Bicentenary of His Death in 1770.* Exhibition, Philadelphia Museum of Art, September 18–November 22, 1970.
Mann catalogue no. 35

Hillier, *Vever*
———. *Japanese Prints and Drawings from the Vever Collection.* Three volumes. London: Sotheby Parke Bernet; New York: Rizzoli, 1976.
Mann catalogue nos. 13, 25, 41, 43, 51, 54, 62, 65, 83, 85, 96, 107, 139

Horioka Chimyo. "An Essay on Sugimura Jihei." *Ukiyoe geijutsu / Ukiyo-e Art* 40 (1973): 17.
Mann catalogue no. 2

Izzard 1983
Izzard, Sebastian. *Hiroshige: An Exhibition of Selected Prints and Illustrated Books.* Catalogue of an exhibition, Pratt Graphics Center, New York, organized by the Ukiyo-e Society of America, February 26–March 19, 1983. New York: Ukiyo-e Society of America, 1983.
Mann catalogue nos. 118.11, 118.14, 119, 124–25, 129, 135–36, 138, 140, 143–44

Izzard 1993
———. With essays by J. Thomas Rimer and John T. Carpenter. *Kunisada's World.* Catalogue of an exhibition, Japan Society Gallery, September 30–November 14, 1993. New York: Japan Society in collaboration with the Ukiyo-e Society of America, 1993.
Mann catalogue no. 98

Izzard 2000
Sebastian Izzard Asian Art LLC. *Japanese Prints, Paintings and Metalwork.* New York: Sebastian Izzard Asian Art LLC, 2000.
Mann catalogue no. 115

———. *Early Images from the Floating World: Japanese Paintings, Prints, and Illustrated Books, 1660–1720.* New York: Sebastian Izzard LLC Asian Art, 2008.

Japan Society Gallery, New York, "Kunisada's World," 1993
Japan Society Gallery, New York, in collaboration with the Ukiyo-e Society of America. Exhibition, September 30–November 14, 1993. Catalogue by Sebastian Izzard.
Mann catalogue no. 98

Japan Society, New York, "The Ledoux Heritage," 1973
Japan Society, New York. "The Ledoux Heritage: The Collecting of Ukiyo-e Master Prints." Exhibition, Japan House Gallery, Japan Society, New York, autumn 1973. Catalogue by Donald Jenkins.
Mann catalogue nos. 75, 144

Japan Ukiyo-e Society. Catalogue of "An Exhibition of Masterpieces of Ukiyo-e by the Japan Ukiyo-e Society / Ukiyoe meihin ten" at Shirokiya Nihonbashi Department Store Galleries, Tokyo, April 5–10, 1963. *Ukiyoe geijutsu / Ukiyo-e Art* 3 (1963): 11 and no. 49.
Mann catalogue no. 16

———. *Masterpieces of Ukiyo-e in Foreign Collections: The Works of Harunobu, Kiyonaga, Utamaro, Sharaku, Hokusai and Hiroshige / Zaigai ukiyoe meisaku ten: Nihon Ukiyoe Kyōkai sōritsu jisshūnen kinen.* Exhibition at Matsuzakaya Department Store Galleries, Tokyo, and travelling exhibition Osaka, Nagoya and other venues in Japan. Tokyo: Japan Ukiyo-e Society, 1972.
Mann catalogue nos. 67, 108

———. *Exposition Toulouse Lautrec et Utamaro.* Catalogue commemorating the 20th anniversary of the Japan Ukiyo-e Society (Nihon Ukiyoe Kyōkai). Tokyo: Mainichi Shinbunsha, 1980.
Mann catalogue nos. 39, 63, 64, 86, 88

Japan, *Vever*, 1975
Pari Beberu korekushon: Ukiyoe meisaku 300 senten / Three Hundred Selected Masterpieces from the Vever Collection. Catalogue of an exhibition organized by Nihon Keizai Shinbun, at Keiō Department Store Galleries, Tokyo, January 4–15, 1975; Hanshin Department Store Galleries, Osaka, February 6–18, 1975; and Sogo Department Store Galleries, Hiroshima, April 21–26, 1975.
Mann catalogue nos. 25, 62, 83

Japan, *Vever*, 1976
Hillier, Jack, Suzuki Jūzō and Adachi Toyohisa. *Ukiyoe Beberu korekushon / Ukiyo-e from the Vever Collection.* Tokyo: Nihon Keizai Shinbunsha, 1976.
Mann catalogue nos. 25, 83

Jenkins, *The Primitive Period*
Jenkins, Donald. *Ukiyo-e Prints and Paintings: The Primitive Period, 1680–1745.* Chicago: The Art Institute of Chicago, 1971. Catalogue of an exhibition in memory of Margaret O. Gentles, November 6–December 26, 1971.
Mann catalogue nos. 2, 10

Jenkins 1973
———. *The Ledoux Heritage: The Collecting of Ukiyo-e Master Prints.* New York: Japan Society, Inc., 1973. Catalogue of an exhibition, Japan House Gallery, Japan Society, autumn 1973.
Mann catalogue nos. 75, 144

———. *The Floating World Revisited.* Portland: Portland Art Museum, 1993.

Katz, Janice and Mami Hatayama, eds. *Painting the Floating World: Ukiyo-e Masterpieces from the Weston Collection.* Chicago: The Art Institute of Chicago, 2018.

Kegan Paul, *Japanese Prints*, 1967
Kegan Paul, Trench, Trubner & Co., London. *Japanese Prints, Drawings and Paintings.* October 1967.
Mann catalogue nos. 22, 155

Kende Galleries at Gimbel Brothers, New York, November 30, 1946. *Japanese Color Prints, Roll Paintings, Books Sold by Order of Pratt Institute.*
Mann catalogue no. 14

Keyes, Roger. With contributions from Robert L. Feller, Mary Currans and Catherine W. Bailie. *Japanese Woodblock Prints: A Catalogue of the Mary Ainsworth Collection at the Allen Memorial Art Museum, Oberlin College.* Oberlin, OH: Allen Memorial Art Museum, 1984.

———. "Hokusai's Illustrations for the '100 Poems.'" In *The Art Institute of Chicago Centennial Lectures,* no. 10 in the series *Museum Studies.* Chicago: Contemporary Books, 1983.

———. *The Male Journey in Japanese Prints.* Catalogue published on the occasion of the exhibition "Rage, Power and Fulfillment: The Male Journey in Japanese Prints," Achenbach Foundation for the Graphic Arts, June 10–August 20, 1989. Berkeley: University of California Press in association with The Fine Arts Museums of San Francisco, 1989.
Mann catalogue no. 23

———. "Pink Fuji: The Print Hokusai Saw." *Impressions,* The Journal of the Japanese Art Society of America, 29 (2007): 69–75.

———. "A Conversation with Roger Keyes." *Impressions,* The Journal of the Japanese Art Society of America, 41 (2020): 71–107.

Kishi Fumikazu. *Edo no enkin-hō: Ukie no shikoku* (Edo perspectives: Visions of perspective pictures). Tokyo: Keiso Shobō, 1994.

Kondō 1985
Kondō, Eiko. *Shindora korekushon ukiyoe meihin ten / Masterpieces of Ukiyo-e from the Schindler Collection.* Catalogue of an exhibition sponsored by the Japan Ukiyo-e Society in Tokyo, Okayama and Osaka, October 4, 1985–January 27, 1986. Tokyo: Nihon Keizai Shinbun, 1985.
Mann catalogue nos. 68, 115

Krolik
Sotheby's, London, July 1, 1968. *A Very Fine Collection of Japanese Colour Prints, Property of P. D. Krolik, Esq.*
Mann catalogue nos. 5, 111, 116

Kruml, Richard. *Japanese Prints.* Catalogue 21. London, 1978.
Mann catalogue no. 158

Kuchiki, Yuriko. "The Enemy Trader: The United States and the End of Yamanaka." *Impressions,* The Journal of the Japanese Art Society of America, 34 (2013): 33–53.

Landesmuseum für Kunst und Kulturgeschichte, Münster, "Ausstellung japanischer Holzschnitte: Sammlung Theodor Scheiwe," Exhibition, 1959. Catalogue by Rose Hempel.
Mann catalogue nos. 75, 159

Lane, Richard. *Images of the Floating World: The Japanese Print.* New York: G. P. Putnam's and Sons, 1978.
Mann catalogue no. 13

Ledoux, *Landscapes*
Ledoux, Louis V. *A Descriptive Catalogue of an Exhibition of Japanese Landscape, Bird, and Flower Prints and Surimono from Hokusai to Kyōsai.* Exhibition at The Grolier Club, New York. New York: The Grolier Club, 1924.
Mann catalogue no. 144

Ledoux, Louis V. *Japanese Prints of the Primitive Period, in the Collection of Louis V. Ledoux.* New York: E. Weyhe, 1942.

Ledoux, *Sharaku to Toyokuni*
———. *Japanese Prints, Sharaku to Toyokuni, in the Collection of Louis V. Ledoux.* Princeton: Princeton University Press, 1950.
Mann catalogue nos. 73, 75, 79

Ledoux, *Hokusai and Hiroshige*
———. *Japanese Prints, Hokusai and Hiroshige, in the Collection of Louis V. Ledoux.* Princeton: Princeton University Press, 1951.
Mann catalogue no. 144

Lempertz, December 2, 1995. Kunsthaus Lempertz, Cologne. Katalog 726, *Sammlung Fedor Sibeth, Teil 1.*
Mann catalogue nos. 77, 90

Le Véel 2
Ader, Picard, Tajan, Paris, auctioneers, and MM Portier, specialists. *Collection Ernest Le Véel, Estampes Japonaises et Chinoises (2e vente): Primitifs . . . Utamaro, Choki . . . Hokusai . . . Surimono.* Catalogue of an auction at Nouveau Drouot, Paris, October 24, 1980.
Mann catalogue nos. 39, 46, 64, 86, 88, 89, 113, 125

Le Véel 3
———. *Collection Ernest Le Véel, Estampes Japonaises (3e vente): Importante Collection d'Estampes par Kiyomasu, Masanobu . . . Kiyonaga . . . Utamaro, Choki . . . Hokusai . . . Surimono.* Catalogue of an auction at Nouveau Drouot, Paris, November 5, 1981.
Mann catalogue no. 63

Lewis, R. E., Inc. *Twentieth Anniversary Catalogue*. San Francisco: September 1972.
Mann catalogue no. 80

———. *Fine Japanese Prints*. Nicasio, CA: December 1974.
Mann catalogue no. 43

———. *Old Japanese Prints*. San Rafael, CA: April 1986.
Mann catalogue no. 52

Link, Howard. *The Theatrical Prints of the Torii Masters: A Selection of Seventeenth and Eighteenth-century Ukiyo-e*. Honolulu: Honolulu Academy of Arts; Tokyo: Riccar Art Museum, 1977.

———. With the assistance of Juzō Suzuki and Roger S. Keyes. *Primitive Ukiyo-e from the James A. Michener Collection in the Honolulu Academy of Arts*. Honolulu: The University Press of Hawaii, 1980.

Little, Stephen. "The Richard Lane Collection," *Orientations* 36 (2): 93.

London Gallery, Ltd. *Important Japanese Prints from Kegan, Paul, Trench & Trubner, London*. Tokyo, May 6–10, 1969.
Mann catalogue no. 38

Mann, *Impressions*
Mann, H. George. "Passionate Pursuit: My Adventures in Ukiyo-e," *Impressions*, The Journal of the Ukiyo-e Society of America, 25 (2003): 77–91.
Mann catalogue nos. 3, 14, 16, 22, 67, 73, 79, 83, 120, 144, 149

———. "Osamu Ueda (1928–2001)." *Impressions*, The Journal of the Japanese Art Society of America, 33 (2012): 113–18.

Marks, Andreas. *Japanese Woodblock Prints in 200 Masterpieces from Ukiyo-e to Shin Hanga, 1680–1938*. Cologne: Taschen, 2019.
Mann catalogue nos. 1, 14, 15, 27, 45, 46, 50, 54, 58, 60, 68, 72, 74, 78, 83, 95, 98, 107, 117, 120, 153, 162, 165

Maroni
Kende Galleries at Gimbel Brothers, New York, April 3, 1948. *The Albert Maroni Collection of Japanese Prints*.
Mann catalogue nos. 47, 58, 61

Masterpieces of Ukiyo-e in Foreign Collections
Japan Ukiyo-e Society. *Masterpieces of Ukiyo-e in Foreign Collections: The Works of Harunobu, Kiyonaga, Utamaro, Sharaku, Hokusai and Hiroshige / Zaigai ukiyoe meisaku ten: Nihon Ukiyoe Kyōkai sōritsu jisshūnen kinen* (Exhibition commemorating the 10th anniversary of the founding of the Japan Ukiyo-e Society). Exhibition at Matsuzakaya Department Store Galleries, Tokyo, and travelling exhibition Osaka, Nagoya and other venues in Japan, 1971. Catalogue by Narazaki Muneshige.
Mann catalogue nos. 67, 108

McVitty
Parke-Bernet Galleries, New York, February 28, 1950. *Etchings & Engravings by Old and Modern Masters . . . A Small Choice Group of Japanese Prints . . . the Collection of the Late Albert E. McVitty*.
Mann catalogue no. 60

Meech, Julia. *Frank Lloyd Wright and the Art of Japan: The Architect's Other Passion*. New York: Japan Society and Harry N. Abrams, 2001.

———. "Edwin Grabhorn: Printer and Print Collector," *Impressions*, The Journal of the Japanese Art Society of America 25 (2003): 55–70.

———. "Richard Lane (1926–2002): Scholar and Collector." *Impressions*, The Journal of the Japanese Art Society of America, 26 (2004): 107–13.

———. "Who Was Harry Packard?" *Impressions*, The Journal of the Japanese Art Society of America, 32 (2011): 83–113.

———. "Edwin Grabhorn: Passionate Printer and Print Collector." In *The Printer's Eye: Ukiyo-e from the Grabhorn Collection*. Edited by Laura W. Allen and Melissa M. Rinne. San Francisco: Asian Art Museum, 2013, 11–20.

Meech, Julia and Jane Oliver, eds. *Rare Correspondence: Letters from Harry Packard to Edwin Grabhorn, 1950–64*. Impressions, The Journal of the Japanese Art Society of America, 36, companion issue (2015).

Melikian, Souren, Saleroom report of Le Véel 2 auction at Nouveau Drouot, Paris. *International Herald Tribune*, November 1–2, 1980.

Mellor
Sotheby's, London, July 9–11, 1963. *The Very Important Collection of Japanese Colour Prints and Illustrated Books*. Collection of John Mellor.
Mann catalogue no. 22

Michener, James. *Japanese Prints: From the Early Masters to the Modern*. Rutland, VT and Tokyo: Charles E. Tuttle Company, 1959.

Musée des Arts Decoratifs, Paris. Exhibitions 1909–14, see Vignier & Inada, 1909 . . . .

Musée des Arts Decoratifs, Paris, "Images du Temps qui Passe," 1966
Musée des Arts Decoratifs, Palais du Louvre. "Images du Temps qui Passe—Peintures et Estampes d'Ukiyo-e." Exhibition, June 1–October 3, 1966. Catalogue organized by Nihon Keizai Shinbun and L'Union Central des Arts Decoratifs, with contributions from Suzuki Jūzō, Harry Packard et al.
Mann catalogue nos. 15, 20

Museum of Decorative Arts, Copenhagen. The Denmark–Japan Society. *Hokusai: The Denmark–Japan Society's Exhibition of Wood-Block Prints by Hokusai in the Museum of Decorative Art in Copenhagen*. Catalogue of an exhibition, June 27–August 31, 1975.
Mann catalogue no. 113

Nagata Seiji. *Ukiyoe saikyō retsuden: Edo no meihin seizoroi––Santafe rī dākusu korekushon / Popular Impressions: Japanese Prints from the Lee E. Dirks Collection*. Edited by Iwakiri Yuriko. Tokyo: Nihon Keizai Shinbun (Nikkei, Inc.), 2018.

Narazaki Muneshige. *Moronobu, Jihei, Kiyonobu, Kaigetsudō, Masanobu . . . .* Vol. 1 of *Ukiyoe taikei* (Compendium of ukiyo-e). Tokyo: Shūeisha, 1974.

Nihon Keizai Shinbun and Ukiyo-e Society of Japan, eds. *Orinpikku Tōkyō taikai sōshiki iinkai kyōsan geijutsu tenji / International Exhibition of Ukiyo-e Masterpieces Depicting the Manners and Customs of Old Japan / Ukiyoe fūzoku ga meisaku ten*. Catalogue of an exhibition, Tokyo, Shirokiya Nihonbashi Department Store Galleries, October 9–21, 1964. Presented by Nihon Keizai Shinbun and Ukiyo-e Society of Japan to commemorate the 1964 Olympic Games in Tokyo. Expanded catalogue published in 1969 (see Shibui et al., *Masterpieces*).
Mann catalogue nos. 15, 20, 67

Nihon Keizai Shinbun and L'Union Central des Arts Decoratifs. *Images du Temps qui Passe*. With contributions from Suzuki Jūzō, Harry Packard et al. Catalogue of an exhibition, Musée des Arts Decoratifs, Palais du Louvre, Paris, June 1–October 3, 1966.
Mann catalogue nos. 15, 20

Nihon Keizai Shinbun, ed. *Pari Beberu korekushon: Ukiyoe meisaku 300 senten / Three Hundred Selected Masterpieces from the Vever Collection*. Exhibition at various venues, Japan 1975 (see Japan, *Vever*, 1975). Tokyo: Nihon Keizai Shinbun, 1975.
Mann catalogue nos. 25, 62, 83

Ōta Memorial Museum of Art, Tokyo, *The Mann Collection*
Ōta Memorial Museum of Art, ed. *Man korekushon ukiyoe meihin ten / The Mann Collection*. Catalogue of an exhibition, October 1–November 26, 1994. Tokyo: Ukiyo-e Ōta Memorial Museum of Art, 1994.
Mann catalogue nos. 2–6, 8–14, 16, 17, 20–23, 27–32, 35–43, 45, 46, 48–65, 67, 69, 70, 71, 73, 74, 76, 79–82, 84–87, 93, 95, 98, 99, 101–14, 116, 117, 118.1–14, 119, 120, 123–46, 148–51, 153, 155–58, 162, 163

Ōta Nanpo. *Various Thoughts on Ukiyo-e (Ukiyo-e ruikō)*. 1790.

Perry, Lilla S. "Introduction to a Catalogue: The Perry Collection of Japanese Prints." *Impressions*, The Official Publication of the Ukiyo-e Society of America, 14 (Spring 1988): 8–11.
Mann catalogue no. 8

Philadelphia Museum of Art, "Harunobu," 1970
"Suzuki Harunobu: An Exhibition of His Colour Prints and Illustrated Books on the Occasion of the Bicentenary of His Death in 1770." Exhibition, Philadelphia Museum of Art, September 18–November 22, 1970. Catalogue by Jack Hillier.
Mann catalogue no. 35

Pins, Jacob. *The Japanese Pillar Print: Hashira-e*. London: Robert G. Sawers Publishing, Ltd., 1982.
Mann catalogue nos. 11, 15

Popper
Sotheby Parke Bernet, New York, October 5–6, 1972. *The Hans Popper Collection of Japanese Prints*.
Mann catalogue nos. 30, 35, 67, 108

Pratt Graphics Center, "Hiroshige," 1983
"Hiroshige." Exhibition, Pratt Graphics Center, New York, organized by the Ukiyo-e Society of America, Inc., February 26–March 19, 1983. Catalogue by Sebastian Izzard.
Mann catalogue nos. 118.11, 118.14, 119, 124–25, 129, 135–36, 138, 140, 143–44

Royal Academy of Arts, London, "Hokusai," 1991–92
"Hokusai: Prints and Drawings." Exhibition, Royal Academy of Arts, London, November 15, 1991–February 9, 1992. Catalogue by Matthi Forrer.
Mann catalogue nos. 105, 107–09, 113

Royal Academy of Arts, London, "Hiroshige," 1997
"Hiroshige: Prints and Drawings." Exhibition, Royal Academy of Arts, London, July 3–September 28, 1997. Catalogue by Matthi Forrer, with essays by Suzuki Jūzō and Henry D. Smith II.
Mann catalogue nos. 118.7, 118.10, 118.14, 119, 125, 130, 133, 134, 136, 137, 142, 144, 146, 148

Rumpf, Fritz. *Sharaku*. Berlin: Lankwitz, Würfel Verlag, 1932.

Salomon
Lair-Dubreuil, F. and Henri Baudoin, auctioneers. *Objets d'Art du Japon & de la Chine: Laques Japonais, Bronzes et Cloisonnés Chinois . . . Poteries Japonaises, Netzuke . . . Estampes, Peintures, Livres Japonais*. Catalogue of an auction at Hôtel Drouot Paris, June 9–11, 1926. Included property from Raymond Koechlin, Edmond and Marcel Guérin and Charles Salomon.
Mann catalogue no. 4

Sawers, Robert. "Swiss Bliss." *Impressions*, The Journal of the Japanese Art Society of America, 25 (2003): 71–75.

Scheiwe 1
Christie's, New York, March 21, 1989. *Japanese Prints, Paintings, Illustrated Books and Drawings from the Collection of the late Theodor Scheiwe, Part I*.
Mann catalogue nos. 76, 159, 162

Scheiwe 2
———, October 16, 1989. *Japanese Prints and Drawings from the Collection of the late Theodor Scheiwe, Part II*.

"Schindler Collection," Japan, 1985–86
"Shindora korekushon ukiyoe meihin ten / Masterpieces of Ukiyo-e from the Schindler Collection." Exhibition sponsored by the Japan Ukiyo-e Society shown in Tokyo, Okayama and Osaka, October 4, 1985–January 27, 1986. Catalogue by Kondō Eiko.
Mann catalogue nos. 68, 115

Schraubstadter
Parke-Bernet Galleries, New York, January 19–20, 1948. *Fine Japanese Color Prints, Including an Extensive Repertoire of Noted Subjects by Hiroshige, and Important Works by . . . Collection of the Late Carl Schraubstadter*. Part 1. Part 2 held March 8–9, 1948.
Mann catalogue nos. 45, 136

Schwab, Dean J. *Osaka Prints*. New York: Rizzoli, 1989.
Mann catalogue nos. 157–58

von Seidlitz 1910
Seidlitz, Woldemar von. *Geschichte des Japanischen Farbenholzschnitts: Verlag von Gerhard Kühtmann*. Dresden: n. p., 1910.
Mann catalogue no. 13

von Seidlitz 1911
———. *Les Estampes Japonaises*. Paris: Hachette, 1911.
Mann catalogue nos. 13, 25

Shibui Kiyoshi, "Masanobu's Sumiye." *Ukiyoe no kenkyū*, vol. VI, no. 3 (March 1929): 56.
Mann catalogue no. 8

Shibui et al., *Masterpieces*
Shibui Kiyoshi et al. English text by Charles H. Mitchell. Nihon Keizai Shinbun and Japan Ukiyo-e Society, eds. *Masterpieces of Ukiyo-e*. Expanded catalogue of the exhibition "International Exhibition of Ukiyo-e Masterpieces Depicting the Manners and Customs of Old Japan" at Shirokiya Nihonbashi Department Store Galleries, Tokyo, held October 9–21, 1964 in commemoration of the Tokyo Olympic Games. Tokyo: Nihon Keizai Shinbun, 1969.
Mann catalogue nos. 15, 20, 67, 76

Shirokiya Nihonbashi Department Store Galleries, Tokyo, "An Exhibition of Masterpieces of Ukiyo-e by the Japan Ukiyo-e Society / Ukiyoe meihin ten." Exhibition April 5–10, 1963. Catalogue published in *Ukiyoe geijutsu / Ukiyo-e Art* 3 (1963).
Mann catalogue no. 16

Shirokiya Nihonbashi Department Store Galleries, Tokyo, "Masterpieces," 1964
"International Exhibition of Ukiyo-e Masterpieces Depicting the Manners and Customs of Old Japan / Ukiyoe fūzokuga meisaku ten." Exhibition organized by Nihon Keizai Shinbun and Japan Ukiyo-e Society, October 9–21, 1964, in commemoration of the Tokyo Olympic Games. Catalogue by Shibui Kiyoshi and Adachi Toyohisa; English text by Charles H. Mitchell.
Mann catalogue nos. 15, 20, 67

Smart Museum of Art, "Awash in Color," 2012–13
"Awash in Color: French and Japanese Prints." Exhibition, Smart Museum of Art, University of Chicago, October 4, 2012–January 20, 2013. Catalogue by Chelsea Foxwell, Anne Leonard, David Acton et al.
Mann catalogue nos. 7, 13, 14, 26, 30, 32, 118.11, 121

Sotheby's, London, October 8–9, 1962. *Japanese Colour Prints and Works of Art*. Included property of Mrs. M. A. Wilkinson.
Mann catalogue no. 111

———, July 11, 1966. *Japanese Colour Prints, Reference Books, Maps and Paintings*. Included prints from the collection of Lilla Simmons Perry.
Mann catalogue no. 8

———, November 5, 1968. *Japanese Colour Prints, Drawings, Illustrated Books, Japanese and Chinese Paintings*.
Mann catalogue no. 149

———, June 30, 1969. *Japanese Colour Prints, Chinese and Japanese Paintings: The Property of the Late Mrs. E. A. Ritchie (Sold by Order of the Executors) and the Property of Various Owners*.
Mann catalogue no. 95

———, June 28, 1972. *Fine Japanese Colour Prints, Chinese and Japanese Paintings, Including the Property of Various Owners*.
Mann catalogue nos. 4, 28, 80

———, October 24, 1977. *Fine Japanese Prints, Drawings, and Paintings, and Japanese Screens, the Property of Various Owners*.
Mann catalogue no. 69

———, April 2, 1980. *Fine Japanese Prints, Japanese Illustrated Books and Screens, Chinese and Japanese Paintings, the Property of Dame Albertine Winner, D.B.E. and the Property of Various Owners*.
Mann catalogue no. 129

Sotheby's, London, December 8, 1987. *Fine Japanese Prints, Paintings and Screens.*
Mann catalogue no. 67

———, November 15, 2001. *Japanese Works of Art, Prints and Paintings.*
Mann catalogue no. 1

Sotheby's, New York, January 17, 1981. *Japanese Prints.*
Mann catalogue no. 11

———, June 26, 1981. *Japanese Prints and Paintings.*
Mann catalogue nos. 20, 150

———, November 30, 1982. *Important Japanese Prints and Important Tibetan, Nepalese and Southeast Asian Works of Art.* Included prints from the collection of Otto Laporte, MD.
Mann catalogue no. 6

———, May 13, 14, 1983. *Fine Japanese Works of Art.*
Mann catalogue nos. 47, 58

———, November 9, 1984. *Fine Japanese Prints and Decorative Works of Art.*
Mann catalogue nos. 59, 109–10

———, March 25, 1998. *Japanese Works of Art.*
Mann catalogue no. 100

Sotheby Parke-Bernet. *Art at Auction 1971–72.* London: Philip Wilson Publishers, 1972.
Mann catalogue no. 80

Sotheby Parke-Bernet, New York, October 2–3, 1973. *Japanese Color Prints, Books, Paintings and Screens.* Included property of Gertrude Wickes Snellenburg.
Mann catalogue no. 84

Staley, Carolyn. *Hiroshige Masterworks.* Seattle: Carolyn Staley Fine Prints, November 1997.
Mann catalogue no. 121

Stoclet 1965
Sotheby's, London, May 3, 1965. *Important Japanese Prints . . . the Property of Mr. Philippe R. Stoclet (from the Collection of the late Adolphe Stoclet).*

Stoclet 1966
Sotheby's, London, June 7, 1966. *Important Japanese Colour Prints, The Property of Madame Michele Stoclet* (formerly in the collection of Adolphe Stoclet).
Mann catalogue no. 27

Stoclet 2004
———, June 8, 2004. *Important Japanese Prints, Illustrated Books & Paintings from the Adolphe Stoclet Collection.*
Mann catalogue nos. 7, 24, 26, 154

Straus-Negbaur
Cassirer, Paul and Hugo Helring, auctioneers. *Sammlung Tony Straus-Negbaur, Berlin: Japanische Farbenholzschnitte des 17. bis 19. Jahrhunderts.* Catalogue of an auction, Berlin, June 5–6, 1928. Catalogue by Fritz Rumpf.

Suzuki Jūzō. *Utagawa Hiroshige.* Tokyo: Nihon Keizai Shinbunsha, 1970.
Mann catalogue nos. 118.1–14

Takano
Parke-Bernet Galleries, New York, January 8, 1952. *Important Japanese Color Prints . . . from the Collection of H. Takano, Tokyo, with a Few Selections from the Collection of Julius Derenberg.*
Mann catalogue nos. 12, 84, 97

Tannenbaum
Christie's, New York, March 20, 1985. *Important Japanese Prints from the Collection of the Late Sidney A. Tannenbaum.*
Mann catalogue no. 51

Tokyo Olympics "Masterpieces," 1964
"Orinpikku Tōkyō taikai sōshiki iinkai kyōsan geijutsu tenji / International Exhibition of Ukiyo-e Masterpieces Depicting the Manners and Customs of Old Japan / Ukiyoe fūzokuga meisaku ten." Exhibition, Tokyo, Shirokiya Nihonbashi Department Store Galleries, October 9–21, 1964. Presented by Nihon Keizai Shinbun and Ukiyo-e Society of Japan to commemorate the 1964 Olympic Games in Tokyo. (Expanded catalogue published in 1969; see Shibui et al., *Masterpieces.*)
Mann catalogue nos. 15, 20, 67

Tokyo National Museum, "Sharaku"
Tokyo National Museum. *Sharaku.* Tokyo: Tokyo National Museum, Tokyo Shinbun and NHK Promotions, 2011. Catalogue of an exhibition, Tokyo National Museum, May 1–June 12, 2011.
Mann catalogue nos. 80, 81, 83, 85

Tuke
Sotheby's, London. Sotheby, Wilkinson & Hodge, April 4, 1911. *Japanese Colour Prints from the Collection of S.* [Samuel] *Tuke.*
Mann catalogue no. 80

Ukiyoe geijutsu / Ukiyo-e Art 3 (1963). See Shirokiya Nihonbashi Department Store Galleries, Tokyo, "Masterpieces," 1963.
Mann catalogue no. 16

Ukiyoe shūka
Ukiyo-e shūka (Collected masterpieces of ukiyo-e). 18 volumes and index. Tokyo: Shōgakukan, 1978–85.
Mann catalogue nos. 25 (vol. 12), 39 (vol. 14), 40 (vol. 12), 57 (vol. 14), 95 (vol. 9)

Ukiyoe taikei
Ukiyoe taikei (Compendium of ukiyo-e). 17 volumes. Tokyo: Shūeisha, 1973–76.
Mann catalogue nos. 16 (vol. 1), 67 (vol. 5), 76 (vol. 6)

Ukiyoe taisei
Yoshida Teruji. *Ukiyoe taisei* (Compendium of ukiyo-e). 12 vols. Tokyo: Tōhō Shoin, 1930–31.
Mann catalogue nos. 11 (vol. 3), 40 (vol. 5), 77 (vol. 7), 83 (vol. 8)

Vever 1
Sotheby's, London, March 26, 1974. *Catalogue of Highly Important Japanese Prints, Illustrated Books and Drawings, from the Henri Vever Collection: Part 1.*
Mann catalogue nos. 13, 41, 43, 65, 85, 139

Vever 2
———, March 26, 1975. *Catalogue of Highly Important Japanese Prints, Illustrated Books, Drawings and Fan Paintings, from the Henri Vever Collection: Part II.*
Mann catalogue nos. 51, 54, 62, 96, 107

Vever 3
———, March 24, 1977. *Catalogue of Highly Important Japanese Prints, Illustrated Books, Drawings and Paintings from the Henri Vever Collection, Part III.*

Vever 4
———, October 30, 1997. *Highly Important Japanese Prints from the Henri Vever Collection: Final Part.*
Mann catalogue nos. 25, 83

Vignier & Inada, 1909
Vignier, Charles and Inada Hogitarō. *Estampes Japonaises Primitives, Tirées des Collecions de MM. Bing, Blondeau* [and others] *. . . et Exposées au Musée des Arts Decoratifs en Fevrier, 1909.* Paris: n. p., 1909.
Mann catalogue no. 13

Vignier & Inada, 1911
———. *Kiyonaga, Bunchō, Sharaku, Estampes Japonaises, Tirées des Collections de MM. Bing, Bouasse-Lebel, Comte de Camondo, Mme. E. Chausson* [and others] *. . . et Exposées au Musée des Arts Decoratifs en Janvier, 1911.* Paris: Musée des Arts Décoratifs, 1911.
Mann catalogue no. 83

Villa Hügel, Essen. "Ukiyo-e: die Kunst der heiteren vergänglichen Welt; Japan 17. - 19. Jahrhundert, Sammlung Scheiwe." Exhibition, March 17–June 30, 1972. Catalogue by Rose Hempel.
Mann catalogue nos. 76, 159, 162

Walpole Galleries, New York, April 11, 1919. *Japanese Prints from Several New York Collections: Bird and Flower Prints, surimono, Watercolor Drawings, Specimens of Old Brocades, Three Fine Prints by Kiyonaga, Evening Snow, Kambara and Others by Hiroshige, Buncho, Hokusai, Harunobu, Utamaro, Shunsho, Yesui.*
Mann catalogue no. 40

———, November 10–11, 1922. *Japanese Color Prints from The Art Museum, Bremen*, Part 2.
Mann catalogue no. 79

———, February 11–12, 1924. *Japanese Prints: The Collection of Nearly Thirty Years Growth of Isaac Dooman. . . .*
Mann catalogue no. 95

Ward, Sidney. *One Hundred Japanese Prints.* Privately published, 1975.
Mann catalogue no. 82

———. *One Hundred Surimono.* Privately published, 1976.

Welch, Mathew and Yuiko Kimura-Tilford. *Worldly Pleasures, Earthly Delights: Japanese Prints from the Minneapolis Institute of Art.* Minneapolis: Minneapolis Institute of Art, 2011.
Mann catalogue no. 4 (note)

Yonemura, Ann. With contributions from Donald Keene, C. Andrew Gerstle, Elizabeth de Sabato Swinton and Joshua Mostow. *Masterful Illusions: Japanese Prints in the Anne van Biema Collection.* Catalogue of an exhibition, Arthur M. Sackler Gallery, Smithsonian Institution, September 15, 2002–January 19, 2003. Washington, DC: Arthur M. Sackler Gallery, Smithsonian Institution in association with University of Washington Press, Seattle, 2002.

———. *Hokusai.* Two-volume catalogue of an exhibition, March 4–May 14, 2006, co-organized by Freer Gallery of Art and Arthur M. Sackler Gallery, Smithsonian Institution and Nihon Keizai Shinbun, Inc., in cooperation with Tokyo National Museum. Washington, DC: Freer Gallery of Art and Arthur M. Sackler Gallery, Smithsonian Institution, 2006.
Mann catalogue nos. 101, 105, 109, 113

GLOSSARY

aiban, a paper format between *chūban* and *ōban* and used more rarely than either, approximately 34 x 23 cm

aizuri-e, "picture printed in blue," referring to prints made with Prussian (Berlin) blue pigment, which was introduced to Japan in the 1820s

allusive picture, see *mitate-e*

aratame, "inspected," censor's seal

baren, a disc-like tool of braided cord, paper and bamboo with loop handle used in the printing of Japanese woodblock prints to rub the back of the print's paper that has been applied to an inked wood block in order to transfer the ink onto the paper

bedding kimono, see *yogi*

beni, a pink color extracted from the safflower plant

beni-e, "pictures with beni," prints with hand coloring in which *beni* is predominant

benizuri-e, prints with woodblock-printed color, usually of *beni* and green, and sometimes printed with yellow, blue or gray, each color printed from an individual wood block

bokashi, a shading or gradation in the depth of a color on a woodblock print produced by wiping the wood blocks after the application of the pigment, using brushes with varying saturations of color or rubbing the wood block with a damp cloth before applying the pigment

chūban, paper format of mid-size, approximately 28 x 20 cm

chūtanzaku, paper format approximately 38 x 12.5 cm

e, "picture," used as a suffix or prefix, such as in *egoyomi* or *mitate-e*

Edo, the old name for Tokyo and the capital of the Tokugawa shogunate 1615–1868

egoyomi, "picture calendar," a print in which symbols for the long and short months of a given Japanese year in the premodern period are worked cleverly into the design

eshi, "master of painting," artist, often used in signatures on early ukiyo-e prints and paintings

ga, "drawn by," "designed by" after an artist's name; also, the word for "picture" or "painting"

giga, "drawn for pleasure," following an artist's name

hashira-e, "pillar picture," a paper format for a long and narrow print approximately 66 x 10 cm to 68.5 x 15 cm made by pasting together vertically two sheets

hitsu, "from the brush of" following an artist's name, meaning it was designed by that artist

hosoban, paper format for prints of narrow size, approximately 31.5 x 15 cm

kakemono-e, "hanging-scroll picture," a large vertical print approximately 75 x 23 cm

kaomise, "face showing," the premiere of the kabuki season, at which the theater presents its new troupe, who perform together, after two weeks of rehearsal, for the first time; in Edo, the season premiere took place between the first day of the eleventh lunar month and the tenth day of the twelfth lunar month

kappazuri-e, an image with stenciled coloring

kiwame, "certified," a seal used by a censor of prints between 1791 and 1842

kotatsu, a Japanese brazier-type room heater with cloth cover

kyōka, "crazy verse," light verse rife with word play in thirty-one syllables that was extremely popular among the artistic set in the late eighteenth and early nineteenth centuries

large-head picture, see *okubi-e*

mitate-e, "allusive picture," a literary term used in ukiyo-e to mean an image that adapts a classical or widely known theme, figure, work or expression using contemporary Edo figures

Noh, Japan's oldest theatrical tradition, since the fourteenth century, involving music, dance and drama

ōban, a paper format, approximately 35.6 x 25.4 cm oriented either vertically (*tate-e*) or horizontally (*yoko-e*)

ōkubi-e, "large-neck picture," a bust portrait generally called a "large-head picture"

ōōban, "extra-large print," a paper format from two sheets of paper that combine to approximately 54.5–64.5 x 30.5–33 cm

ōtanzaku, paper format, approximately 38 x 17 cm

perspective print, see *uki-e*

pillar print, see *hashira-e*

season premiere, the play that starts the kabuki season and introduces the new troupe of actors; see *kaomise*

Shibaraku, "Wait a Moment!," a highly dramatic scene in the kabuki repertoire enacted by a superhero, usually by an actor of the Ichikawa line

shōhitsu, drawn by, brushed by, designed by, after an artist's name

shunga, "spring picture," an erotic image

sumizuri-e, "black-ink printed picture"

surimono, "printed thing," a print emphasizing text, often thirty-one-syllable light verse (*kyōka*), that usually has accompanying imagery, frequently privately commissioned and distributed and often printed with deluxe techniques, such as hand shading, embossing and metallic embellishments

tan-e, "picture printed with *tan*," an orange-red pigment

uki-e, "floating picture," a perspective picture

ukiyo-e, a term now in the English lexicon from the Japanese *ukiyo* (floating world) and *e* (picture), the general term for paintings and prints of people, activities and entertainments in popular culture of the Edo period (1615–1868)

urushi-e, "lacquer picture," a print hand-applied with transparent deer-hide glue (*nikawa*) mixed with black pigment to give a lacquerlike gloss and/or sprinkled with decorative mica or metallic filings, usually of brass or bronze

yakko, a footman, a low-level retainer in a samurai household

yogi, a thickly padded bedding kimono

Yoshiwara, the best known of Edo's licensed pleasure quarters

za, theater

zu, "picture," meaning "drawn by," "designed by" after an artist's name

INDEX

Note: Page numbers in italics refer to illustrations.